Introduction to IT Privacy

A Handbook for Technologists

D0877716

Executive Editor
Travis Breaux, CIPT

Contributors
Chris Clifton
Lorrie Faith Cranor
Simson Garfinkel
David Gordon
Malcolm Harkins
David Hoffman, CIPP/US
Aaron Massey
Stuart Shapiro, CIPP/US, CIPP/G
Manya Sleeper
Blase Ur

An IAPP Publication

©2014 by the International Association of Privacy Professionals (IAPP)

Copy editor: Sarah Weaver
Compositor: Ed Stevens, Ed Stevens Design
Indexer: Jan Bednarczuk, Jandex Indexing

ISBN: 978-0-9885525-5-5
Library of Congress Control Number: 2013956484

About the IAPP

The International Association of Privacy Professionals (IAPP) is the largest and most comprehensive global information privacy community and resource, helping practitioners develop and advance their careers and organizations manage and protect their data.

The IAPP is a not-for-profit association founded in 2000 with a mission to define, support and improve the privacy profession globally. We are committed to providing a forum for privacy professionals to share best practices, track trends, advance privacy management issues, standardize the designations for privacy professionals and provide education and guidance on opportunities in the field of information privacy.

The IAPP is responsible for developing and launching the only globally recognized credentialing programs in information privacy: the Certified Information Privacy Professional (CIPP), the Certified Information Privacy Manager (CIPM) and the Certified Information Privacy Technologist (CIPT). The CIPP, CIPM and CIPT are the leading privacy certifications for thousands of professionals around the world who serve the data protection, information auditing, information security, legal compliance and/or risk management needs of their organizations.

In addition, the IAPP offers a full suite of educational and professional development services and holds annual conferences that are recognized internationally as the leading forums for the discussion and debate of issues related to privacy policy and practice.

Contents

CHAPTER 7

David Hoffman, CIPP/US, Malcolm Harkins

FIGURE LIST

TABLE LIST

Acknowledgments

The IAPP is pleased to present *Introduction to IT Privacy: A Handbook for Technologists*, which provides technology professionals with the necessary knowledge to understand the privacy risks associated with the ever-increasing use of personal data, and the skill and practices to safeguard data and support the privacy goals of their organization.

This book would not have been possible without the leadership and guidance of its executive editor, Travis Breaux, CIPT. In addition to assembling many of the top contributors to the field, he led the book through all stages of content development—from chapter outline to final manuscript. I thank Travis for his vision and dedication to this project.

We were fortunate to have an outstanding team of contributing authors on this project—Travis Breaux, Chris Clifton, Lorrie Faith Cranor, Simson Garfinkel, David Gordon, Malcolm Harkins, David Hoffman, CIPP/US, Aaron Massey, Stuart Shapiro, CIPP/US, CIPP/G, Manya Sleeper and Blase Ur. These individuals represent important voices in scholarship and practice in privacy and information technology, and we are enormously thankful for their contributions to this project.

The manuscript was reviewed by Shaun Bush, Gilles Fourchet, CIPT, Rebecca Herold, CIPP/US, CIPT, CIPM, John Howie, CIPP/US, CIPT, Laura Lazarcyk, Debi Lohr, CIPT, Mary Morshed, CIPP/G, CIPT, Javier Salido, CIPP/US, CIPT and Ed Yakabovicz, CIPT, CIPM. I am grateful for their suggestions and insights, which helped bridge this project from draft to final manuscript. To Derek Jones and Meghan Myers, who validated facts and citations throughout the manuscript, thank you.

Editorial and design professionals ensure that the published text is of the highest quality. My appreciation to Sarah Weaver, who copyedited this text; Will Sweeney, who provided illustrations in Chapter 3; and Ed Stevens, who designed and laid out the interior text.

Thank you to all of the professionals who contributed to this invaluable resource for the IT community.

Marla Berry, CIPT
Certification Director
International Association of Privacy Professionals

Introduction

Technology is a persistent driving force shaping the world in which we live. Since man first used spears to hunt prey, through agricultural and industrial revolutions, right through our current computer revolution, technological innovation has brought increases in efficiencies and productivity, improved goods and services and enriched the quality of human life immeasurably. History demonstrates that we can count on constant technological evolution, but it is equally clear that each new wave of innovation looks a little different from those that preceded it.

Today much of our innovation is emerging from a set of conditions that are unique to this moment in history. For the first time we are able to connect with one another, as well as with product and service providers around the world, with unprecedented ease. This is bringing about huge cultural shifts in how we communicate and is changing our expectations for the products and services we receive. As a by-product of this communication, we are also generating massive amounts of data—much of it personal in nature—that is collected and stored in databases around the world.

Personalization, profiling and other forms of predictive analytics, which continue to grow in importance to organizations both large and small, are possible only through the use of these data stores of personal information. In fact, they have grown to such an important part of our economic ecosystem that an entire industry is forming to provide tools, services and information to assist organizations in leveraging this data. For those of us tasked with providing these services or managing the data they require, it is both an exciting and a challenging time.

The challenge grows as the public increasingly expresses discomfort over unexpected use of personal data and as lawmakers and industry regulators are taking notice. Consequently, we see rapid growth in legal and regulatory attempts to address these concerns. In the United States these include the creation of the U.S. Privacy Bill of Rights, more aggressive protection of consumer privacy rights by the FTC and revisions to U.S. laws that protect health information and minors. Parts of Europe have enacted legislation to add transparency to third-party tracking, and the European Union is writing a broad regulation governing all uses of personal information. Many other areas of the world, including Asian and Latin American countries, are following suit.

As a result, not only is personal information an increasingly valuable commodity, but tightening regulation also presents real risks to organizations that do not properly steward the personal information they obtain. Given the complexity with which modern organizations handle data—the collection, protection, storage and use of personal information—it can be difficult for those without a technical background to fully grasp these implications. Therefore, information technology professionals of all stripes are increasingly asked to help manage privacy risks for their organizations.

With the growing importance of personal information in all manner of business environments, the rising number of methods for acquiring and using personal data and the public's growing unease with profiling, the challenge of protecting privacy has grown exponentially. An IT professional with privacy responsibilities must have a broad understanding of the multitude of ways a simple misstep can create a privacy violation.

If you are new to privacy or want a deeper understanding of how technology and privacy interplay, this book is an excellent starting point. Editor Travis Breaux has tapped some of the leading minds in the field of privacy to highlight the most critical areas of concern. While the text is carefully organized so that it can be read from cover to cover, each chapter stands on its own as a reference that can be revisited as needed. I am very excited about this book because it addresses the real need to educate IT professionals on how technology and privacy intersect. The future for IT professionals, particularly those involved with security, audit and governance issues, will include responsibilities for managing and mitigating privacy risks. This book is an important primary resource from which those professionals will build a foundation and identify areas requiring further education.

Jeff Northrop, CIPP/US, CIPT
Chief Technology Officer
International Association of Privacy Professionals

CHAPTER 1

Introduction to Privacy for the IT Professional

Travis Breaux, CIPT

Information technology (IT) continues to revolutionize modern life through increasing automation and innovation. Automation includes transforming existing, often paper-based, practices into electronic processes that aim to save time and reduce waste. The migration from paper-based medical records to electronic health records and the transition to electronic voting are just two examples of IT automation. IT innovation occurs when new services are realized that were never before in reach due to technological limitations. Recently, social networking and handheld mobile devices have led to extensive innovation by bringing data and information into the context of personal and professional activities. These two examples alone have led to a paradigm shift in how we manage and interact with information on a daily basis. The challenge for modern IT, however, is that new types of system quality and value are now necessary to sustain this emerging ecosystem. Whereas the early days of IT were driven by value produced primarily from improved performance, better reliability and stronger integrity, modern IT systems must increasingly contend with value produced from better usability, security and privacy. In particular, privacy concerns increase as personal information is collected, processed and transferred in new ways that challenge existing legal and social norms.

To prepare IT professionals with the skills they need to support the privacy goals of the organization, this book serves as a road map to navigate the complex IT ecosystem from the viewpoint of an IT administrator or developer. As a road map, the book cannot reasonably cover every detail needed to train an IT professional to become an expert in privacy. However, the book does include several important *signposts* that direct IT professionals to more easily identify and understand critical terminology for discovering and incorporating privacy and security best practices into their workplace responsibilities. This terminology can later be studied in depth in a manner commensurate with the role and responsibilities of IT professionals in their larger organizations. Furthermore, the book aims to prepare the professional to identify common pitfalls that have previously led to privacy harms—in some cases costing companies millions of dollars in fines and lost revenue. In this chapter, we begin by defining what we mean by an IT *professional* and making the case for why some IT professionals *must become privacy experts*. We conclude by providing a brief, multi-viewpoint definition of privacy and laying out an initial privacy framework that IT professionals can use to contextualize content from the remaining chapters as they work to become privacy experts. After studying this book, IT professionals should be knowledgeable about how privacy integrates into their daily practices and the daily practices of others around them, and with whom they should coordinate to improve privacy throughout their information systems.

1.1 Who Should Use This Book?

Today, IT has evolved into a rich ecosystem of stakeholders who participate in the development, acquisition and administration of IT systems. Together, these stakeholders ensure that IT systems are sustainable over time and continue to deliver value to customers and others. In this book, we focus on these three broad categories of IT professionals:

- IT *Developers*: Personnel who are responsible for researching, designing, developing and testing IT systems to meet broad market demand, or to more narrowly satisfy an organization's business needs. For many organizations, IT development includes translating customer or other stakeholder requirements into system specifications. For other organizations, a separate research and development group is responsible for envisioning "leap ahead" technologies that can surface new, unforeseen privacy risks. In either situation, privacy concerns are less expensive to address in the early stages of development than during the later stages.

- IT *Acquisition*: Personnel who are responsible for acquiring open source or commercial software and hardware to fulfill their organization's business needs. The IT professional should be able to identify privacy-enabling and privacy-threatening product features and their relationship to privacy risks. When IT professionals are working on the potential acquisition of IT systems, they are responsible for reviewing contracts to ensure that the necessary privacy requirements are included in the system targeted for acquisition.

- IT *Administration*: Personnel responsible for installing, configuring and maintaining IT systems. These professionals sustain and manage the connection between IT and business functions, often finding ways to adapt existing systems to meet the unique needs of their organizations. Similar to IT acquisition personnel, administrators need a strong vocabulary for describing the technologies that concern privacy. However, administrators are more similar to IT developers when they are required to integrate technology into their infrastructures and command the technical details of various technologies, sometimes refactoring or gluing systems together to share information in new ways.

This book aims to cover these three perspectives in different ways. Chapter 2 describes engineering practices for IT developers who design and construct their own IT systems. These practices include methods to identify privacy requirements from a variety of recognized sources, trace these requirements into system design and implementation and, finally, test these systems for conformance to privacy. Strategies for identifying and managing privacy risk that build on legal and philosophical foundations of privacy are also presented in Chapter 2. Integrators, administrators and acquisition staff should use these risk management practices when assessing privacy-preserving technology in an off-the-shelf product.

The next three chapters cover specific technologies that IT developers may use in their designs, such as technologies to support confidentiality and encryption in Chapter 3, identifiability and access control in Chapter 4, and tracking and surveillance in Chapter 5. These three chapters are relevant to IT acquisition and IT administration personnel, who can use this information when selecting and evaluating products and systems to support privacy in their organization. Chapter 6 describes the consequences of interference that can arise when IT systems use personal information to yield outcomes that are potentially privacy-invasive. Because individuals often cannot see how their information is used, this chapter provides specific coverage to "behind-the-scenes" privacy issues that may arise, such as system personalization based on consumer preferences and cloud computing. This chapter is organized as a series of case studies to illustrate the effects of poorly designed IT systems that failed to preserve privacy. Chapter 7 describes privacy governance, risk and compliance terminology and best practices. These techniques address the human dimension of IT management, including the role of privacy policies and notices, and several techniques that mature organizations use to manage privacy compliance through IT asset management, training and incident response.

The topics presented in this book may be applied to any system that processes personal information. This coverage ranges from general business systems, such as customer relationship management (CRM) systems, human resources (HR) systems (e.g., payroll, benefits), and enterprise resource planning (ERP) systems, to domain-specific systems, such as electronic medical records, online storefronts and industry-specific, self-service kiosks. One challenge for IT professionals is understanding when information is personal and when it describes a data subject. Examples of personal information include an individual's contact information, account numbers and unique biometric or health data. In this case, payroll systems, workplace computers that may be used for personal reasons and corporate wikis all contain personal information.[1] Less obvious examples are information that describes personal preferences, such as political or lifestyle preferences, and information generated by systems that may be uniquely linked to an individual, such as a personal vehicle or mobile computer. We cover in depth issues of identifiability in Chapter 4, and how technology can be used to track and surveil individuals in Chapter 5.

1.2 What Is Privacy?

Privacy has a rich history in law and philosophy that can meaningfully inform how IT professionals think about privacy in their IT systems. Because many definitions of privacy consider one or more separate perspectives, the IT professional should be prepared to work in a *privacy pluralistic world*. In other words, a privacy expert is prepared to distinguish between different definitions of privacy and recognize when another person is using a particular definition to review and analyze an IT system. Each definition is not exclusive of the other; rather, the definitions serve to highlight specific issues. To briefly illustrate, we consider a few prominent viewpoints on privacy that have served to define privacy in different ways:

- *Alan Westin's Four States of Privacy:* These are *solitude* (the individual stands by himself, separate from the group, and remains free from the observations of others); *intimacy* (the individual is part of a small unit, wherein trust, information sharing and the rules of secrecy are negotiated with members of the unit); *anonymity* (while the individual is in public, he maintains freedom from identification and surveillance) and *reserve* (while the individual is in a large group, he maintains the ability to withhold communication or disengage from others to create a psychological barrier against unwanted intrusion).[2] These four states can be used to characterize individual expectations of privacy and how works to achieve or conflict with those expectations.

- *Helen Nissenbaum's Contextual Integrity:* Privacy can be expressed as norms that should govern information access. Norms are domain specific; for example, the norms governing banking information differ from the norms governing medical information. In addition, norms are context specific, such that individuals can have their own reasons for controlling access to their information in specific situations based on their own expectations that govern those situations.[3] This viewpoint presents a challenge to IT professionals: how to identify relevant norms and preserve norms when professionals introduce new or modify existing technology.

- *Daniel Solove's Taxonomy of Privacy:* Privacy is understood through the activities and mechanisms that violate privacy. This includes activities such as interrogation and surveillance to compel information disclosure, secondary use, and appropriation or distortion, especially of another's image.[4] These activities can be used to determine when IT enables privacy-threatening outcomes (see Chapter 2 for more discussion of the individual activities and risks posed to individuals).

- *Ryan Calo's Harm Dimensions:* Objective harms, wherein a person's privacy has been violated and a direct harm is known to exist, are measurable and observable. Subjective harms exist without an observable or measurable harm, but an expectation of harm exists.[5] Subjective and objective harms may have the same impact on individual privacy, because the individuals take similar steps to protect themselves. For IT professionals, the challenge is to recognize that the perception of harm is just as likely to have a significantly negative impact on individual privacy as experienced harms. Thus, IT professionals may need to rely on privacy notice and privacy controls to build and retain trust from individuals.

Information technology provides the capability to shift the states of privacy as defined by Westin for a particular individual. For example, IT can be used to interrupt one's solitude, reveal an intimate moment, identify a person in a crowd or infer and expose an individual's attitudes and opinions despite his or her active reserve. This may occur in social networking environments, where others have the freedom to disclose intimate details about another person, or where participation is preconditioned on easing access to information about oneself. Finally,

Solove's taxonomy and Calo's dimensions both reflect the risks that can result when an IT system violates a person's privacy or creates the perception of a potential violation. While these concepts form a strong philosophical foundation for privacy, the IT professional bears the unique responsibility of translating these concepts into IT system features that work to protect an individual's sense of privacy.

1.3 What Are Privacy Risks?

In the context of this book, privacy risks concern the *likelihood* that a privacy threat will exploit an IT vulnerability and the *impact* of this exploit on the individual and the organization that retains information on the individual. The source of a threat, called the threat agent, may be internal to an organization (i.e., an *insider threat*) or external. Common insider threats include malicious threats, such as when an employee steals personal customer information and uses it to conduct fraudulent transactions on that person's behalf, called **identity theft**. According to the 2012 Javelin Strategy & Research Report on identify theft, 11.6 million U.S. adults were victims of identity theft in 2011.[6] The average out-of-pocket cost of identity theft to the consumer was $354 per incident and the average time required by the individual to resolve the incident was 12 hours.[7] With respect to the companies that host personal information, the Ponemon Institute reports that U.S. companies lose on average $194 per customer record as a result of a data breach, which includes costs from legal defenses.[8] In addition, companies that experienced a data breach also experienced an average 3.2 percent customer churn as a result of the breach.[9]

Celebrities or high-profile customers are subject to a different kind of insider threat, where employees steal personal details about the customers or their families and plan to sell this information to tabloids and newspapers. This risk is especially high in hospitals, where medical details of a celebrity's newborn or psychological assessment are purchased for publication and outing of these personal details.

Nonmalicious insider threats can be due to carelessness, mistakes, insufficient training, weak security policies or ineffective controls, to name just a few. Lost or stolen mobile devices are frequently a source of gross data losses. This situation arises when laptops taken from the office for business or other travel purposes are lost, misplaced or stolen. If the laptop hard drive is unencrypted, then anyone who discovers the laptop can more easily gain access to the company files. This is particularly threatening to individual privacy when those files contain sensitive personal information, such as Social Security numbers, financial account numbers or medical information. Other examples of lost or stolen devices are unencrypted USB flash drives and unencrypted backup drives and tapes that are stored in offsite locations, which may be less secure than the primary work location.

External threats employ many of the same techniques to steal information that IT security analysts aim to prevent. These techniques include phishing, which is a form of social engineering that uses a routine, trusted communication channel to capture sensitive information from an unsuspecting employee. Phishing occurs most commonly in e-mail messages that appear to be authentic and encourage employees to click on a link or respond to the message by disclosing their personal information, such as passwords, birth dates and/or financial account numbers. When clicking a link, employees may be led to a website that collects the information, or they may unknowingly install malicious software on their computers that aims to collect the information. Phishing is called spear-phishing or whaling when the activity targets high-profile personnel, such as corporate executives or HR managers who have more extensive access or access to more sensitive information. To reduce these risks to an organization's IT infrastructure, IT staff must combine a technical understanding of the available privacy-enabling and privacy-threatening technology (described in this book) with strategies for managing data through IT governance (discussed further in Chapter 7).

For individuals, threats may exploit how the individual uses a broad range of computing devices. For example, individuals may install otherwise innocuous browser plug-ins or personal software, such as file-sharing software, on their computers that engage in covert collection of personal information. This can affect IT staff as well, because workplace computers are vulnerable to the same threats when employees use their work computers for both work-related and personal reasons. Throughout this book, we explore in greater detail the kinds of threats that affect individuals with respect to various dimensions of privacy, including confidentiality in Chapter 3, identifiability in Chapter 4, tracking and surveillance in Chapter 5 and interference in Chapter 6.

1.4 Privacy, Security and Data Governance

Within an organization, privacy is commonly situated in the legal department or other group responsible for data governance. This creates a challenge for IT professionals, as the focus on privacy has often followed compliance with laws and regulations, which generally hold a narrower view of how privacy impacts individuals than how those individuals view their privacy. Furthermore, weak or infrequent communication between legal and IT departments is problematic, as legal needs to communicate the goals of privacy protections to IT, and IT must be allowed to determine the appropriate IT controls to support those goals. Chapter 2 aims to bridge traditional engineering practices used to develop IT systems with privacy goals to enable IT professionals to engage legal personnel in meaningful and frequent communication and in relevant IT decisions that affect privacy.

Before privacy became a more prominent focus in IT, security had been receiving increasing attention within IT departments. Evidence for the increasing focus on security exists in the rising number of companies with a dedicated security executive position, reported at 29 percent in 2008, 44 percent in 2009 and 53 percent in 2011.[10] Security is traditionally defined as activities that support three different quality attributes: *confidentiality*, which ensures that information is accessible only by authorized individuals; *integrity*, which ensures that information has not been unintentionally modified; and *availability*, which ensures that information is readily available whenever it is needed.

Some have argued that privacy is simply a subset of security, because privacy includes restricting access to information and ensuring confidentiality. This is convenient as it suggests that organizations that practice good security practices have already addressed privacy. For example, one might argue that existing security standards, such as the ISO 27000 series, already cover privacy concerns.[11] However, multiple privacy theories show that privacy is much broader than security. For example, the well-respected jurist Charles Fried argues that people do not always enjoy more privacy when others know less about them, which means confidentiality or restricting access to personal data alone cannot increase a person's sense of privacy.[12] While privacy certainly includes an individual's ability to grant and deny access to his or her information, it also concerns an individual's ability to control the granularity of information that others can access. The privacy scholar Julie Cohen further expounds upon the value of privacy to individual autonomy, noting that the ability to make "first moves" and "false starts" is necessary to develop individual identity.[13] Recent research on "regrets" illustrates how individuals will willingly share information, only to later regret that this information will be permanently remembered and made available by technology.[14] Whereas a security expert will see "access control" in these examples, a privacy expert will see a broader range of issues that concern information access, including surveillance, interrogation, feelings of insecurity and being exposed, appropriations and distortions of one's image and so on.[15] Despite this gap in perspectives, IT security professionals are well positioned to extend their expertise with an additional focus on privacy. IT security experts have the technical knowledge of IT administration and development practices required to integrate privacy into IT systems, as well as the understanding of risk management practices that can be adapted to privacy, as we discuss in Chapter 2.

In addition to IT security departments, U.S. regulations and international standards have led to the development of data governance groups within an organization. Regulations and standards that affect data governance and can support internal, organizational privacy standards include:

- Sarbanes-Oxley (SOX), which aims to improve corporate accounting
- Basel II, which aims to improve credit risk calculations
- The Health Insurance Portability and Accountability Act (HIPAA) Privacy Rule, which requires accounting for medical information disclosures

These rules affect data management practices, and thus organizations respond by developing internal data governance policies to comply. Data governance policies are implemented by IT managers and leverage many of these same practices in the pursuit of improved privacy, such as identifying data assets and mapping regulatory controls onto IT systems that store governed data. In Chapter 7, we discuss how governance, risk and compliance practices can be extended to include compliance with privacy regulations. However, data governance policies are only complementary to a strong privacy program, and IT professionals must also develop a risk management strategy, such as those discussed in Chapter 2, and account for specific privacy-preserving and -threatening technologies, such as those discussed in Chapters 3–6.

1.5 Privacy Principles and Standards

The privacy profession is led by established principles and standards that should be used to guide IT professionals, particularly developers in requirements, design and testing, toward better privacy-preserving systems. Privacy principles have their origin in the fair information practices (FIPs), which were first established by the Health, Education and Welfare Advisory Committee on Automated Data Systems in 1973.[16] Today, there are several interpretations and extensions to the original FIPs, and recent calls for "privacy by design" have sought to use the FIPs as the foundation for an early integration of privacy into software.[17] The more prominent principles that developers should be familiar with include:

- *The Fair Information Practice Principles* (FIPPs), adopted by the U.S. Federal Trade Commission (FTC) and used as guidance to businesses in the United States[18]

*ıidelines on the Protection of Privacy and Transborder Flows of
l Data (1980)*, published by the Organisation for Economic
ration and Development (OECD)

- *The Privacy Framework (2005)*, published by the Asia-Pacific
  Economic Cooperation (APEC)

- *The Generally Accepted Privacy Principles (GAPP, 2009)*, published
  by the American Institute of Certified Public Accountants (AICPA)
  and the Canadian Institute of Chartered Accountants (CICA)

- *Appendix J, the Privacy Control Catalog in Special Publication 800-
  53, Revision 4 (2013)*, published by the U.S. National Institute of
  Standards and Technology (NIST)

The 1980 OECD Guidelines provide a foundational and international
standard for privacy. The guidelines contain principles that are not found
in the FTC's FIPPs, such as the collection limitation principle, and the
GAPP largely refine the guidelines into more concrete privacy controls in a
manner similar to the NIST privacy controls. The following guidelines are
from the OECD website:[19]

1. **Collection Limitation Principle:** There should be limits to the
   collection of personal data and any such data should be obtained by
   lawful and fair means and, where appropriate, with the knowledge
   or consent of the data subject.

2. **Data Quality Principle:** Personal data should be relevant to the
   purposes for which they are to be used, and, to the extent necessary
   for those purposes, should be accurate, complete and kept up-to-date.

3. **Purpose Specification Principle:** The purposes for which personal data
   are collected should be specified not later than at the time of data
   collection and the subsequent use limited to the fulfillment of those
   purposes or such others as are not incompatible with those purposes
   and as are specified on each occasion of change of purpose.

4. **Use Limitation Principle:** Personal data should not be disclosed,
   made available or otherwise used for purposes other than those
   specified . . . except: (a) with the consent of the data subject; or (b)
   by the authority of law.

5. **Security Safeguards Principle:** Personal data should be protected by
   reasonable security safeguards against such risks as loss or unauthorized
   access, destruction, use, modification or disclosure of data.

6. *Openness Principles:* There should be a general policy of openness about developments, practices and policies with respect to personal data. Means should be readily available of establishing the existence and nature of personal data, and the main purposes of their use, as well as the identity and usual residence of the data controller.

7. *Individual Participation Principle:* An individual should have the right: (a) to obtain from a data controller, or otherwise, confirmation of whether or not the data controller has data relating to him; (b) to have communicated to him, data relating to him within a reasonable time; at a charge, if any, that is not excessive; in a reasonable manner; and in a form that is readily intelligible to him; (c) to be given reasons if a request made under subparagraphs (a) and (b) is denied, and to be able to challenge such denial; and (d) to challenge data relating to him and, if the challenge is successful to have the data erased, rectified, completed or amended.

8. *Accountability Principle:* A data controller should be accountable for complying with measures which give effect to the principles stated above.

The principles provide a common language through which to speak about privacy: chief privacy officers and the legal department should have a reasonable understanding of the meaning of purpose specification, but IT professionals are more likely to know the technical details of tracing data through various databases and server and client applications to ensure that data is not repurposed. Moreover, the principles work in tandem, and IT professionals can apply the principles in a systematic manner to their systems by using the data lifecycle, a topic we discuss next.

1.6 The Data Lifecycle

As we explore further in Chapter 2, privacy-preserving systems exist in a rich ecosystem with a diversity of actors who have different viewpoints: Lawyers aim to maintain a defensible position in a court of law, IT developers focus on developing robust, extensible and useful software, IT managers aim to deliver value to their customers and so on. The unifying theme across all these professions is how data "lives" in the IT ecosystem and how the IT developer can take steps that protect the privacy of that data in a manner consistent with these other viewpoints. To this end, we present the data lifecycle and refer to activities in the lifecycle throughout this book.

The data lifecycle (see Figure 1-1) provides a generic, high-level overview that describes how data flows through an organization, including through its business processes and supporting IT systems. The lifecycle is generic so it can be adapted to different situations; however, the technical details—of how data is collected or used, for example—can vary widely based on the technology, and thus these details can introduce additional considerations not captured by the lifecycle. Despite this limitation, the lifecycle provides a means for an IT professional to think about end-to-end privacy protection.

In the data lifecycle, it is the responsibility of a privacy-respecting organization to specify the purpose for which information will be used and to maintain consistency between actual uses and stated uses. The challenge for IT professionals is that the users of the data determine the purposes, and these purposes will evolve as the organization evolves its business practices. Under the European Union (EU) Data Protection Directive, for example, the maintainers of data are the data controller and the users of data are the data processors.

Figure 1-1: The Data Lifecycle

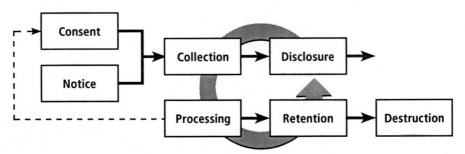

Data collection occurs at various points within an information system. Types of data collection include (1) first-party collection, when the data subject provides his personal data directly to the collector (e.g., in a web-based form that is submitted only when the data subject clicks a button); (2) surveillance, when the collector observes data streams produced by the data subject without interfering with the subject's normal behavior; (3) repurposing, which occurs when the previously collected data is now assigned to be used for a different purpose (e.g., reusing a customer's shipping address for marketing); and (4) third-party collection, when previously collected information is transferred to a third party to enable a new data collection.

Each of these four collection types may be either active, which occurs when a data subject is aware of the collection, or passive, when the data subject is unaware. Various consent mechanisms exist to engage the data subject in the collection activity and make the collection more overt.

The best practice is to obtain consent prior to the collection, to avoid any misconceptions and allow the data subject to opt out of or opt in to the collection before it occurs. In an *explicit consent*, the individual is required to expressly act to communicate consent. Examples of an explicit consent include:

- Clicking a checkbox that appears alongside the collection disclosure statement in a web-based or other data-entry form (e.g., "By clicking this checkbox you agree to allow us to collect . . . ")

- Clicking a button to acknowledge the receipt of a privacy notice, which may be displayed above the button or made obtainable through an additional step, such as a hyperlink or file download (e.g., "By clicking this button you agree to the terms and conditions stated in . . . ")

- Responding to an automatically generated e-mail or other type of private communication to indicate receipt of the privacy notice (e.g., "This notice was sent to you by e-mail, because . . . " and "Please click the link in this e-mail to acknowledge . . . ")

Passive or implied consent is generally obtained by including a conspicuous link to a privacy notice that describes the collection activities. These links may appear at the foot of a web page, for example, or be embedded in installation instructions or a user manual. However, no actions are taken by the IT system to engage the individual with the notice, and instead use of the system is assumed to imply consent.

The extent to which the data subject obtains the privacy notice and infers the specific types of collections taking place determines whether the collection is overt. For example, a privacy notice may describe that collections are performed for marketing purposes (e.g., to enable a third-party collection by a marketing service). Such general purposes may not lead a data subject to believe he or she would be the subject of online behavioral advertising through this type of collection. If collection disclosure statements are intentionally or unintentionally vague and the data subject cannot anticipate scope of collection, the collection may reasonably be viewed as covert.

IT professionals should ensure that the purposes for which data is collected trace to appropriate uses and disclosures of that data throughout their information system. The act of *repurposing* occurs when data is collected for one purpose and then reused for an entirely different purpose. This can be a source of privacy harms to the individual and may be illegal under some regulatory frameworks. Examples include collecting airline passenger data directly from passengers to schedule airline travel, and then reusing this information to develop a terrorist threat detection system; and collecting a mobile user's location to provide a route between two locations, and then reusing repeated location samples to develop general profiles of traffic patterns.[20] While repurposing is not always viewed negatively by data subjects, it is important to assess the risk to privacy before proceeding to repurpose data.

Finally, IT professionals should consider how long data is retained by their system, and, when retention is no longer needed, how they choose to destroy the data. Data may be retained to fulfill ongoing business needs or legal obligations. For example, an airline must retain consumer travel information for its bookings at least until the traveler has completed his or her flight; however, this information may be retained longer to comply with government regulations, to fulfill the internal requirements of customer loyalty programs, to profile its customers for marketing purposes or to offer customers improved services. However, this data may eventually have limited value to any of the company's existing practices, at which point the company may consider destroying the data to reduce the risks associated with retaining it. The U.S. NIST Special Publication 800-88, Appendix A, describes several media-appropriate techniques for sanitizing storage devices and destroying data that range from clearing the data by overwriting it with pseudorandom data, to degaussing electromagnetic devices, to incinerating the physical media. The level of destruction required is determined by the sensitivity of the data, and in many situations simply deleting the data offers adequate protection.

The data lifecycle is shaped by the privacy objectives and business practices of an organization, and the systems the company develops will be adapted to meet these objectives. Table 1-1 presents the data lifecycle from two extreme perspectives: (1) a maximize information utility objective, which views data as the basis for monetization and new revenue and seeks to collect and retain as much data as possible, and (2) a minimize privacy risk objective, which views data as potentially toxic, with inherent risks that can result in significant, irreversible privacy harms. Depending on the data type, a single organization may prefer to mix these two cultures in its philosophical approach to engineering privacy-preserving systems.

As we see in Table 1-1, organizations have different viewpoints based on their business objectives. In the maximize information utility culture, information is broadly collected and shared and retention persists up to the physical limits of the organization's storage devices. In the minimize privacy risk culture, collection and retention are driven by need, and new uses are planned commensurate with consent from the data subject. While both of these views are extreme, they may be practiced separately for different types of data within the same organization.

Table 1-1: Envisioning Two Data Lifecycle Extremes from the Perspective of the Data Collector

	Maximize Information Utility	Minimize Privacy Risk
Collection	Collect any data that is available, as the value will be realized later when we envision new services and products; post generic privacy notices to accommodate broadly defined future collections.	Collect data for established purposes only and always collect consent from data subjects for sensitive data; allow data subjects to opt out of services they deem unnecessary and before collecting the data, when possible.
Processing	Ensure open access to data within the organization; easy access drives innovation, and creative new uses lead to increased utility and market competitiveness.	Use data only for the purpose of the original collection; any new uses require additional consent from the data subject and/or sending new privacy notices.
Disclosure	Enable disclosures with third parties to leverage new marketing and outsourcing opportunities, or to enable previously unplanned third-party services.	Limit disclosures to those purposes for which data was originally collected; any new disclosures require additional consent from the data subject and/or sending new privacy notices.
Retention	Retain data as long as reasonably practical; long-term retention enables longitudinal analysis of data subjects to better accommodate their long-term needs and build lifetime services.	Destroy data when it is no longer needed to complete the transaction; any new uses that motivate longer retention periods require additional consent from the data subject and/or sending new privacy notices.
Destruction	Avoid destruction by using long-term backups, or reduce access to data but retain original data or a summary of the data for future uses or for reinstating services.	As soon as data is no longer needed, ensure the data and any derivatives are removed from all systems using appropriate methods to prevent recovery.

1.7 Individual Expectations of Privacy

Individuals, whether they are employees, students, customers or citizens, are concerned about their privacy. In a privacy study by Acquisti and Grossklags, we learned that 73 percent of individuals believe they do not have enough privacy.[21] An overwhelming majority of those surveyed (more than 90 percent) define privacy as control over their information, with more than half viewing privacy as necessary to preserve their personal dignity (61.2 percent) and to develop personal autonomy (50.4 percent). However, it was further discovered that individuals do not behave in a manner consistent with what they say—in other words, while individuals value privacy, they may be observed freely exchanging their privacy for services and other conveniences. Acquisti and Grossklags effectively argue that bounded rationality limits the human ability to acquire, memorize and process all relevant information when making privacy choices. This includes information about the long-term impact of sharing personal details with others, about all the various ways that personal information might be used, and how that use can affect the person's long-term desire to feel safe from outside interference and surveillance and to remain free to express himself within a private community. Even with complete information, such as the information that could be gleaned from an extensively detailed privacy notice, individuals are still inclined to weigh losses heavier than gains, miscalculate their own future preferences, draw inaccurate conclusions from past experiences and trade future utility for immediate gratification. These behaviors may lead individuals to assume that a given situation is private, because their past experiences did not include the new technologies that change how sensitive, personal details are collected. An individual who suffers a privacy harm could also reject a service indefinitely—never trusting that the technology can be adapted to protect their privacy in the future.

For IT professionals, these insights present important ethical and risk-related challenges to how technology is used to collect and protect personal information. One approach is to transfer control to the individual whenever possible to allow people to manage their own privacy risks. Though this approach requires designing systems to expose this level of control to users, the underlying premise is that individuals know their unique privacy risks better than outsiders, whereas IT professionals may misjudge the risk or be unfamiliar with the individual's personal circumstances. However, this cannot be the whole solution, as individuals can still miscalculate their long-term preferences. Thus, IT professionals must be vigilant to observe privacy harms and refactor their systems with privacy controls to prevent these harms in the future. Often, to protect an individual, more information (e.g., gender, age, lifestyle, etc.) must be collected to determine the person's privacy risks, which only further exposes this individual to additional privacy threats. Thus, IT professionals must strike the right balance between respect for individual expectations of privacy and the business needs for the data.

1.8 Chapter Summary

In this chapter, we provided a general overview by identifying who should read this book, by comparing alternative definitions of privacy and by illustrating a few sources of privacy risk to organizations and individuals. In addition, we briefly introduced a framework for IT professionals that

can be reused across the remaining chapters of the book. The framew
defines the relationship between privacy and security, which explains
that security can be used to support privacy, but security alone does n
ensure IT privacy. Rather, privacy requires that IT professionals coordinate
technology and policy to construct a holistic solution. This framework
includes the privacy principles, which have become the foundation for
discussing privacy in a domain-independent manner and which can be
used to evaluate technology and policy to identify and mitigate privacy
risks. For IT professionals, the privacy principles are most meaningful in
the context of the data lifecycle. We discussed how the data lifecycle can
be used to envision two extreme perspectives on personal information use:
the maximize information utility culture and the minimize privacy risk
culture. These two perspectives illustrate the trade-offs that organizations
face when making choices about privacy-enabling and privacy-threatening
technology and policy—choices that impact the acquisition, development
and deployment of IT systems. Finally, we closed by discussing the inherit
conflict in how individuals view their personal privacy: on the one hand,
freely exchanging very private details for convenient products and services;
and on the other hand, wishing they had more privacy. As stewards of
personal data, IT professionals must grapple with this tension throughout
the data lifecycle and recognize when to invoke ethical decision making as
an individual's personal rewards exceed the personal protections afforded
by IT and IT policy.

Endnotes

1 "Wiki: a Web site that allows visitors to make changes, contributions, or corrections," Merriam-Webster.com, accessed October 17, 2013, www.merriam-webster.com/dictionary/wiki.
2 Alan Westin, *Privacy and Freedom* (New York: Atheneum, 1967), 31–32.
3 Helen Nissenbaum, *Privacy in Context: Technology, Policy, and the Integrity of Social Life* (Stanford Law Books, 2009).
4 Daniel J. Solove, "A Taxonomy of Privacy," *University of Pennsylvania Law Review* 154, no. 3 (2006): 477–564.
5 M. Ryan Calo, "The Boundaries of Privacy Harm," *Indiana Law Journal* 86, no. 3 (2011): 1131–1162.
6 Javelin Strategy & Research, "2012 Identity Fraud Report: Consumers Taking Control to Reduce their Risk of Fraud," February 2012.
7 Ibid.
8 Ponemon Institute, LLC, "2011 Cost of Data Breach Study: United States," March 2012.
9 Ibid.
10 PriceWaterhouseCoopers, "2010 Global State of Information Security: Trial by Fire," October 2009; PriceWaterhouseCoopers, "2011 Global State of Information Security: Respected—but Still Restrained," 2010.

11 "An Introduction to ISO 27001, ISO 27002, . . . ISO 27008," The ISO 27000 Directory, 2013, www.27000.org/.

12 Charles Fried, "Privacy," Yale Law Journal 77, no. 3 (1968): 475–493.

13 Julie E. Cohen, "Examined Lives: Information Privacy and the Subject as Object," Stanford Law Review 52, no. 5 (2000): 1426.

14 Yang Wang et al., "'I Regretted the Minute I Pressed Share': A Qualitative Study of Regrets on Facebook" (paper presented at Symposium on Usable Privacy and Security, Pittsburgh, Pennsylvania, July 20–22, 2011).

15 Daniel J. Solove, "A Taxonomy of Privacy," University of Pennsylvania Law Review 154, no. 3 (2006): 477–564.

16 U.S. Department of Health, Education and Welfare, Secretary's Advisory Committee on Automated Personal Data Systems, Records, Computers, and the Rights of Citizens (Washington, DC: Government Printing Office, 1973).

17 Ann Cavoukian, Privacy by Design: Take the Challenge (Ontario: Office of the Information and Privacy Commissioner, 2009), www.ipc.on.ca/images/Resources/PrivacybyDesignBook.pdf.

18 www.ftc.gov/reports/privacy3/endnotes.shtm#N_27_.

19 Organisation for Economic Co-operation and Development, "Guidelines on the Protection of Privacy and Transborder Flows of Personal Data," updated in 2013, www.oecd.org/internet/ieconomy/oecdguidelinesontheprotectionofprivacyandtransborderflowsofpersonaldata.htm.

20 Annie I. Antón, Qingfeng He and David L. Baumer, "Inside JetBlue's Privacy Policy Violations," IEEE Security and Privacy 2, no. 6 (2004): 12–18.

21 Alessandro Acquisti and Jens Grossklags, "Privacy and Rationality in Individual Decision Making," IEEE Security and Privacy 3, no. 1 (2005): 26–33.

CHAPTER 2

Engineering and Privacy

Travis Breaux, CIPT; Stuart Shapiro, CIPP/US, CIPP/G; David Gordon

In this chapter, we examine the role of software engineering in protecting personal privacy and explore how IT developers can integrate privacy in software development. Software engineering is a disciplined approach to the construction of software. While considerable amounts of software are created by end-user programmers who initially work to solve a personally familiar problem, these personal projects quickly become large-scale endeavors developed and maintained by hundreds, if not thousands, of professional engineers.[1] The emerging complexity that results from scaling small software projects into large projects requires a sophisticated software ecosystem consisting of well-trained professionals and well-established processes.[2]

IT professionals should consider how their systems affect privacy whenever these systems contact personal information. Information-intensive systems include web-based retail, hospitality and travel reservation systems, banking systems, electronic health records and social networking, to name a few. However, under the privacy theories of autonomy and freedom, privacy also concerns systems that may not directly collect or use personal information but still affect the personal development, free expression and movement of individuals throughout society.[3] This includes transportation systems, electronic voting systems and systems that provide citizens with information about the activities of their local and national government. Because of the personal nature of privacy, it is critical that IT developers consider the role that software plays in privacy and take steps to design systems to protect individual privacy. In Section 2.1, we examine the larger privacy ecosystem and discuss how it relates to different software development models. This section illustrates how various professions play an important role in privacy-preserving software engineering and also presents a brief introduction to the software engineering practice. In Section 2.2, we introduce the fundamentals of risk management and demonstrate how risk can drive decisions to increase or decrease a project's investment in privacy. Sections 2.3 through 2.6 address specific techniques for managing privacy during all stages of software engineering, including requirements, design, testing, deployment and beyond.

2.1 Privacy in a Software Ecosystem

A useful way of thinking about how privacy is situated within a large IT project is to consider the broader software ecosystem, which consists of multiple professions that all interact during the development and use of software.[4] In addition to the developers who write the software, the surrounding privacy ecosystem includes other roles that hold a stake in how the software is developed (see Figure 2-1). These roles include:

- *Project managers,* who ensure that adequate resources are available to construct the software and that team members communicate effectively during construction, deployment and maintenance.

- *Marketing and sales,* who work with customers to establish new requirements and promote the software in the marketplace. Salespeople should understand how their software protects the privacy of individuals at an appropriate technical level for their clientele.

- *Lawyers,* who track regulatory issues relevant to the software's function or manner of construction. This includes monitoring privacy legislation developments in markets where software is deployed, monitoring emerging threats to privacy that could reshape the regulatory environment or consumer trust and communicating these issues to developers who are responsible for aligning software with legal and social norms.

- *Requirements engineers,* who collect, analyze and manage requirements.

- *Designers,* who translate software requirements into an architecture or design. Designers are responsible for tracing privacy-related requirements, such as anonymity, confidentiality and integrity requirements, throughout the software architecture.

- *Programmers*, who translate software design into source code using best practices and standard libraries and frameworks.

- *Testers*, who validate that the software conforms to the requirements. Testers must discover ways to "break the system" or ways in which privacy may be violated by a misuse or abuse of the software's functionality.

- *Users*, who operate or interact with the software to perform their daily work or recreation. Users who are also data subjects must be aware of and informed about how software uses their personal information, and they must be provided a reasonable degree of control over that information.

- *Administrators*, who install and maintain the software. Administrators, who may also be users, have responsibilities to ensure that operational assumptions behind the software's design are implemented, whether these assumptions are in the physical environment or in the operating system. Administrators rely on adequate documentation to ensure software is properly installed and maintained.

Figure 2-1: An Incomplete View of the Software Ecosystem for Privacy

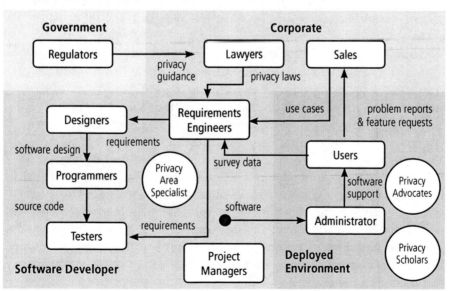

2.1.1 The Area Specialist for Privacy

The diversity of stakeholders in the software ecosystem can be managed by appointing an *area specialist* who serves as a repository of knowledge and works to tailor this knowledge for the different stakeholders. In our experience, this specialist begins as a software developer and later becomes a software project manager before taking on the role of area specialist. The area specialist has several responsibilities: to collect critical regulatory requirements from lawyers; to validate that marketing requirements are consistent with laws and social norms; to meet with designers to discuss best practices when translating requirements into design specifications; and to collect user feedback and monitor privacy blogs, mailing lists and newspapers for new privacy incidents. As a privacy practitioner, the area specialist develops a *community of practice*— "a collective process of learning that coalesces in a shared enterprise," such as reducing risks to privacy in technology.[5]

The community of practice includes professionals outside the specialist's organization. For example, prominent bloggers, including privacy law scholars and nonprofits, track emerging issues and report on newsworthy items that affect their profession. In June 2012, emerging state legislation on driverless vehicles and autonomous aircraft (drones) was closely monitored by Ryan Calo, a prominent privacy scholar at University of Washington. The Center for Democracy and Technology also maintained policy research and analysis on a range of privacy-sensitive topics, such as behavioral advertising, location, identity management, data breaches and more. In addition, regulators often provide guidelines to industry that inform how to interpret various regulations. The U.S. Federal Trade Commission (FTC) regulates privacy using its statutory authority to pursue unfair and deceptive trade practices. In privacy, such practices arise from a misalignment between privacy policies, which promise a level of privacy protection to consumers, and broken information practices that violate those policies. Through decades of experience, the FTC has published case highlights, guidelines, reports and workshop summaries that privacy area specialists can integrate under the constraints of their software enterprise to explore where consensus is forming around emerging issues in privacy. Finally, organizations such as the International Association of Privacy Professionals sponsor workshops and training seminars to improve the privacy profession by enabling networking opportunities across industries and government. By monitoring these varied sources of information and by learning about prominent thought leaders, area specialists can remain current as to how privacy evolves in response to technology and learn to improve how they deliver relevant input into their organization's software engineering process.

2.1.2 Software Process Models

Since the 1968 North Atlantic Trade Organization conference on software engineering that produced the "Garmisch" report, software engineers have employed software process models and methods to manage engineering complexity and coordinate the steps in constructing software.[6] Software process models define the various stages of software development and the conditions by which development is allowed to transition from an early stage to a later stage, as well as the artifacts produced at each stage. These models may also designate developer roles and responsibilities. Today, one can choose from a variety of software processes: Plan-driven methods, such as the waterfall and spiral models, emphasize up-front documentation and planning, in contrast to lighter-weight, agile methods, such as Extreme Programming and Scrum, which emphasize personal communication and small, dynamic development teams.[7] There is even a middle ground, such as the Team Software Process, which emphasizes process measurement and team building early on.[8] This is not an exhaustive list, but independent of the process one uses, software developers will address the following six activities in some capacity:

- *Requirements Engineering:* The activity that yields requirements that describe constraints on the software system. Requirements include environmental factors, stakeholder goals and functional and behavioral properties of the system, including privacy, performance and reliability.

- *Design:* The activity that yields software designs and architectures, which describe how a particular system will operate and may include modular "components" with assigned functionalities as well as "connectors" that link components, such as an information flow between a client and a server.

- *Implementation:* The activity of writing the source code to implement a particular design, including the development of the setup and configuration process to support the system for the very first time.

- *Testing:* The activity of verifying that the runtime system conforms to the requirements. This includes developing test cases, which test specific functions in the software, and conducting user testing to discern how users operate the software.

- *Deployment:* The activity of installing and configuring the software in its operational environment. This may include user training to ensure users can operate the software.

- **Maintenance:** The activity of extending and fixing software over the course of its lifetime, either to repair bugs after deployment or to provide users with new functionality.

In plan-driven and agile software development methods, software development activities are coordinated at different development stages and levels of developer commitment. In Figure 2-2, the spiral model requires multiple iterations of development that yield working prototypes to manage engineering risk. Going from the center of the spiral outward, this model shows how developers begin with an inform concept of operations (CONOPs) and proceed to refine these ideas into requirements, design and eventually code and test cases. At each iteration point, the development team reassesses project risks such as: Are the requirements correct? Is the system design feasible? In the Scrum model, developers employ time-boxing (in 24-hour and 30-day cycles) to achieve similar effects on controlled portions of functionality within a limited time frame: Requirements, called user stories, are contained in a product backlog managed by the product owner; the team, which generally excludes the product owner, decides which portion of the backlog to implement in each iteration, taking into account working functionality, priorities and time constraints.

Figure 2-2: Spiral (below) and Scrum (at right) Models of Software Development

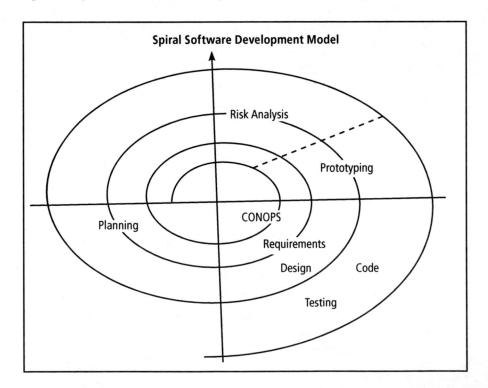

Boehm and Turner characterize the choice between plan-driven or agile methods as determining which types of risk dominate a software project.[9] Privacy can be integrated into either type of method; however, the preservation of legal requirements and the privacy specialist's observations acquired from monitoring the community of practice necessitate a minimum level of planning to respond to privacy risks in a systematic way. In the spiral model, privacy must be considered from the very beginning, at the CONOPs and requirements stage in the center of the spiral. Alternative designs are produced to address privacy requirements before project planning begins in the lower-left quadrant. The risk analysis phase of the upper-right quadrant concerns *project risks*, raising questions such as: Is the scope of planned effort feasible? Which design alternative is best suited to solve a particular problem? Can we explore designs and reduce risks using prototypes of novel or complex functionality? While IT developers can return to or repeat earlier iterations in the spiral model, this type of revision is costly and should be avoided. Therefore, in plan-driven methods, there is a need to address privacy early using a comprehensive toolkit of requirements and design techniques.

As Boehm and Turner argue, even agile methods can include some planning when the risks outweigh the benefits of increased agility. In the Scrum process, for example, the product owner prioritizes requirements, called user stories, which will be developed during an iteration, called sprint. Developers determine how much time is required to implement each story. To bridge Scrum and privacy, the area specialist can participate in developing user stories to help identify privacy risks and harms and then

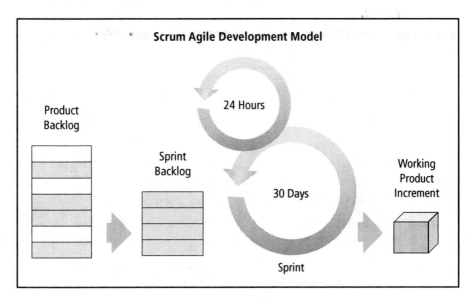

Scrum Agile Development Model

Product Backlog

Sprint Backlog

24 Hours

30 Days

Working Product Increment

Sprint

propose strategies to mitigate those risks. Furthermore, the area specialist may review the sprint backlog, which contains the list of stories that will be implemented during the current sprint, to ensure that the working increment produced by the iteration does not contain major privacy risks. For example, imagine a new web-based product developed for children under 13 that would be governed by the Children's Online Privacy Protection Act of 1998 (COPPA). In an upcoming sprint, the product owner may wish to see a new login facility for the product. To comply with the COPPA, however, this working increment will need to support a parental consent mechanism before collecting the child's personal information. While the login facility could be prototyped without this privacy control, it should not be tested on children without the control in place, since the control plays a critical role in protecting privacy. Therefore, the area specialist can intervene and review the sprint plans to catch dependencies between privacy-enabling and privacy-threatening functionality and suggest changes to the sprint backlog before these functions "go live." In general, the project manager should decide when and where to involve the area specialist to reduce privacy risks during software development and to ensure that other developers respect this person's contributions.

2.1.3 Defect, Fault, Error, Failure and Harm

Our premise is that many functional violations of privacy can be avoided by the correct design, implementation and deployment of software. The IT developer is able to limit privacy violations by carefully managing steps leading up to system failure. The Institute of Electrical and Electronics Engineers (IEEE), one of the largest engineering professional associations, defines software engineering defects, faults, errors and failures as follows; we include the definition of harm as it relates to privacy:[10]

Defect: A flaw in the requirements, design or implementation that can lead to a fault.

Fault: An incorrect step, process or data definition in a computer program.

Error: The difference between a computed, observed or measured value or condition and the true, specified or theoretically correct value or condition.

Failure: The inability of a system or component to perform its required functions within specified performance requirements.

Harm: The actual or potential ill effect or danger to an individual's personal privacy, sometimes called a hazard.

A functional violation of privacy results when a system cannot perform a necessary function to ensure individual privacy. For example, this occurs when sensitive, personally identifiable information is disclosed to an unauthorized third party. In this scenario, the *defect* is the one or more lines of computer source code that do not correctly check that an access attempt is properly authorized, and the *fault* is the execution of that source code that leads to the error. The *error* is the unauthorized access, which is an observed condition that is different from the correct condition—"no unauthorized access will occur." The *failure* is the unauthorized third-party access; failures are often described outside the scope of source code and in terms of business or other practices. Privacy harms may be objective or subjective: An *objective harm* is "the unanticipated or coerced use of information concerning a person against that person;" a *subjective harm* is "the perception of unwanted observation," without knowing whether it has occurred or will occur.[11] In public reports, we frequently learn about a system failure and subjective privacy harms, or potential for harm. Less often do we hear about the underlying errors, faults and defects that led to the system failure, and occasionally we learn about specific individuals who suffered objective harms.

Daniel Solove has identified four risk categories of privacy harm: information collection, information processing, information dissemination and invasion.[12] Solove writes that information collection harms resulting from surveillance and interrogation may lead to a degree of coerciveness. Observing a user click on age-relevant website links (e.g., links to music from a particular age-specific era) is an example of surveillance, whereas asking a user to provide his or her age as a condition of using a service is a form of interrogation. We discuss Solove's harms in further detail in Section 2.2.1.4 under risk management. While these harms can overlap in practice, a robust privacy design applies special consideration to each of these harms to avoid unintended threats to an individual's privacy.

When a privacy incident occurs, the reported description often refers to the failure or harm. Because individuals personally experience harms and share these experiences with others, the engineer may discover harms reported in news articles or blogs. In addition, regulatory agencies conduct investigations in response to reported harms and, as a consequence, regulatory enforcement actions can detail additional evidence in the form of errors or failures that link the software's operation and installation to the reported harm. As we discuss in Section 2.3, there are techniques that IT developers can use to anticipate and mitigate the risk of potential harms based on regulatory enforcement reports and news articles. In addition, there are techniques for identifying and removing defects from design documents and programs, which we discuss in Sections 2.4 and 2.5 on high- and low-level design, respectively.

2.2 Privacy Risk Management

Risk management is an integral aspect of developing reliable software. IT development projects must address multiple types of risk, including programmatic risk, such as the risk of project cost and schedule overruns, and technical risk, which includes the risks associated with specific technologies. Thus, an IT professional may be required to perform the role of a privacy risk analyst.

Risk is defined as a ~~potential~~ adverse impact ~~along with the~~ likelihood that this impact will occur. The classic formulation of risk is an equation: ~~risk = probability of an adverse event × impact of the event~~. In practice, analysts may express probability and impact numerically and compute a numerical result that can be used to compare risk levels across different events. Risk comparisons are used to prioritize risks, nominally on the basis of the risk score, but sometimes based primarily on the highest impact or highest probability. However, it is often the case that a technical or empirical basis for one or both of these numbers is nonexistent, in which case an ordinal measure is used, such as assigning a value of low, medium or high impact to an adverse event. Similar to numerical measures, ordinal measures are subject to the limitations of human perception and bias, and all measures with the same level (e.g., low) remain contextually relative and not easily comparable. One approach is to identify a relative median event that a risk analyst can use to assign values to other events (e.g., event X is higher or lower impact than event Y). However, caution should be used when treating such measures as quantitative data, because normal arithmetic may not be applied to this data: One cannot, for example, take the sum of two or more ordinal values, that is, low + high ≠ medium. Still, the advantage of identifying risks early is that the analyst can develop specific administrative, operational and technical means to manage these risks.

Effective privacy risk management employs a risk model that an analyst ~~uses to identify and align threats with the system vulnerabilities that the threats may exploit to yield ris~~ks, which are adverse events associated with degrees of likelihood and impact (see Figure 2-3). For guidance in applying the risk model, the analyst uses a risk management framework, which is a step-by-step process for identifying threats, vulnerabilities and risks and deciding how best to manage the risks. Conventional risk management options can include (1) accepting the risk as is, (2) transferring the risk to another entity (which is how property insurance works), (3) mitigating the risk by introducing an appropriate privacy control or a system design change or (4) avoiding the risk (e.g., by abandoning particular functionality, data or the entire system). Risk avoidance may be impractical or impossible in many situations. For example, the risk of laptop theft is generally impossible to avoid, and thus assuming this vulnerability will always exist may lead to using encryption as a means to mitigate the loss of private data stored on these devices. Furthermore, any one of these risk management options may introduce a new risk, thus creating a risk-risk trade-off. A risk-risk trade-off is not risk avoidance per se, but the result of interdependent risk mitigation and acceptance decisions.

Figure 2-3: Risk Model Alignments

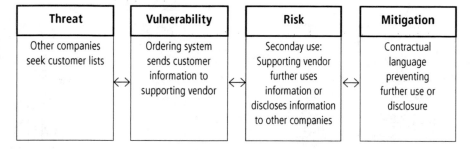

Threat	Vulnerability	Risk	Mitigation
Other companies seek customer lists	Ordering system sends customer information to supporting vendor	Seconday use: Supporting vendor further uses information or discloses information to other companies	Contractual language preventing further use or disclosure

2.2.1 Privacy Risk Models

Privacy risk analysts can now choose from a number of privacy risk models that they may employ individually or in combination. The most frequently used and long-standing privacy risk models are the compliance model and the Fair Information Practice Principles. More recently, other models have been introduced, including Calo's subjective/objective dichotomy, Solove's taxonomy of privacy problems and Nissenbaum's contextual integrity heuristic. We review each of these in the following sections. While this list is not exhaustive, these models are widely recognized and serve to illustrate the variety of options that system developers can incorporate into their projects.

2.2.1.1 The Compliance Model

Most systems that handle personal information do so within a related legal and/or policy regime. Legal regimes, which include statutory and regulatory mandates at any level of government, usually prescribe or proscribe certain aspects of a system in terms of what data it contains, what the system does with that data and how the system protects that data. Statutory and regulatory mandates, such as the Security Rule of the U.S. Health Insurance Portability and Accountability Act (HIPAA), are designed to be flexible and therefore require analysts to make interpretations based on their own security risks and available security controls. This flexibility manifests itself in the Security Rule in the form of prescribed security controls that are "addressable." This means that an organization, if its environment renders such a control unreasonable or inappropriate, may substitute alternative controls that achieve an equivalent level of risk management. The organization can even forgo alternative controls if they are not reasonable and appropriate.

In addition, systems may fall under an organizational policy regime with obligations and prohibitions that must be met. The compliance model is relatively straightforward; risks are delineated as the failure to do what is required or to avoid what is prohibited. For those laws, such as HIPAA, that require a risk assessment or reasonableness standard, however, a privacy risk model can be used to comply with this requirement. Under the compliance model, identification and alignment of threats and vulnerabilities amounts to examining the elements of the system that relate to each specific legal or policy requirement. To maintain a record of compliance, the privacy risk analyst can employ a traceability matrix, as discussed in Section 2.3.3.

2.2.1.2 Fair Information Practice Principles

The Fair Information Practice Principles (FIPPs) often dovetail with the compliance model, as they frequently form the basis of privacy-related legal and policy regimes. For example, the FTC and U.S. Department of Homeland Security (DHS) have both adopted the FIPPs in their privacy risk management recommendations: The FTC recommends the FIPPs to industry, whereas DHS applies the FIPPs to their internal practices, including privacy impact assessments. The presence or absence of an associated compliance regime notwithstanding, the FIPPs can be used in a similar fashion to a law, regulation or policy. FIPPs mostly prescribe, and in some cases proscribe, specific qualities and behaviors of systems that handle personal information. However, because FIPPs sit at a higher level of abstraction than legal and policy strictures typically do and because most of the principles are relative to the *purpose of the system*, significant interpretation by analysts and developers is necessary to determine how the FIPPs should manifest themselves in a given system. Once an appropriate interpretation has been established, that interpretation can be employed as a risk model in much the same way as a legal and policy regime. Identification and alignment of threats and vulnerabilities entails examining the elements of the system that relate to each specific Fair Information Practice Principle.

2.2.1.3 Subjective/Objective Dichotomy

Ryan Calo's subjective/objective dichotomy (S/OD) focuses on privacy harms, which he argues fall into two categories: *Subjective harms* are grounded in individual perception (irrespective of its accuracy) of unwanted observation, while *objective harms* arise out of external actions that include the unanticipated or coerced use of that person's information.[13] The relationship between subjective and objective harms is analogous to the legal relationship between assault and battery. Assault is the threat of unwanted physical contact, while battery is the experience of unwanted physical contact. Similarly, subjective privacy harms amount to discomfort and other negative feelings, while objective privacy harms are actual adverse consequences.

Harms are equivalent to adverse events in terms of risk models. Thus, this model establishes a coarse-grained point of reference for events, to which threats and vulnerabilities must be aligned. Under the S/OD model, any privacy threat that is perceivable by individuals corresponds to a subjective privacy harm. Julie Cohen and Alan Westin argue that the fear of privacy harm can limit an individual's sense of freedom and expression, which may negatively affect the target system, such as a user choosing not to use a system due to a subjective harm.[14] To assess the potential for subjective and objective harm, an analyst may examine elements of the system that relate to individuals' expectations of how their information may be used, actual usage—including surveillance or tracking—and consent or lack thereof to the collection and use of that information.

2.2.1.4 Taxonomy of Privacy Problems

Daniel Solove's taxonomy of privacy problems arose out of specific cases.[15] Rather than promoting high-level privacy precepts (as is done in the FIPPs and S/OD models, e.g.), Solove surveyed specific instances that—based on cultural analysis using historical, philosophical, political, sociological and legal sources—are recognized as problematic from a privacy standpoint. From these observations, he derived a generic set of privacy problems. The taxonomy consists of sixteen distinct privacy problems, organized into four categories: information collection, information processing, information dissemination and intrusion and decisional interference.

Information Collection

- *Surveillance* involves the observation and/or capturing of an individual's activities. Example: An advertising website embeds HTML iframes into multiple third-party news, social networking and travel websites to track users by what pages they visit and what links they click on.

- *Interrogation* involves actively questioning an individual or otherwise probing for information. Example: A website requires a user to enter his or her mobile phone number as a condition of registration, although the website's primary function does not require the phone number and there is no statutory or regulatory requirement to do so.

Information Processing

- *Aggregation* involves combining multiple pieces of information about an individual to produce a whole that is greater than the sum of its parts. Example: A retail company correlates purchases of unscented lotions, large tote bags and prenatal vitamins to infer that a customer is likely pregnant.

- *Identification* links information to specific individuals. Example: A website uses cookies, a recurring IP address or unique device identifier to link an individual's browsing history to his or her identity.

- *Insecurity* results from failure to properly protect individuals' information. Example: A website fails to encrypt private communications, thus exposing users to potential future harm.

- *Secondary use* involves using an individual's information without consent for purposes unrelated to the original reasons for which it was collected. Example: A retailer uses an e-mail address for marketing purposes when the address was originally collected to correspond about a purchase.

- *Exclusion* denies an individual knowledge of and/or participation in what is being done with his or her information. Example: A marketing firm secretly purchases consumer data to advertise to the customer under a different company name without his or her knowledge.

Information Dissemination

- *Breach of confidentiality* results from revealing an individual's personal information, despite a promise not to do so. Example: A platform releases a user's data to a third-party plug-in despite the platform's privacy notice promising not to disclose the data to anyone.

- *Disclosure* involves revealing truthful information about an individual that negatively affects how others view him or her. Example: A private "lifestyle" service discloses a list of members, which is obtained by groups who disapprove of the lifestyle.

- *Distortion* involves spreading false and inaccurate information about an individual. Example: An employment history verification service incorrectly identifies a job applicant as a felon.

- *Exposure* results from the revelation of information that we normally conceal from most others, including private physical details about our bodies. Example: A person's prior purchase of a urinary incontinence product is used as a promotional endorsement and sent to the person's broader social network.

- *Increased accessibility* involves rendering an individual's information more easily obtainable. Example: A children's online entertainment service allows any adult to register and interact with child members, leaving these children accessible to strangers without parental consent.

- *Blackmail* is the threat to disclose an individual's information against his or her will. Example: An overseas medical claims processor threatens to release patient data to the Internet unless new employment conditions are met.

- *Appropriation* involves using someone's identity for another person's purposes. Example: An online dating service uses a customer's personal history, including age, biography and education, to promote its website to new customers.

Intrusion and Decisional Interference

- *Intrusion* consists of acts that disturb an individual's solitude or tranquility. Example: A mobile alert notifies potential customers that they are within the proximity of a sale.

- *Decisional interference* involves others inserting themselves into a decision-making process that affects the individual's personal affairs. Example: A website limits access to negative product reviews to bias a new user toward a specific product selection.

A few of these potential problems, such as breach of confidentiality and blackmail—which amount to harms and adverse events—can be quickly ruled out by well-intended, ethical IT developers. However, the increasing extent to which IT systems are distributed across multiple firms means that IT developers may depend on subcontractors to fully protect the system against these more ethical harms. Moreover, identifying and aligning threats and vulnerabilities for the remaining harms requires a risk analysis that includes an assessment of the likelihood that a particular problem will arise. Similar to the FIPPs, three of Solove's categories correspond to the data lifecycle or how data moves through a system. These categories can be addressed by analyzing the system's data collection, processing and dissemination practices for the risk of these problems.

2.2.1.5 Contextual Integrity Heuristic

Helen Nissenbaum defines *contextual integrity* as maintaining personal information in alignment with informational norms that apply to a particular context.[16] The contextual integrity heuristic posits that privacy problems arise out of disruptions to these informational norms. Contexts are socially constructed settings characterized by, among other things, norms or rules and internal values in the form of purposes or goals. Context-relative, informational norms involve actors (information senders, recipients and subjects), attributes (information types), and transmission principles that govern the flows of information. When an IT system violates or otherwise disrupts a context's informational norms, this can result in a perceived privacy problem. Using the contextual integrity heuristic entails analysis to surface what norms govern a given context. Unlike the preceding risk models, there is no preexisting reference point for privacy risks, such as privacy principles or categories of harm. To apply this heuristic, an analyst must first establish the existing informational norms, and second, determine how the system may disrupt those norms. Once identified, these disruptions can be interpreted as privacy vulnerabilities, thereby enabling a stable reference point from which to identify threats and adverse events.

Consider an example in healthcare. A patient may share information about a medical condition to enable the doctor to provide an accurate prognosis. The doctor expects the patient to be candid, although she may also expect the patient to be cautious during the first encounter. When the doctor has obtained the patient's trust, the doctor and patient will freely exchange information under the norms of this medically necessary engagement. However, the information that the doctor obtains may be shared categorically and electronically with a pharmaceutical company that has treatment options available to the patient. If these treatment options were mistakenly communicated by postal mail to the patient's home or work address, thus unintentionally revealing the presence of the condition to others, then the system would have disrupted the informational norms governing the patient-doctor transaction. To mitigate this risk, the system can explicitly ask the patient to opt in to these communications, or the system may consider exposure risks under Solove's taxonomy and how to mitigate these risks.

2.2.1.6 Combining Models

As the astute reader will have noticed, the models described above are not mutually exclusive. If there is any applicable compliance model for a system—and there often will be at least one, since the compliance model includes policy as well as legal requirements—then use of the compliance model becomes mandatory. Even the most comprehensive compliance models, however, are unlikely to foresee every possible privacy risk for every system envisioned. Similarly, relevant risks can slip past a FIPPs-based model, because the FIPPs model is data purpose-centric. There is no reason to presume that any other model is infallible, either. Because there are likely diminishing marginal returns to integrating each new privacy risk model into an organization's risk management framework, a privacy analyst should instead pursue a limited combination or synthesis.

A limited combination or synthesis of models can have the practical benefit of rendering the risk identification process more manageable when using less prescriptive models. For example, the contextual integrity heuristic can be used to identify vulnerabilities in the form of disruptions to informational norms. However, the analyst must decide how particular threats might exploit those vulnerabilities to yield privacy risks. In contrast, both the S/OD and taxonomy of privacy problems models provide a set of potential adverse privacy events, but do little to assist in finding the threats and corresponding vulnerabilities that could lead to these events. Combining either of these models with the contextual integrity heuristic could provide mechanisms for recognizing both vulnerabilities and events, leaving only threats as an exercise for the analyst.

2.2.2 Privacy Risk Management Framework

Risk management frameworks provide a process for applying a risk model to a specific information system in order to identify and address risks. Risk models directly address the domain-specific issues, while risk management frameworks are more about process and are therefore more generic. ISO 31000 is an example of an existing generic risk management framework. Indeed, ISO 31000 is so generic that it essentially includes construction of a risk model as part of the process. The risk management framework described here is a synthetic framework based on a variety of frameworks across multiple domains and adjusted to better accommodate the different ways in which privacy risk models may be built out. It should be noted that risk management frameworks are far more similar than they are different; as long as a framework is capable of incorporating an appropriate privacy risk model, it should suffice. This framework proceeds in six steps: (1) characterization, (2) threat, vulnerability and event identification, (3) risk assessment, (4) risk response determination, (5) risk control implementation and (6) monitor and review.

2.2.2.1 Characterization

The first stage of any privacy risk management framework involves characterizing the system that is the target of privacy threats in a way that renders it amenable to privacy risk analysis. This includes identifying the purpose of the system, what and how personal information flows throughout and is processed by the system, and what technologies are in place to support this system. The privacy risk analyst may choose to employ the data lifecycle as an additional framework to walk through the various system components that handle the data, or use requirements and design artifacts, such as use cases, goal diagrams or data flow models. For example, Figure 2-4 presents a basic use case template instantiated as a retail website that links customer purchase histories to the customer's social network to personalize promotions of the retailer's products to the customer's friends.[17] This characterization identifies the primary actor (the friend) and assumes that the secondary actor (the original customer who bought the product) is no longer of issue. Because use cases may focus on the primary functional intent (e.g., to promote products), a privacy analyst may need to modify or extend the use case to include additional information about who may be harmed; in this case, the original customer.

Figure 2-4: Example Use Case for Performing Characterization

Name	Personalized Customer Promotions
Description	The system shall share a customer's product purchase with people in his or her social network, called friends
Primary Actor	Friends in the customer's social network
Precondition	The customer has purchased a product
Trigger	The customer's friend visits a product previously purchased by the customer

Fortunately, the choice of risk model may determine the amount of additional context that is required during the characterization stage. For example, the contextual integrity heuristic specifically targets the human-computer interactions between the system and its environment. These interactions include the various stakeholders that interact with each other and the norms that govern those interactions. Under contextual integrity, the original customer may expect that the retailer may use his or her purchase information only for the purpose of completing the transaction and will not share this information and the customer's identity with third parties, even friends. Similarly, the S/OD and taxonomy of privacy problems models both concern the data subject and his or her perceptions of privacy risk. Accounting for those perceptions will require characterizing stakeholders outside the system's physical boundary and data flows, but will enable the next stage in risk analysis.

2.2.2.2 Threat, Vulnerability and Event Identification

Risk models may emphasize a particular reference point in the form of threats, vulnerabilities or adverse events. In practice, vulnerabilities and events tend to be more commonly used than threats. The latter become risks when associated with some notion of impact and likelihood (possibly based on threats and/or vulnerabilities). To the extent the events or vulnerabilities are specified, each one acts as an initial fixed or quasi-fixed point from which the analysis can extend out to identify and incorporate the specifics of the other elements for a given system. For example, once we know a given event, we can work backward to identify the relevant vulnerabilities and threats. The S/OD and taxonomy of privacy problems models emphasize adverse privacy events (what can go wrong), whereas the contextual integrity heuristic emphasizes vulnerabilities (which information norms can be disrupted). Thus, the analyst begins by identifying the elements that correspond to the privacy risk model in use.

Returning to the use case in Figure 2-4, the events may be characterized using Solove's taxonomy. This includes disclosure and exposure, depending on what products the customer has purchased. Products that are linked to lifestyle choices or that are used to treat misbehaving bodily functions, for example, could lead to harassment or embarrassment when revealed to the customer's coworkers. Alternatively, the coworkers may view this information as an unwanted intrusion. The use case also leads to an appropriation event, because the company is using the customer's likeness to market the product. In all cases, the threat is the implementation of the use case wherein the customer would not want to be associated with certain products.

Once the risk model's elements have been identified, the privacy risk analyst then proceeds to complete the risk analysis. If vulnerabilities were identified under the contextual integrity heuristic, then the analyst proceeds to identify the threats that seek to exploit those vulnerabilities and the adverse events that would result from a successful exploitation. At this point, combining multiple privacy risk models that complement each other may be helpful. After identifying a vulnerability, the analyst may, for example, apply the taxonomy of privacy problems to discover potential events.

2.2.2.3 Risk Assessment

Risk assessment is the process of assigning likelihoods and impacts to previously identified events, which yields risks. Likelihood may be expressed as an ordinal value (low, medium, severe) or as a numerical value (0.0–1.0). Likelihood is sometimes assumed to mean the probability that the vulnerability would be exploited to yield the given event. Where specific threats can exploit specific vulnerabilities, the likelihood associated with that risk is significant. Where a vulnerability does not align with any specific threat, the likelihood may be less significant. The ability to identify threats depends on an analyst's knowledge of a variety of political, social and economic issues that change over time (i.e., threats may be functionally required by the system to process information, or they may be motivated by politics, social groups or economics). Thus, the inability to identify a specific threat doesn't imply that the threat does not or will not eventually exist.

While impact may also be expressed numerically, this is a subjective judgment in the absence of metrics such as calculated or statistical financial cost or loss. Using a numerical scale for purely subjective judgments could be an exercise in misleading or false precision. Similarly, likelihood could be treated as a numerical value as well in the absence of any objective basis for its estimation. It can be argued that a less misleading approach is to use ordinal values to measure likelihood and impact. However, this can produce its own problems when attempting to "multiply" or "average" these values to score the risk. Depending on the circumstances, assigning a combined ordinal value of low, moderate or severe may be used to represent a combined judgment regarding the level of concern merited by the risk, though caution should be used when viewing these measures as ground truth.

In Table 2-1, we present a list of threats, adverse events and risk scores. Some threats to personal information arise from conducting normal business, such as determining whether a person is an adult, whereas other threats are external, such as law enforcement access. Still other threats arise from the imperfect design of systems (e.g., restoring from outdated backups as a patch to a periodically failing system or database). The events in Table 2-1 were identified using Solove's taxonomy of privacy problems as the risk model: Other events could have been identified for these same threats. For example, law enforcement access to data could also produce insecurity (exposure to possible future harm due to the failure to protect a person's information) and secondary use (using information for purposes other than those for which it was originally collected).

Table 2-1: Example Assessments That Link Threats and Events to Risk Scores

Threat	Adverse Event	Risk
Law enforcement may request that we disclose a user's IP address from web server logs	*Identification:* The disclosure allows others to link pseudo-anonymous comments to a person's real identity	Low
We collect a person's date of birth to determine if he or she is over 18, which is a condition of using our service	*Interrogation:* The person may not wish to provide date of birth	Moderate
We periodically refresh our financial database from weekly backups when we encounter a system crash	*Distortion:* The backup may introduce data errors that misrepresent a person's financial history	Severe

We now discuss how to respond to identified risks.

2.2.2.4 Risk Response Determination

After the risks have been assessed, the privacy risk analyst can determine how to respond. The type of response must account for real-world resource constraints, such as time, money and people in addition to the risks themselves. Recall, the analyst has four choices when responding to a risk:

- *Accept the Risk:* If the risk is low, then it may be reasonable and necessary to accept the risk. In Table 2-1, if the disclosure reveals only consumer reviews about products, then privacy risk of identification may be minimal. The person may suffer from other risks—for example, the risk of being connected to a crime for reasons outside the scope of the system. However, accepting the risk may make sense for a low-level risk. Another reason to accept risk is when the cost to transfer, mitigate or avoid the risk is too high.

- *Transfer the Risk:* If there are other entities that can do a better job managing the risk, transferring the risk may be the best option. For example, using third-party services that can manage payroll, payment and other financial services using high privacy and security standards may be preferable to developing an equivalent system from the ground up. This is especially important when using a compliance model, where these third-party services have been engineered to conform to specific privacy laws, such as the variety of data breach notification laws. While the original organization may still bear ~~ultimate legal responsibility~~, it has nonetheless transferred relevant risks in part to the third-party service, as it is the service that must contend with those risks at an ~~operational level~~.

- *Mitigate the Risk:* Mitigation is the best option when the IT developer can implement privacy controls that reduce the risk. This may be through a software component or through a change in business processes. In Table 2-1, the distortion risk may be mitigated by performing daily backups and consistency checks on the data or remedied by allowing the person access to correct errors in his or her data. We discuss this mitigation in more detail in the following section.

- *Avoid the Risk:* Avoidance occurs when one can avoid the adverse event by changing the system design or business process. In Table 2-1, the interrogation risk can be avoided by ~~replacing the function~~ that collects the person's date of birth with a function that asks a yes/no question: "Are you over 18 years of age?" This change is sufficient to address the original requirement (determine if the user is a legal adult by local law) and avoid the specific event of probing to reveal a person's date of birth or exact age.

2.2.2.5 Risk Control Implementation

Risk controls fall into three categories: *administrative controls*, which govern an organization's business practices; *technical controls*, which govern software processes and data; and *physical controls*, which govern physical access to hard copies of data and the systems that process and store electronic copies. In privacy, example administrative controls include:

- Appointing a privacy officer who is responsible for organization-wide privacy practices

- Developing and documenting privacy and security procedures

- Conducting personnel training in privacy

- Creating an inventory of personal information to track data practices

We discuss administrative controls in more detail in Chapter 7, which covers governance, risk and compliance.

Technical controls target information systems and should be the focus of IT developers in designing privacy-preserving systems. These include:

- Implementing access control mechanisms
- Auditing information access
- Encrypting sensitive data
- Managing individual consent
- Posting privacy notices

The National Institute of Standards and Technology (NIST) publishes a Privacy Control Catalog for U.S. federal information systems as Appendix J in the Special Publication 800-53, Revision 4.[18] This control list covers both administrative and technical controls. In addition to other privacy standards, such as the Generally Accepted Privacy Principles (GAPP), the privacy analyst may employ these controls as a standard means to mitigate several classes of privacy risk. For example, the NIST Privacy Control IP-1 on consent requires the system to provide individuals a mechanism to authorize the collection of their personal information, where feasible. This control may address a class of adverse privacy events, such as exclusion, which occurs when the individual does not have knowledge of, or participate in, the use of their personal information. If this use is made overt and the individual is permitted to authorize the use of his or her information for this purpose, then this risk to the individual is mitigated.

2.2.2.6 Monitor and Review

Information systems evolve over time and so do the risks to personal privacy. Thus, it is imperative that privacy risk management frameworks include periodic reviews. An effective framework includes automatic triggers that require a subsequent review before a change can be initiated. In systems engineering, these triggers may be linked to modifying critical program code segments or configuring critical services. For example, before modifying any consent mechanism or before adding new tables to a personal information database, a privacy risk review is required.

In addition, there is a need to monitor the existing set of controls. This requires collecting sufficient information to trigger awareness of a control failure or probing individuals to test their knowledge of failures. Certain privacy controls may serve this goal directly, including personnel training controls that include performance tests or assessments, and complaint collection and resolution mechanisms that may surface an individual's report of a privacy harm.

2.3 Requirements Engineering for Privacy

Requirements describe constraints on software systems and their relationship to precise specifications that change over time and across software families.[19] For IT professionals, understanding and applying privacy requirements is important both when creating new system designs and when selecting a proprietary or open source component to address a particular problem.

Whether the requirements are formally documented in a software requirements specification (SRS), expressed in a mathematical model or briefly summarized in an Agile user story, requirements provide engineers an early opportunity to capture critical privacy properties prior to embarking on design and other deep technological commitments. Barry Boehm, an expert on the economics of software engineering, found that the cost to fix a requirements defect during implementation increases a hundredfold over fixing the defect during the requirements or design phase.[20] This guideline is also true for privacy: Any changes to reengineer a software application in response to a known privacy threat will be more costly than addressing the privacy threat during requirements engineering. Thus, it is critical for engineers to capture privacy requirements by participating in the community of practice and monitoring existing sources of information about privacy.

In this section, we will review techniques for acquiring, eliciting, managing and analyzing privacy requirements.

2.3.1 Documenting Requirements

Requirements engineers often distinguish between two types of requirements: functional and nonfunctional. Functional requirements describe a specific function of the intended information system. A product tester can evaluate a running system to verify the following functional requirements: "The system shall provide a link to a privacy notice at the bottom of every page" and "the system shall encrypt credit card numbers using AES 256-bit encryption." Nonfunctional requirements describe a constraint or property of the system that an engineer can trace to functional requirements or design elements. Examples of nonfunctional requirements: "The system shall not disclose personal information without authorization or consent" and "the system shall clearly communicate any privacy preferences to the data subject." In the first nonfunctional requirement, the designer must trace this requirement to all uses of personal information to ensure authorization or consent is verified before disclosure; in the second requirement, the analyst must trace this requirement to any functional requirements that are governed by the data subject's privacy preferences (e.g., the use of user e-mail addresses or activities for marketing purposes). In addition to a requirements statement, the engineer should provide context for understanding the requirement and attempt to answer any critical questions to aid designers in applying the requirement to their designs.

Requirements are collected in an SRS that uses a standard format or template for presentation. IT professionals can reuse and adapt existing formats to their purposes. Figure 2-5 illustrates a generic example of a requirements template that describes an authorization and consent requirement. The template header includes summary information, such as a unique requirement ID that may be used to cross-reference the requirement, the requirement statement in the optative mood "shall," the author who can be contacted for additional information, the revision number that is used to track changes to the requirement, the release date

Figure 2-5: Example of an Instantiated Requirements Template

Requirement ID:	REQ-68
Requirement Statement:	The system shall not disclose personal information without authorization and consent
Author:	Sam Brown, System Specialist III
Revision:	1.1
Release Date:	January 1, 2014
Keywords:	Confidentiality, Consent, Access
Legal Compliance:	HIPAA Privacy Rule §164.506, §164.508; EU Directive 95/46/EC (30)

Scenario Description:

Whenever an *agent* attempts to access *personal information*, the system will check that the agent is authorized to access this information based on the agent's assigned *user role* or the *data purpose* for which the data will be used. If consent is required prior to disclosing this information to this recipient, the system will check that the *data subject* has previously provided consent for disclosure based on this *user role* or *data purpose*.

Design Assumptions:

The system maintains a list of approved user roles and data purposes.

The system maintains linkages between data subjects, types of personal information and consent decisions and data purposes.

and the keywords that can be used to identify related requirements across the SRS document. In this example, the legal compliance section provides legal cross-references to related regulations that this requirement attempts to fulfill. These and similar cross-references are typically included in trace matrices, which we discuss in Section 2.3.3 and which are used to show conformance among various software artifacts. The template body describes a scenario in which the requirement appears and several design assumptions that underlie a successful implementation of the requirement.

In addition to requirements, the SRS document includes a technical glossary that provides standard definitions to be reused across requirements. Figure 2-6 presents a sample glossary for requirement REQ-68 above: The term *agent* may be defined as a user or process, to denote that this requirement applies to both types of objects in the system design. This glossary also contains the term **personal information**, which is refined into a list of appropriate data types: the combination of a person's name and address, or the person's e-mail address, telephone number or credit card number. In addition to standardizing terminology, the technical glossary provides the engineer a mechanism to collect and negotiate descriptions of the system in text before committing to more specific descriptions in design and source code. Designers can ask critical questions based on definitions in the glossary, such as "Should all requirements be applied to personal information equally, or should a separate category of information, called sensitive personal information, be created for a subset of these requirements, such as encryption requirements?"

Figure 2-6: Example of a Requirements Glossary Used to Standardize Terms

Agent means a user or process that performs a function within the system.

Data purpose means the approved work-related activities for which data will be collected, used or disclosed. The complete set of approved roles or purposes consists of product or service fulfillment, internal operations, fraud prevention, legal compliance, first-party marketing, third-party marketing and product research.

Data subject means the identified or identifiable, natural person about whom information is related (see EU Directive 95/46/EC, Article 2, paragraph (a)).

Personal data is any information that relates to a data subject. This includes the data subject's first and last name, physical or mailing address, electronic mail address, telephone number or credit card number.

Requirements can be written to be reusable across multiple systems. Reusable repositories of privacy requirements allow the area specialist to coordinate standard approaches across their organization and to discern strategies for handling exceptions, such as a novel technology that deviates from traditional norms. As we discuss in Section 2.4, designers translate requirements into system designs and consider alternative designers to fulfill requirements. For example, designers may distinguish between different types of consent. Under a website's privacy policy, certain types of information may be collected, such as browsing history, whereby use of the site corresponds to passive consent. In this context, the consent record is inferred from the website's access log: A user agent request for a web page that is linked to the privacy policy corresponds to consent to collect information described in the policy, such as the visitor's IP address, browser type, operating system and so on. Alternatively, the designer may choose to use an explicit checkbox at the start of a transaction with at least two design choices: (1) recording the date and time of the selection in a database or (2) restricting the transaction to those who select the checkbox, in which case evidence of the collected data subsequent to the checkbox can exist only if the checkbox was selected (i.e., the checkbox is required and not optional, and no other workflow leads to the data collection). The decision about which approach is best may depend on the need for retaining and exhibiting evidence of consent to auditors.

In addition to textual documentation, privacy requirements may be specified using visual models. These include process diagrams, information flow diagrams, role and permission matrices and state diagrams, to name a few.[21] These models serve to make relationships between the objects of discourse (actors, data, systems and processes) explicit and enable additional analysis. We describe a few analytics that rely on these models in Section 2.3.4.

2.3.2 Acquiring and Eliciting Requirements

Privacy requirements may be acquired from multiple, diverse sources. This includes eliciting requirements from stakeholders using interviews, case studies and focus groups, as well as by extracting or "mining" text documents—such as contracts, standards, laws, newspapers and blogs—for requirements. There are standard elicitation techniques for working with subject-matter experts. Interview and survey techniques have been established for conducting surveys and focus groups.[22] In addition to elicitation, the privacy standards, such as the FIPPs and the NIST Privacy Control Catalog, serve as a source of requirements (see Chapter 1). For example, the use limitation principle stating that "personal data should not be disclosed, made available or otherwise used for purposes other than those specified" may be directly adapted to a nonfunctional requirement using the template above. Similarly, NIST Privacy Control AR-8, which requires organizations to "keep an accurate accounting of disclosures of information held in each system of records under [their] control," can be adapted to any IT system and not only to those systems governed by the U.S. Privacy Act of 1974.[23]

While standards and guidelines are formatted for easier consumption by software developers, the format of less structured texts, such as laws and regulations, requires analysis to infer requirements. Regulations are publicly available, and IT professionals can work with their legal counsel to identify relevant privacy regulations that govern their industry. Regulations may be generic or specific in their description of principles and processes that software engineers should employ. *Legal standards* refer to nonfunctional requirements or properties that cut across a system's design and functionality.[24] The HIPAA Privacy Rule includes the minimum necessary standard, which requires covered entities, such as hospitals and health insurance companies, to disclose only the minimum information necessary to complete a transaction (see HIPAA §164.502). Alternatively, *legal rules* describe specific steps that should be taken to ensure compliance with a privacy law. Consider the following excerpt from the Children's Online Privacy Protection Rule (COPPA Rule):[25]

§312.5 Parental Consent.

(a) *General requirements.*

    (1) *An operator is required to obtain verifiable parental consent before any collection, use, and/or disclosure of personal information from children . . .*

(b) *Mechanisms for verifiable parental consent.*

    (1) *An operator must make reasonable efforts to obtain verifiable parental consent . . .*

    (2) *Methods to obtain verifiable parental consent that satisfy the requirements of this paragraph include: providing a consent form to be signed by the parent and returned to the operator by postal mail or facsimile; requiring a parent to use a credit card in connection with a transaction; having a parent call a toll-free telephone number staffed by trained personnel; using a digital certificate that uses public key technology; and using e-mail accompanied by a PIN or password obtained through one of the verification methods listed in this paragraph.*

In this excerpt, the COPPA Rule describes specific steps to obtain consent before collection, including details about approved methods for obtaining consent. These rules frequently include statements with modal verbs, such as *may* and *must*, which indicate discretionary and mandatory

requirements, respectively.[26] In addition, they contain terms of
definitions are needed to determine legal coverage; in the exa   *Level*
"verifiable parental consent" is a term of art that is defined in
§312.5(b)(2). From this example, a requirements engineer can extrac~
or "mine" the regulatory ~~text to yield a corresponding requirement~~. The
following requirement was derived by tracing phrases from paragraphs (a)
(1), (b)(1) and (b)(2):

> **REQ-72:**   The system shall obtain verifiable parental consent
> by having the user complete a credit card transaction prior to
> collecting a child's personal information.

PCI-DSS.

In this requirement, the engineer commits to one of the five
mechanisms permitted by COPPA §312.5(b)(2) in the above excerpt.

Regulatory enforcement actions, newspapers and blogs provide insight
into "what went wrong" when a system fails to meet a privacy requirement.
Travis D. Breaux and David L. Baumer performed a ~~retrospective~~ analysis
~~on the FTC's regulatory enforcement actions~~.[27] This analysis yields several
security requirements that could have been used to avoid system failures
that violated consumer privacy policies and the Gramm-Leach-Bliley Act.
Alternatively, the IT professional or privacy area specialist can monitor
newspapers and blogs for early indications of potential privacy risks. For
example, the International Association of Privacy Professionals' *Daily
Dashboard* provides daily updates on emerging legislation and events in
the press. In addition, the *Wall Street Journal's* "What They Know" series
periodically publishes in-depth analysis covering privacy-invasive practices,
such as online trackers, and new technologies that introduce new,
previously unforeseen privacy risks. By watching what other companies do,
and how the press and the public interpret these privacy-related practices,
software engineers can avoid privacy pitfalls in their own systems.

2.3.3 Managing Privacy Requirements Using Trace Matrices

The requirements engineer uses trace matrices for encoding relationships
between requirements and other software artifacts. Each trace link has a
special type that describes the meaning of the link. For example, a trace
link from a requirement to a privacy law means the requirement *implements*
the law, whereas a trace link to a design element, such as a role-based access
control mechanism, means the requirement *is implemented by* the design
element. These trace links are many-to-many relations, as a requirement
can simultaneously have different relationships to multiple laws, design
elements and test cases. Consider the four requirements numbered REQ-32
through REQ-35:

REQ-32: The system shall only disclose the minimum information required to complete a transaction

REQ-33: The system shall restrict uses of personal information to only those purposes for which the information was collected

REQ-34: The system shall only disclose information for purposes that the data subject has provided explicit or implicit consent

REQ-35: The system shall provide law enforcement access to personal information by administrative subpoena

In Figure 2-7, we present a trace matrix that links the above requirements to privacy laws and standards (listed down the first column) and to software requirements (listed along the top row). Where a trace link means the requirement implements the standard or law, an "X" appears in the matrix. We observe that some requirements implement multiple standards and laws, such as REQ-32, which implements both the HIPAA Privacy Rule's minimum necessary standard and the Organisation for Economic Co-operation and Development's use limitation principle. Other standards or laws may be implemented by a conjunction of multiple requirements, such as the GAPP standard 5.2.1, which simultaneously limits the uses of personal information to specific purposes (REQ-33) and requires consent for all disclosures (REQ-34), but has an exception for law enforcement purposes (REQ-35).

Figure 2-7: Example Trace Matrix Linking Regulations to Requirements

Privacy Laws and Standards	REQ-32	REQ-33	REQ-34	REQ-35	. . .
Data Minimization					
HIPAA Privacy Rule, 45 CFR §164.502(b), Minimum Necessary Standard	X				
OECD Use Limitation Principle	X	X			
GAPP 5.2.1 Use of personal information		X	X	X	
Government Access					
Stored Communications Act, 18 U.S.C. §2703 (b)(1)(B)(i)				X	
Gramm-Leach-Bliley Act Privacy Rule, 16 CFR §313.15(a)(4)				X	

Because software engineers and legal experts must interpret standards and laws when creating trace links in the trace matrix, the engineer may keep track of the rationale for each link to record these interpretations for future reference. When conducting a traceability exercise, one can use the rationale to answer the question, "Why is this trace link important?" Figure 2-8 presents an example where the rationale is recorded for REQ-35, which allows law enforcement access to personal information by administrative subpoena. The trace link rationale for GAPP 5.2.1 explains that this link is an exception, which describes how requirement REQ-35 should be viewed in the context of REQ-33 and REQ-34. In advanced trace matrices, these exceptions are encoded into separate tables to ensure that a designer who implements REQ-33 integrates the exception into his or her design. The trace link rationale for the Gramm-Leach-Bliley Act (GLBA) Privacy Rule includes the cross-reference from the GLBA to the Right to Financial Privacy Act of 1978 that the engineer had to follow to discover this exception.

Figure 2-8: Example Trace Link Rationale

Source	Target	Rationale Description
REQ-35	GAPP 5.2.1	The GAPP 5.2.1 provides an exception for any disclosure that is required by law or regulation.
REQ-35	GLBA Privacy Rule, 16 CFR §313.15(a)(4)	An administrative subpoena is permitted by cross-reference to the Right to Financial Privacy Act, 12 U.S.C. §3405.

While the examples shown above cover upstream tracing of requirements to their origin in laws and regulations, separate trace matrices are also used to trace requirements to downstream artifacts, such as software designs, source code and test cases. In privacy, trace matrices should also trace requirements to user agreements, such as privacy policies, terms of use (ToU) agreements, end-user license agreements (EULA) and so on. Whenever a requirement or IT system component changes, the trace matrices should be consulted to determine the impact of the change on other parts of the system, including privacy policies.

2.3.4 Analyzing Privacy Requirements

Requirements analysis describes activities to identify and improve the quality of requirements by analyzing the system and deployment environment for completeness and consistency. This includes identifying relevant stakeholders to ensure no one was overlooked and examining user stories and requirements for ambiguities, conflicts and inconsistencies. In this section, we focus on two activities that concern privacy: completeness arguments and threat analysis.

2.3.4.1 Developing Privacy Completeness Arguments

For systems of any reasonable size, requirements documents are never complete: There is always some description of the intended system that has been overlooked or only partially described. This incompleteness provides designers flexibility, because they are able to "fill in the gaps" with different technical approaches based on prevailing technology and other business needs. However, some omissions lead to unwanted behavior, such as privacy harms. To improve requirements quality in general, we recommend constructing completeness arguments that ensure limited aspects of the requirements are complete. These arguments are constructed using step-wise analyses to ensure that a finite list of concerns has been reviewed in its entirety. For privacy, this includes reviewing requirements trace matrices to ensure that all privacy standards, guidelines and laws have been traced to a requirement. Completeness arguments can be used to cover every step in the data lifecycle for especially sensitive data types, and to expand one's interpretation of a privacy law or regulation, which we now discuss.

Is tracing complete? Completeness arguments can be constructed for privacy policies, wherein the argument determines whether the tracing is complete from privacy policy statements to software artifacts that implement those statements. A privacy policy is a promise to users that their personal information and their privacy will be respected according to certain rules. Misalignment of privacy policies with information practices is a great source of concern and can lead to privacy violations.[28] Goal-based analysis can be applied to privacy policies to identify protections, which are statements that aim to protect a user's privacy, and vulnerabilities, which are statements that threaten a user's privacy.[29] Consider this except from Google's Privacy Policy, which was last modified on June 24, 2013:[30]

> We may collect device-specific information (such as your hardware model, operating system version, unique device identifiers, and mobile network information including phone number). Google may associate your device identifiers or phone number with your Google Account.
> . . .
> We encrypt many of our services using SSL.
> We offer you two step verification when you access your Google Account, and a Safe Browsing feature in Google Chrome.

The first two statements in the excerpt describe a general permission allowing Google to collect device-specific information, such as mobile phone numbers, and link this information to a user's Google account. These statements are potential vulnerabilities, because they enable surveillance and tracking of a user's movement and linking to other information through the account. For example, this vulnerability enables Google's passive collection of the mobile phone unique device identifiers of Android and iPhone users when the user accesses wireless routers, as well as Google's active collection of mobile phone numbers when users log in to their Google account online.[31] Any changes to the policy affecting these collections should be traced to these technologies, and vice versa.

The last two statements describe protections. The use of the secure sockets layer (SSL) to encrypt communications, such as access to Gmail, and an optional two-step verification that consists of (1) supplying the username and password and (2) supplying a code sent to the user by text message or voicemail. The first statement improves confidentiality and reduces the likelihood that a third party can read a user's e-mail when he or she uses an unencrypted wireless connection. The second statement provides users a higher level of assurance that third parties cannot access their account without also obtaining access to their mobile phone or to the wireless networks used to send messages to their mobile phones.

Protections and vulnerabilities can be traced to other downstream software artifacts to promote alignment between the privacy policy and system functionality and behavior. Whenever privacy policies change, due to changing laws or new business practices, these changes should be propagated into the trace matrices to determine what aspects of the system have been affected by the policy change. When policies are managed in this way, the IT developer can argue that a software artifact accounts for each privacy statement in the company's privacy policy. However, the issue of quality, or the issue of how well that artifact satisfies the policy statement, may require a more advanced, risk-based argument.

Is the lifecycle complete? Completeness arguments can be constructed for a specific data lifecycle, wherein the argument asserts that *every step in the data lifecycle was visited* for a particular data element or dataset. At each step in the data lifecycle for a specific data type, the engineer considers whether the data type requires special consideration. Does a shopping history have special retention requirements, for example, based on either business needs (to service refunds or warranties) or law enforcement needs (to investigate crimes)? The IT developer may choose to develop only these arguments for especially sensitive data elements, such as financial account numbers or detailed purchase histories. To construct the argument, the IT developer begins by (1) selecting the data element to trace and (2) for each data lifecycle stage, identifying requirements in the SRS document that cover the data element. Figure 2-9 illustrates the outcome of this tracing for the data element "credit card numbers" in a fictitious system that processes online shopping orders. The lifecycle stages appear in the first column, followed by the ID and Requirement Statement in subsequent columns. Because requirements describe data at different levels of abstraction (from data elements to datasets), the IT developer must map the data element of interest to the datasets that contain this element. The technical glossary can aid the engineer when performing this mapping, assuming that terminology has been standardized across the SRS. In Figure 2-9, the italicized phrases for customer orders, customer's payment method, billing information and credit card numbers all refer to data or datasets that contain a credit card number.

This example analysis yields two interesting findings for the IT developer. First, the credit card number is not observably shared with third parties, because no requirements that map to data disclosures were discovered. Unwanted disclosures may still occur, but this finding suggests such disclosures are not required. Second, the need to retain billing information is potentially too broad (see REQ-63). While billing information is needed to process certain requests, such as refunds or warranties, this does not include the credit card number. For refunds, the company may retain an approved one-way hash of the credit card number and ask the customer to resupply the number only when he or she requests a refund. Thus, the IT developer can modify REQ-63 to exclude the credit card number from this retention requirement, and introduce a new requirement to retain only the one-way hash of the credit card number.

Figure 2-9: Example Matrix for a Data Lifecycle Completeness Argument for "Credit Card Numbers"

Lifecycle Stage	ID	Requirement Statement
Collection	REQ-31	The system shall process *customer orders* and ship products to customers within 3 business days.
Use	REQ-47	The billing agent shall charge the purchase amount using the *customer's payment method.*
Disclosure	None	
Retention	REQ-63	The system shall retain *billing information* for 2 years.
Destruction	REQ-89	The system shall destroy *credit card numbers* immediately after completion of the payment transaction.

Is our legal interpretation complete? Completeness arguments can be constructed for compliance with regulatory requirements. While it is impossible to completely cover every prospective interpretation by an auditor, regulator or judge, there are steps that engineers can take to broaden the scope of their interpretations to capture missed requirements. Travis D. Breaux et al. identified five patterns to analyze legal requirements extracted from laws and regulations to improve completeness of the SRS.[32] These patterns were discovered through empirical analysis of a large manufacturer's SRS and a national technology law. The patterns are applied directly to requirements statements acquired from either laws or standards and can yield new, potentially missing requirements for the system. The patterns are presented below with examples from U.S. data breach notification laws.

Remove or generalize preconditions. Preconditions include phrases in a requirement statement that must be satisfied before a requirement is applied in the system design. These phrases can be recognized by if and when keywords. Removing or generalizing preconditions for obligations and prohibitions causes the statement to generalize; in other words, the engineer must apply the requirement to more situations than were originally intended. A more general form of this pattern is to apply a requirement to a broader class of stakeholders than legally required, or to a broader class of data and information types. For example, Nevada law governing the security of personal information requires businesses that conduct business in Nevada to take reasonable measures to destroy personal information.[33] Applying this pattern to this requirement would entail generalizing this requirement so that it applies to any personal information, regardless of whether the information concerns practices conducted in Nevada or any other state. This pattern has the benefit of streamlining business practices at the cost of extending those practices to other situations where they may not be otherwise required by law or standards.

Preclude preconditions, assume exceptions. In legal compliance, some privacy requirements concern specialized situations that can be avoided by writing product or service requirements that assume the exception, which may be a higher standard of care. For example, the Virginia data breach notification law defines a "breach of security of the system" as unauthorized access to unencrypted computerized data.[34] In the event that an organization detects a data breach, notices are sent to consumers and others to comply with this Virginia law only if the data was not encrypted.

By ensuring that this data is encrypted in transit and in storage, the IT developer *assumes the exception* and defines the system as not covered by this legal requirement. Privacy scholars have also called this exception the "encryption safe harbor."

Ground legal terms in the domain. Legal terms determine when a privacy regulation applies and are often purposely written to be abstract so as to make laws flexible and adaptable to new situations or technologies. Based on a company's products and services, these terms may be grounded in industry-specific terminology or product or trademarked names. For example, California Civil Code §1798.29 requires protecting access codes that can be used to access a personal financial account. This code chapter does not define "access code" or "financial account," thus leaving the interpretation to IT developers and their legal counsel. In computing, accounts that allow users to conduct financial transactions during routine use of the system may be subject to these rules. As new technologies arise, traditional interpretations of banking are evolving. In 2008, the U.S. Internal Revenue Service explored the tax implications of virtual currencies in online games.[35] If the IRS determines these virtual currencies and other property to be taxable, would California state data breach notification law cover the user's account and password? IT developers should consider the various ways these legal definitions apply to their systems and document when these terms both increase and decrease their perception of coverage by privacy laws.

Refine by refrainment. Privacy laws often describe goals to be achieved or obligations about what a covered organization must meet. In software systems, however, there are activities that can create obstacles to compliance or yield privacy-threatening outcomes that are not explicitly prohibited by the law. This pattern concerns identifying what should not occur as a means to reinforce compliance with mandatory privacy requirements. Under Code of Virginia §18.2-186.6(A), the act of stealing the cryptographic keys that can be used to decrypt encrypted personal information is not included in the definition of a security breach. However, because this outcome can enable a privacy-threatening scenario, wherein a data thief can now decrypt encrypted personal information, the IT developers can choose to adopt a refrainment, or prohibition, that requires that systems not make these keys accessible to unauthorized users. By expressing this prohibition explicitly, IT developers can conduct analysis on the system to check whether the design violates this requirement.

Reveal the regulatory goal. The rules in privacy laws serve to achieve a broader privacy goal or norm. For example, a privacy goal may be to protect an individual from public embarrassment by an unwanted disclosure, or to protect an individual's freedom to travel without fear of excessive surveillance. While an IT developer can seek to "comply with the letter of the law," the alternative is to comply with the goal of the law to acquire longer-term benefits, and often the area specialist can help identify these goals. By identifying the regulatory goal and then broadly applying this goal to their systems, IT developers can discover new requirements that are not described in a law. These new requirements may reflect novel technologies in their systems that were not previously foreseen by regulators, or they may leverage emerging interpretations of privacy goals that did not exist when the original regulation was written. This approach may have the added benefit of aligning these technologies with broader privacy expectations of users, or of heading off new regulation earlier in the software engineering lifecycle. For example, treating online gaming accounts as virtual financial accounts and sending out data-breach notices in accordance with privacy law may benefit users. The users can take steps to protect those accounts and review account histories for suspicious activity, which is consistent with how users react to more traditional financial accounts.

2.3.4.2 Identifying Privacy Threats

IT developers use threat analysis to identify risks to the system based on concrete scenarios. Threat analysis considers the negative outcomes enabled by a threat agent. While this analysis has grown out of security engineering, the same techniques may be used to detect privacy harms, such as Daniel Solove's harms described in Section 2.2.1.4. There are several examples of security threat analysis artifacts and methods available to the engineer, such as anti-goals and misuse and abuse cases, that can be adapted to privacy.[36]

Anti-goals are an attacker's own goals or malicious obstacles to a system.[37] Goal-oriented analysis to identify anti-goals begins with the engineer identifying the system's positive goals, before identifying anti-goals that describe how an attacker could limit the system's ability to maintain or achieve the positive goals. For example, in a hospital, an electronic health records system has the goal of ensuring that doctors and nurses access patient medical records only for authorized purposes. A prospective anti-goal includes a nurse who accesses a patient medical record to steal Social Security numbers or to reveal the name and gender of a celebrity's expected or newborn baby.[38] The procedure begins as follows:

(1) Identify the anti-goals that obstruct relevant privacy goals, such as confidentiality and integrity goals; (2) identify the attacker agents who would benefit from each anti-goal; (3) for each attacker agent and anti-goal pair, elicit the attacker's higher-level goal that explains why he or she would want to achieve this anti-goal (this step continues in a series of how and why questions to elaborate the anti-goal graph); (4) derive anti-models that identify the attacker, object of the attack and anti-goals; and finally, (5) operationalize the anti-model in terms of potential capabilities that the attacker agent may use in this scenario.

In Figure 2-10, we illustrate an example anti-goal hierarchy: The blocks represent goals and anti-goals, and the arrows point from subgoals that achieve higher-level goals. The initial anti-goal is that an insider, such as a nurse, steals a celebrity patient's birth record. This theft is intended to fulfill the attacker's goal of selling the record data to tabloids. To accomplish this attack, the insider must know the patient's name and doctor. The system designer, realizing this information cannot be restricted in the healthcare setting, chooses to use technology to mitigate this anti-goal by limiting access and logging accesses. While limiting access may prevent unauthorized insiders, the additional goal of logging access improves the chances of identifying authorized insiders after the attack has occurred.

Figure 2-10: Example Anti-Goal Hierarchy with Mitigating Goals

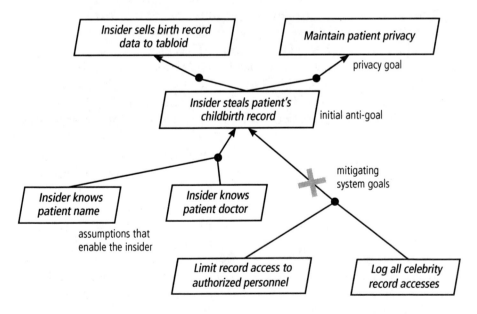

Goals and anti-goals are expressible in first-order logic to yield a more precise specification; however, this may be too cumbersome or time-consuming for broad adoption in every situation. For IT developers preferring a lighter-weight method, misuse and abuse cases were developed to adapt the existing use case methodology to describe negative intents. Similar to anti-goals, an abuse case describes a complete interaction between a user and the system that results in a harmful outcome.[39] Although misuse and abuse cases were originally developed to describe security attacks, the same notation can be used to describe potential privacy pitfalls. In Figure 2-11, we present an example misuse case. The white actor is the user, and the shaded actor is the misuser. It should not be assumed that the shaded actor in a privacy setting is a bad actor; rather, he or she is an actor who may be prone to misusing personal information in a privacy-threatening manner. Thus, the products and services provided by the misuser are often desirable by some actors, with privacy-threatening side effects that are undesirable by other actors. In the example, actions appear as ovals and are linked to other actions by arrows. The <<includes>> keyword indicates links to an action that is a part of another action, a similar meaning to how subgoals link to goals. The <<threatens>> keyword indicates when an action threatens another action, and the <<mitigates>> keyword indicates when an action serves to reduce the privacy threat from an action.

The Google Street View service is enabled by automobiles that are driven along public streets to capture images of streets and adjacent scenery. The project provides significant value to consumers, because they can use Street View to preview their routes on a computer before driving to their final destination. However, this service raised privacy concerns because unsuspecting individuals had their photographs taken in public and published online. In addition, the Street View automobile collects wireless packet data from public Wi-Fi networks to provide more precise geolocation to Wi-Fi users who access these networks. Many wireless routers remain installed in the same location, which improves the reliability of this dataset. As the Street View automobile passes by a public Wi-Fi network, the vehicle collects the wireless packet data to determine the wireless router's service set identification (SSID), or unique device identifier, and the media access control (MAC) addresses of any machines connected to the network. During this collection, the car also intentionally or unintentionally captures user login credentials that are sent over the network while a user accesses other Internet services, such as online shopping and e-mail accounts.

This collection threatens a mobile Internet user's goal to securely and privately bank online and send personal e-mails. In Figure 2-11, we capture this threat by coloring the action "Collect Wi-Fi packets" black. The IT developer can mitigate this threat by introducing a new action, "Sanitize packet data," which removes all unwanted, personally identifying data. What about the "Photograph streets" action? What actor does this affect and how would the engineer mitigate this threat?

Figure 2-11: Example Misuse Case Applied to Unwanted Collection of Wi-Fi Data

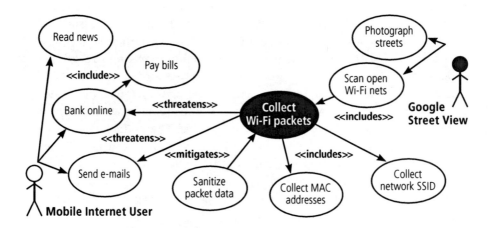

As previously mentioned, the "Photograph streets" action threatens the ability of individuals to perform daily activities without the fear of surveillance. These individuals might approach surveillance differently, either by dressing differently or avoiding the area altogether. To mitigate this threat, the engineer can use face detection technology to blur faces or allow individuals to report unwanted intrusions that can be remedied by blurring the threatening images.

2.4 High-Level Design

Whereas requirements describe what functional and nonfunctional behaviors the system is supposed to exhibit, designs begin to describe how the system is supposed to implement those behaviors. Designs are generally expressed using notations that define the processes and the data that those processes operate upon, as well as the high-level components that serve to group these processes and data together into categories of functionality. This includes the Unified Modeling Language (UML), which provides object-oriented diagrams, sequence diagrams, state diagrams and more for describing composition and temporal relationships between elements in the design.[40] Expert designers will use sophisticated architecture component-and-connector diagrams, architectural styles and other techniques to manage the complexity of working with larger and larger information systems.[41] In this section, we briefly introduce common IT architectures, quality attributes and design representations for reflecting on Privacy by Design.

2.4.1 Common IT Architectures

During the past several decades, architectural paradigms have emerged to describe the relationship among software components. These paradigms serve to orient developers by communicating how their contributions integrate with those components under development by other members of the development team. To orient developers, each architectural paradigm encapsulates a limited viewpoint of the overall system design. Figure 2-12 presents a simple illustration of the various paradigms that we cover here.

Figure 2-12: Common IT Architectures That Describe Different System Viewpoints

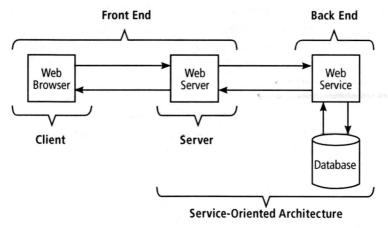

The front end is the part of the system that the user experiences. It includes user interface elements that mediate between the user and the rest of the system. This includes converting user actions into something that is understandable by the system and converting system responses into something understandable by the user. In Figure 2-12, the front end consists of a web browser that a user employs to search for a particular product on an e-commerce site. The search request is translated into a database query by the web server or web service. The response from the database is appropriately formatted and returned to the user for display by his or her browser. In this example, the database and any intermediary services that encapsulate the database and are not directly connected to the user's experience constitute the *back end*. The back end contains the information stores—products, orders, accounts, etc.—that underlie the activities that the user and the site owner engage in. The front end facilitates communication and manipulation of that information, but is essentially a façade, in the same way as any storefront.

Privacy affects these two viewpoints in different ways. Ensuring privacy in a system design requires designers to attend to the usability of the front end: Are users effectively notified about the company's privacy practices? Are users able to express their consent about the use of their information, for example, by effectively opting in or out of secondary uses? Poor design practices or frequently changing the front-end design can cause the user to become confused or to incorrectly express privacy preferences. Agile designs that rapidly evolve in response to competitive markets, such as Facebook's changing façade, can be accompanied by online tutorials, one-time introductions to features, and other contextual tips that help users navigate new and evolving privacy settings. Back-end components concern what data is collected, when data is used or for what purposes, to whom data is shared and how long data is retained, among other practices. In this case, designers may consider how to map the privacy principles, such as use limitation or data minimization principle, to their back-end services.

Client-server architecture describes the relationship between the *client*, which is typically a program that runs on a local computer, and the *server*, which is the program that runs on a remote computer. The client-server architecture commonly describes the relationship between a user's website and a remote website (see Figure 2-12). The designer may choose to define the boundary of the server to include any back-end services that facilitate the client-server interaction; however, the server is typically the computer process that responds to client requests. Thus, the back-end architecture may be composed of multiple client-server arrangements (e.g., a web server is a client to a database server).

One advantage of this architectural paradigm is that it allows the service to store computer data on the client side for the purpose of completing transactions. Because the web is asynchronous—that is, the hypertext transfer protocol (HTTP) does not maintain shared data between the client and server and each request is independent—designers use creative mechanisms to track client behavior across multiple HTTP requests through the use of cookies (see Chapter 5), or session identifiers used in each communication request from browser to server. Storing data on the client may introduce privacy risks if the client data is insecure, or if the storage of this data is not clear to the user and serves the purpose of surveillance or identification, when the user would otherwise prefer to remain anonymous. Session identifiers, when used, may be guessable or stolen, allowing an attacker to interact with the server as though he or she were the victim.

Service-oriented architectures are similar to client-server architectures in that they aim to decouple services from large-scale servers. This enables reuse and separation of concerns and, for increasingly larger systems, improved load balancing by allowing designers to replicate services across multiple machines. Last, *peer-to-peer architectures* are an extreme alternative to client-server architectures whereby each peer is both a client and a server. To enable this distributed scenario, peers often use a directory service to find other peers. This is how peer-to-peer networks, such as BitTorrent, operate. Peer-to-peer architectures can improve performance by reducing the need to work through intermediaries, but the emergent nature of the network allows for peers to be largely anonymous. Anonymity in this context is both a benefit to privacy and a burden, because peers may be malicious and users may be unsuspecting when they transfer their personal information to these anonymous intermediaries in the peer-to-peer network.

In addition to client-server architecture, a *plug-in-based architecture* can be used to extend an application with new features. Modern web browsers support plug-in-based architectures and application platforms, such as Facebook's Application Developer API and the Apple iOS or Android platforms, allow third-party developers to extend a user's experience with new programs, called apps. Plug-in-based architectures and especially app platforms can introduce new privacy risks for users. These risks emerge because the user has a direct relationship with the platform; the platform developer has a vested interest in protecting its user base to widen the adoption of the platform. For example, a user of an iPhone or Android phone has a relationship with Apple or Google, which owns, develops and maintains the platform. However, the platform owner has a third-party relationship with the app developer, who delivers the app to a repository, sometimes called a marketplace, from where the user can then acquire the app. To enable these apps to interact with the user and his or her data, the platform exposes services to the app. In the case of mobile phones, these services may include the user's location, contact list or address book, and mobile web browser history. Privacy risks arise when the app accesses information in a manner that is undesirable, either by violating the privacy policy of the platform or by exceeding the privileges required by the app. For designers, the challenge arises in how they enforce the user's privacy settings provided through the platform in the behavior of their services and the behaviors of the apps themselves. A recent enforcement case by the U.S. Federal Trade Commission highlights these risks.[42]

Cloud-based computing describes the shift of client-based services or services typically run on a company's Intranet to an off-site third party. "Clouds" refer to the collection of services, which may be accessible by anyone (public clouds), restricted to a particular organization (private clouds) or some hybrid of these two options. NIST defines multiple levels of cloud services: infrastructure as a service (IaaS), platform as a service (PaaS) and software as a service (SaaS).[43] Organizations may choose to outsource their infrastructure or hardware, and install, administer and maintain their own platforms or software. The challenge for privacy is that users of a cloud must relinquish control to the third party to protect their data. For example, a cloud provider could have access to data on the clouds that it operates, unless a sophisticated cryptographic scheme was used to decrypt the data once it returned to the client's intranet. Enforcement of privacy in clouds managed by third parties is typically achieved through contract language. In public clouds, users may be required to accept the terms and conditions or privacy policy of the cloud provider, whereas private clouds may be purchased and customized by the client to fit specific needs. A European company that wishes to purchase a private cloud operated in the United States, for example, may seek to use a model contract under Article 26(4) of Directive 95/46/EC of the European Parliament and the Council on the protection of individuals with regard to the processing of personal data and on the free movement of such data (the Data Protection Directive) to ensure that the cloud provider employed sufficient safeguards. Ultimately, it is the responsibility of the designer to ensure these safeguards are implemented through privacy and security controls in software and hardware.

Federated architectures and systems combine multiple distributed resources to be used together, while keeping these systems under the autonomous control of the system owners. Federated search, for example, enables a search to be performed across multiple distributed databases without integration of their content or without centralized control of the databases. Instead, the search query is decomposed and parceled out based on the logical organization of the constituent databases. Each database responds to its specific piece of the query, and the results are then integrated and presented as a single result. A more specific example of a federated system is a virtual data warehouse, in which a functional data warehouse can be developed without actually bringing together and integrating the data from multiple data sources. Integration in response to specific queries permits different policies to be applied to different collections of data and mitigates some privacy risks related to comprehensive aggregation. The privacy impact of federation concerns what information can be learned from aggregated data that was originally collected with the purpose of storing the data separately. This also can affect surveillance, as data points are linked together to track a person's behavior over time and across multiple, separate data sources.

2.4.2 Design Representations

Designers use notations to identify and organize various system elements and express critical relationships between these elements. This includes object models, which describe the discrete entities (servers, program modules, data elements, etc.), and process models and data flow diagrams, which describe the order of operations and data exchanges within the system. Historically, entity-relationship (ER) diagrams provided the basis for these representations. Today, there are multiple notations tailored to the specific tasks of high-level and low-level architectures, such the Unified Modeling Language (UML), database schemas, and component-and-connector (C&C) diagrams. We now discuss a few of these representations using industry standard notations.

2.4.2.1 Object and Data Models

Object models are used to describe elements of a system and the compositional relationships between these elements. The UML object-oriented class diagram is a commonly used notation for describing object models, because of the wide variety of supporting tools available to draw these diagrams and because some of these diagrams can be used to generate program code. UML class diagrams describe classes, their data elements and functions over that data, as well as associations between objects when one class contains a reference to another class. Privacy analysts can use object models as a lingua franca to enable developer discussions about how personal information will reside in the system, what fidelity the data will be stored at and shared at, how to support pseudo-identification, and how to segregate information to limit or avoid unwanted inferences across large datasets that reveal private details about a person.

Figure 2-13 presents a UML diagram for a customer class. The customer class is named "Customer" and the class has a data element "customer_id," which is a type of integer, abbreviated as "int." This class also has a function called get_sales() that returns an array of type Sale. The dashed line between the Customer class and the Sale class denotes that each Customer has a relationship to zero or more Sale objects. In this design, the designer chose to use **information hiding**, which is a common object-oriented design practice, to separate the personally identifiable information into a subclass, called IdentifiedCustomer in Figure 2-13; the arrow points from the subclass to the superclass. For large systems where developers reuse these classes across their components, one developer can design an interface that shares only PseudoAnonymous objects with outsiders, and internally operates on the IdentifiedCustomer object to limited unwanted accesses to personal information at runtime. Because the PseudoAnonymous class still inherits the customer_id from its superclass Customer, the PseudoAnonymous customer objects can be used to uniquely identify customers without revealing their personal names or other sensitive information contained in the IdentifiedCustomer class.

Figure 2-13: Example UML Diagram for a Customer Purchase History

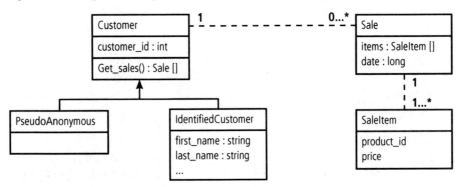

The wide use of databases to store information has led to the development of database schemas. Databases consist of tables containing columns that describe the data elements and rows that describe the data records. Tables may include distinct keys to cross-index records among multiple tables. Figure 2-14 illustrates a database schema for a customer purchase history. The schema includes two tables: CustomerProfile, which contains the customer's personal information, and PurchaseHistory, which contains records of purchases indexed by a sale_id. The key symbol in the CustomerProfile means that this schema element is unique, that is, each customer has only one unique customer_id. Unlike the above UML diagram, this schema is simple and keeps the customer information in a single table. However, the purchase history is still separated into a second table. The link between the two tables is the customer_id; thus to cross-reference data, a program requires access to both tables and this id. In this design, designers can limit access to customer information by granting access only to the PurchaseHistory table; this table describes the customer's purchases, some of which may still be sensitive, but does not disclose the customer's personal information. To gain access to that information, the program would need to use the customer_id to access the CustomerProfile table containing the customer's address, phone number, etc. Commercial database systems include access control features that allow developers to restrict access to tables, and in some cases individual cells (i.e., row-column locations). This topic is discussed more in Chapter 4.

Figure 2-14: Example Database Schema for a Customer Purchase History

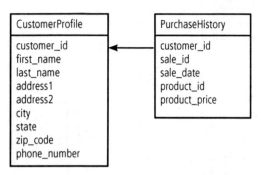

Finally, as designers consider how to map requirements into the design, they should pay special attention to the data dictionary and special requirements pertaining to each data type. The trace matrices that map legal requirements to data types may limit how data can be used, and it is the designer's responsibility to ensure those limits are translated into their design. This translation can be further expressed using process models, discussed next.

2.4.2.2 Process Models

Process models complement data models by representing what will be done with that data. Flowcharts are a simple type of process model. Flowcharts represent the system's operations and the sequencing of those operations, including conditional decision points. Figure 2-15 presents a flowchart fragment to express how a user registers for a service. Because some users may be under age 13, the legal age of children under the U.S. Children's Online Privacy Protection Act (COPPA), the system must obtain verifiable consent from the parents of those children. This flowchart has two critical design features that are necessary (but not sufficient) to comply with COPPA: First, only if the user is under age 13 and the parent provides verifiable consent will the system collect more information from the child other than name, age and e-mail address; and second, if the parent does not consent, or if a response to the consent request is not received within a reasonable time (i.e., the request has expired), then the system will delete the child's information, including the user's name, age and e-mail address. The COPPA allows for some other exceptions that are not represented here, but this example demonstrates how a designer can model the regulatory process in his or her system design prior to implementation.

Figure 2-15: Example Flowchart Describing a Partial COPPA-Compliant User Registration Process

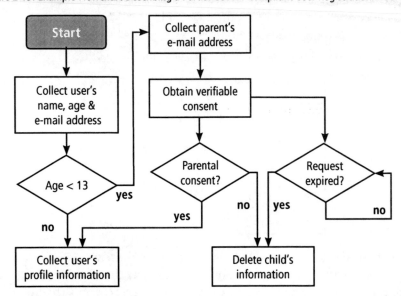

In addition to flowcharts, designers may use UML sequence diagrams or other notations to express the order of operations for functions in a UML class diagram. Furthermore, they may use flowcharts or similar diagrams to describe data flows among components.

2.4.2.3 Design Patterns

Erich Gamma, Richard Helm, Ralph Johnson and John Vlissides introduced design patterns into mainstream software engineering through object-oriented programming.[44] Design patterns describe recurring problems through a shared solution that can be repeatedly reused to solve the problem. These design patterns proposed by Gamma et al. serve to improve program code maintenance by providing developers with a common mental model when approaching a recurring problem. They identify four elements of a design pattern:

1. A *pattern name* that enables easy reference to, and communication of, the pattern.

2. A *problem description* that the pattern is intended to solve. This includes sufficient information to recognize when the pattern applies.

3. A *solution* that describes the elements of the design, their relationships, their roles and how they interact. The solution may be presented as a template that the designer must instantiate in the context of the design through some modification or extension.

4. The *consequences* that describe the results from applying the pattern and any trade-offs that occur by using or not using the pattern. This information assists the designer in determining whether the pattern's benefits are an improvement to the design.

Recently, work has been done in academia to identify privacy patterns.[45] Researchers at the University of California–Berkeley School of Information maintain the privacypatterns.org website, which disseminates information on emerging privacy patterns. For example, the ambient notice pattern, which appears in this online repository, describes a general solution to the problem of providing unobtrusive, ongoing notice of real-time location tracking. The challenge with location tracking for mobile users is they may not realize when their location is being monitored, or how often it is monitored, and providing intrusive notices can be as disruptive to the user's privacy as monitoring the user's movement through private settings.

Patterns in the repository are grouped by topic, including notification, minimization, access and transparency, among other topics, and presented in a format similar to the common pattern format described above. In addition to reuse, an added benefit of design patterns is the ability to combine multiple patterns to yield more robust solutions. For example, the ambient notice pattern may be combined with the privacy dashboard pattern, which provides an individual with an overview of all the information that an organization maintains on that person. This combination provides both specific indications of when information is used in a nonintrusive manner, as well as an overview of how different pieces of information are used together by a broad range of services.

2.4.3 Quality Attributes

In addition to translating requirements into designs to show how a system implements a client's need, designers must pay special attention to quality attributes. Quality attributes in software engineering describe crosscutting concerns that cannot be addressed by a single function. Privacy is an example of a quality attribute, as are security, usability and accessibility. In security, some quality attributes, such as confidentiality and integrity, are also called security objectives. Because of the complex nature of implementing quality attributes, different designs embody different priorities or emphasize different properties. The next sections discuss several quality attributes required to improve privacy in design.

2.4.3.1 Identifiability

Identifiability concerns the extent to which a person can be identified within a system. Sarah Spiekermann and Lorrie Faith Cranor conceptualize a four-stage scale running from "identified" (stage 0) through "pseudonymous" (stages 1 and 2) all the way to "anonymous" (stage 3).[46] In each progressive stage, the linkability of data to personal identifiers decreases and privacy protections are based increasingly on technical rather than policy mechanisms. From a privacy perspective, less identifiability is preferable to greater identifiability. While collecting no personal information reduces privacy risk, personal information may be necessary to provide business value; thus, storing personal data separately from other information when no requirement exists to keep this information together is a strategy to reduce identifiability.

Identifiability is manifest in many forms. Information can be identifiable in the absence of a single identifier. Latanya Sweeney demonstrates through k-anonymity (see Chapter 4) that the combination of gender, birth date and zip code can likely uniquely identify 87 percent of the population in the United States.[47] If such quasi-identifiers can be applied to different databases with other personal information such as name and address, then a degree of identifiability exists in the system. Therefore, when assessing identifiability, one must examine combinations of nonunique identifiers and evaluate how their system design isolates the collection and use of these identifiers to limit drawing unwanted inferences from the data in a privacy-threatening manner. Another example is browser "fingerprinting," in which the configuration attributes of a user's browser (operating system and version, browser version, browser settings, etc.) combine to act as a unique identifier and link information together when they are sent in the HTTP request header to the server.[48] This type of identification constitutes pseudonymity, because the identifier is a substitute for the person's real identity. To reduce this level of identification, web server log files can be configured to record less information from the HTTP request header. Care must be taken to ensure that the design of the system is actually consistent with goals and assertions regarding identifiability.

2.4.3.2 Network Centricity

Network centricity concerns the extent to which personal information remains local to the client.[49] When using a client-server architecture, for example, the designer may choose to retain personal information on the client side and transfer this information only for the limited purpose of completing a transaction. Weighting personal information and processing toward the client rather than the server can reduce inappropriate or unwanted disclosure and secondary use, among other risks, and enhance individuals' control over their personal information. This may create new challenges, however, because the designer must distribute application logic across the client and server, as opposed to centralizing this processing on the server side. One consequence may be frequent updates to the client application to offer new value-added services.

While systems that are network centric can pose privacy risks by consolidating data in server-oriented architecture, a middle ground exists that potentially offers privacy benefits. For example, if network centricity enables personal information to be disaggregated while still making the information available for legitimate uses, the end result may be positive. Federated systems, which distribute personal information across multiple systems but provide clients with a single interface, can potentially mitigate inappropriate dissemination and use, since any given database contains only some fraction of each individual's personal information. This benefit assumes that appropriate policy and technical controls are in place to prevent inappropriate aggregation; without such controls, network centricity can yield more risk than it serves to mitigate. Moreover, in situations where the client is insecure, network centricity may be desired to avoid a breach of security on the client side.

2.4.3.3 Confidentiality

Confidentiality refers to the extent to which personal information is accessible by others. Access control lists that specify who is allowed access, role-based access control mechanisms that assign sets of permission to generic roles, which are then assigned to individuals, and attribute-based access control mechanisms that base access decisions on particular characteristics of the requester are just a few design choices that can be used toward this end (see Chapter 4). Access can also be controlled using data encryption and tokenization, such as format-preserving encryption that maintains the readability of some but not all of the data (see Chapter 3). For the designer, determining when to use confidentiality mechanisms depends on tracking business needs throughout the design and aligning authorization with these needs. Tax processors at the U.S. Internal Revenue Service, for example, are authorized to access personal information, but only in the context of the specific tax returns being processed. "Browsing" or "snooping" on other returns is expressly prohibited. Complex systems can be designed to cross-reference access logs with role or work assignment logs to identify confidentiality breaches. More generally, confidentiality requires that access control schemes align with business functions and responsibilities. Poor alignment results in excessive accessibility and correspondingly increased risk of compromised confidentiality. If poorly segmented role-based access control is used, for example, users will have to be assigned many roles in order to carry out their tasks, providing access to personal information that is too broad in scope.

2.4.3.4 Availability

Availability is typically referred to as a security property and the need to ensure that information is available to satisfy business needs. While confidentiality may naturally fit with privacy by restricting access, one might view availability as inherently in conflict with privacy. When choosing to lock down data, the designer should consider whether emergency access to personal information is a requirement. This requirement arises in healthcare situations and is expressly permitted in the U.S. HIPAA Privacy Rule when a patient requires immediate treatment but is incapable of consenting to the access of his or her medical records. In such situations, strong auditing is recommended as a compensating design control that ensures whenever emergency access is invoked, logs record this access so that any inappropriate uses may be investigated after the emergency is addressed. Because of the potential for misuse, the structure of such mechanisms should be carefully considered. The designer should consider the means to scope emergency access: Who is allowed to invoke this access? What information is made available during this access? How long should this access be available (what are the exit conditions to access)? And who is responsible for reviewing audit logs or approving access after the incident?

Availability should also be considered with regard to data persistence across the entire system, including on- or off-site backup and storage. Although data may have been deleted from a production database, that data can persist in the form of backups, replication sites and archives. The total time required to delete personal information from the system must be considered as well as the risk implications of data persistence, which may allow data to be accessible outside the scope of normal confidentiality controls. While persistence can provide a safety net—that is, it enables recovery of information in the event of a failure or forensic investigation—it can also provide an opportunity for inappropriate use and disclosure. Establishing retention requirements in the early phases of system development and then tracing these requirements to design and implementation using the data lifecycle viewpoint is a means to mitigate such risks during development.

2.4.3.5 Integrity

Integrity refers to the extent that the system maintains a reliable state, including the quality of data as being free from error. For data, integrity can be broken down into three cross-cutting concerns: *Accuracy* concerns whether the information is correct and free from errors; *completeness* concerns whether there is missing information; *currency* concerns whether the information is up-to-date. Inaccurate data can lead to decisional interference—a privacy harm in Solove's taxonomy discussed earlier. For example, in February 2000, a Kentucky woman named Ms. Boris made several insurance claims to the Kentucky Department of Insurance.[50] The back-end data broker, ChoicePoint, incorrectly recorded these claims and later fed false information to the insurance department that caused Ms. Boris to lose her coverage due to decisions based on incorrect data. Similarly, incomplete information can lead to privacy harms. Missing or outdated information in a person's medical record can lead to misdiagnosis. To address these risks in design, the designer should consider how data is collected and restored: Is data entry manual, and if so, are there cross-checks in place so the data entry specialist can verify the entries are correct? Is the data restored from backups, and if so, are there mechanisms to ensure that corrections propagate to backups or are restored when a backup is pushed online? Allowing individuals to participate in maintaining the accuracy of their data can limit designers' reliance on other mechanisms that may be outside their control or prone to failure.

2.4.3.6 Mobility

Mobility is the extent to which a system moves from one location to another. Mobility has become of increasing importance with improvements in laptop and mobile phone hardware. Increasingly, location data and the manner in which it is collected and used introduce privacy risks. In June 2011, Casey Halverson identified a mobile privacy threat in the Nissan Leaf entertainment system, Carwings.[51] The system included a Rich Site Summary (RSS) news receiver that, upon establishing a remote HTTP request with any server, broadcasts the car's global positioning system (GPS) location, including latitude, longitude and speed. While this information was made available by the new design of the Carwings system, it was not needed to download the RSS feeds. In addition to tracking location, designers should consider the possibility that mobile devices can be lost, misplaced or stolen. Locally storing data on a mobile device may require increased security in the event that the device falls into the hands of an unauthorized individual. Alternatively, minimizing the amount of data stored locally may also reduce this risk.

2.5 Low-Level Design and Implementation

The implementation of software follows from the requirements and design phases to yield working source code that can be tested for conformance to requirements. There are several opportunities to engage engineers in how to improve the quality of their programming practices with respect to privacy. In this section, we briefly review the state of best practice before discussing these opportunities, which include good coding practices and code reviews and reuse of standard libraries and frameworks.

Programmers sit at the center of a software development project. In small projects, the programmer may take on multiple roles, such as requirements engineer, designer and tester; in large projects, they coordinate with these other roles through software development infrastructure, tools and meetings. This includes source configuration management (SCM) systems, such as the stable Concurrent Versions System (CVS) and more modern systems, such as Subversion and several web-based systems designed for Agile teams. All of these systems allow developers to periodically commit files that they are working on, lock files to prevent others from modifying them, and track changes to files with the ability to roll back changes to prior versions. An SCM system can be used to control source code only, or they can be used to control versioning on other software artifacts, including requirements, designs and test cases.

In many development environments, a separate system is used to report and track bugs, which include defects, errors and failures. Companies that provide public access to bug reporting are open to receiving error and failure reports from users. Open source projects that use bug reporting even accept defect fixes by outside programmers. For privacy, software engineers can especially benefit from privacy complaint monitoring (i.e., failure or harm reporting) that includes a detailed description of how the system came to offend a user's privacy. While developers, like any other individual, are not well suited to receiving negative criticism, these reports can provide early feedback that can be used to complement other types of requirements analysis, such as completeness arguments and threat analysis discussed in Section 2.3.4.

2.5.1 Good Coding Practices and Code Reviews

Good coding practices have emerged that improve maintainability of code: Easy maintenance can improve a programmer's ability to improve other qualities, such as privacy. This includes using secure coding practices and an object-oriented programming language that supports information hiding and loose coupling to control information processing. Information hiding is the practice of encapsulating data in classes and restricting access to the data through limited class functions and methods that operate on that data. Programmers can design a class to be an open container that provides other developers complete access and control over the data, including reading data to compromise its confidentiality and rewriting the data to compromise its integrity. Alternatively, a programmer can restrict access to the data using information hiding and allowing only select, approved classes access to the data. While another programmer can circumvent good information hiding practices by modifying the class or creating a class of the type approved for access, a standard SCM system would expose such circumventions. Rather, strong interfaces that hide information by controlling access to data and operations on data are more likely to reduce casual errors and misuse of data.

In addition, programmers can employ loose coupling to reduce information flows. Coupling **tightens** when objects depend on the inner workings of other objects. By loosening coupling, a programmer reduces dependencies among objects. This practice can be used to isolate information processing to a select group of approved classes and reduce the likelihood that other developers can unintentionally repurpose data—for example, when the marketing system reaches into the billing system to collect e-mail addresses by bypassing privacy controls.

Finally, in addition to routine documentation, a programmer can use special codes to annotate source code with privacy attributes. This includes using programming assertions that state compile-time and runtime assumptions about privacy controls. Figure 2-16 illustrates a Java code snippet in which the programmer uses a runtime assertion to check that a user profile permits the system to publish the user's data in a global directory (see line 6). While this check could be made with an if-condition that allowed for a false return value, this programmer assumes this assertion is always true by design. Such assumptions can be made only if the design ensures that no state exists that violates this assumption in the program execution leading up to this point. Thus, if the function consentForPurpose were to return false on line 6, the defect is in the software's design, which has been modified outside the assumptions of the programmer.

Figure 2-16: Example Assertion in Java to Check an Assumed Data Purpose

```
1      // The user has selected the option to publish their profile in

2      // in the global user directory.

3      UserProfile p = profileManager.getUserProfile();

4

5      // User consent for this function is true

6      assert(p.consentForPurpose(ApprovedPurposes.USER_DIRECTORY));

7      publishUserProfile(p);
```

Code reviews are organized by developers to review critical source code for defects. Unlike branch and path testing, wherein an executable test case identifies defects by visiting code branches and paths, code reviews are in-person meetings that can identify defects in logic or poor practices that cannot be found in a standard testing regime. Code reviews are conducted by three to five developers, with special roles to organize the meeting: the *reader*, who reads the code out loud and offers questions to the developer; the *moderator*, who remains independent and serves to mediate disagreements and conflicts; and the *developer*, who authored the code and who listens to the review feedback and answers questions about the code. The developer cannot be the reader or the moderator, because he or she may be prone to take a defensive position to critical feedback. Furthermore, the meetings are best limited to two hours; longer meetings can lead to participant fatigue and reduced quality of feedback.

Code reviews provide an opportunity to involve privacy area specialists in the in-depth discussion about how software implementations satisfy privacy requirements. Unlike privacy legal experts, who typically have a law background, the area specialist has a technical programming background that allows him or her to engage developers in technical discussions about how to write and organize source code. Furthermore, the area specialist is likely to be an independent reviewer with broad experience from participating in multiple projects. This diverse experience translates into design alternatives that the area specialist can introduce to the review, as well as knowledge of existing, reusable privacy frameworks developed by other project teams that may be relevant to the topic of the review.

2.5.2 Reusing Standard Libraries and Frameworks

Programmers can reuse standard application programming interfaces (APIs) and frameworks to reduce defects in source code. Security APIs can be used to improve confidentiality and integrity in support of privacy. Most general-purpose programming languages, such as C++ and Java, and many web-based scripting languages, such as PHP and Python, include standard libraries for performing a variety of critical security functions. Whenever possible, programmers should reuse these libraries and react to critical security vulnerabilities in existing standards.[52] Libraries are available to solve multiple standard privacy and security problems, including:

- Authentication and authorization APIs, including fine-grained and role-based access control

- Encryption algorithms, including standard implementations for 3DES, AES

- Public key cryptography, including key and X.509 certificate management

- Secure communications, including SSL and transport layer security (TLS)

In addition to using standard libraries, programmers can build their own frameworks for addressing privacy principles using a standard protocol. These frameworks should be documented, shared and reused across the organization's products and services. Through reuse, the effort expended to validate these frameworks against legal and standards-based privacy requirements, including review by the in-house legal or privacy office, reduces privacy risk in many ways. Because reuse reduces project costs, it helps ensure that privacy remains a priority as opposed to an intractable expense; when projects run over budget or past deadlines, privacy requirements may receive less attention than the core functionality required to deliver a working product. Reuse also reduces deviation from best practices: Feedback from legal experts and privacy area specialists can help to reduce the defects and incorrect interpretations of privacy requirements in validated frameworks; thus, reuse lowers the likelihood of making common privacy mistakes multiple times across different projects. Opportunities for developing privacy-enabling frameworks include:

- User registration services designed to comply with specific regulations, such as COPPA or the EU Data Protection Directive

- Privacy notice mechanisms, including reusable web-based links and e-mail notification services

- Marketing services that are compliant with the CAN-SPAM Act of 2003

- Report generation services for law enforcement and other requests based on the Electronic Communications Privacy Act of 1986 (ECPA)

2.6 Testing, Validation and Verification

Testing is perhaps the most crucial phase of the software development process with regard to managing privacy concerns. As defined by the IEEE, a test is "[a]n activity in which a system or component is executed under specified conditions, the results are observed or recorded, and an evaluation is made of some aspect of the system or component."[53] In general, testing consists of two sets of activities: *verification*, which ensures that a resultant system performs according to its requirements, and *validation*, which ensures that those requirements themselves satisfy the original needs of the user base for whom the system was developed.[54] While a system may have been designed and implemented with consideration given to privacy-related requirements, it is only through testing that requirements are deemed satisfied.

Like design, implementation and deployment, testing can be broken down into various phases, based upon the object being tested or the purpose for which testing is conducted.[55] This includes unit testing, which covers individual functions and system components; integration testing, which covers the interactions between groups of components; and system testing, which covers completed portions of the whole system. Further levels of testing exist beyond system testing as well, including acceptance testing, which covers requirements validation (do customers accept the system as delivered?), and regression testing, which ensures that changes made to an existing system do not affect (or at the very least, predictably affect) other components within the system.

Although considered a "phase," testing often occurs alongside many of the other phases of the development lifecycle, notably implementation and deployment. However, depending on when testing occurs in this process, the privacy-related concerns will vary. For example, a developer is tasked with writing a function that copies a subset of thousands of user records from one table in a database to another. Ideally, the developer reviewed requirements pertaining to this function in advance and followed any relevant design specifications. When it comes time to test this function (a unit test), the developer must provide it with suitable data. The most representative data yields the best test results, because the data reflects real-world use of the system. In some cases, this data may be obtained from a data vendor or collected from other runtime systems owned or operated by the manufacturer.[56] Usage of real data to test a component prior to deployment raises a number of issues regarding how the data was obtained, who is the dedicated tester performing the test in question and how the data is accounted for during and after completing the testing process.

Testing functions and system components with representative datasets is tremendously valuable, because failures in the system are more likely to reflect real-world use of the system. However, the data supplied, no matter how closely it may represent that of anticipated users, is at best a proxy for "the real thing." To improve testing fidelity, a portion of the system may be exposed to real users through alpha and beta testing. These testing methods involve inviting real users to use the system and provide live data, which raises a number of new privacy issues regarding management of their data and their expectations.

Once beta testing has concluded and further changes or adjustments made to the system, it will be deployed for active use. Testing continues, however, in the form of both new features and updates that may use the testing methods already discussed and runtime monitoring and auditing of the current system. This may include log analysis, issue tracking and testing of APIs, which allow other software and remote services to communicate with a system.

In the following section, we briefly review the more common types of testing (unit, integration, system, acceptance and validation) before devoting our primary discussion to usage of data in testing, alpha and beta testing, and runtime monitoring and auditing.

2.6.1 Common Types of Testing

Unit testing is focused on system components, usually the smallest cohesive or self-contained pieces of the implementation. In software, this includes object classes in object-oriented programming and subroutines or procedures in procedural programming. In addition, a single web page or a database script embedded in a web page can be the unit in unit testing. The fundamental principle in unit testing is to determine whether a unit, given a predefined input, will yield an expected output. For testing purposes, some requirements can be assigned to specific units. For example, a privacy requirement to allow a user to configure a privacy setting can be tested by ensuring that a form submission from a privacy setting configuration web page would yield a change in a database entry that stores this setting. However, additional testing would be needed to ensure the database entry is later read by those parts of the system that must behave in accordance with the setting, such as restricting access to the user's personal information.

Integration testing is focused on testing the individual units as members of a subsystem. Unlike individual units, subsystems enable more complex transactions that can be tested against more complex requirements that describe larger behaviors of the system. Returning to our example in unit testing, a tester may wish to observe the effect of changing a privacy setting on those other units of the system that must behave in accordance with the setting. For example, if the setting restricts sharing the user's e-mail with third parties for marketing purposes, and the system has a unit to generate a list of customer e-mails for an approved third party, the tester can check whether the generated list excludes a user who has configured this setting. While these two units may be tested independently, engineering experience has shown that when components are integrated, additional design assumptions are revealed that lead to failures that would otherwise not be expected. Thus, it is important to incrementally test privacy requirements as portions of the system are completed and delivered rather than waiting to complete the whole system.

System testing is focused on the complete system, including nonfunctional requirements of the system as a whole that cut across individual units and subsystems. System testing activities include security, performance and stress testing. Privacy requirements that relate to the gross behavior of the system can also be tested at this time. For example, a requirement to ensure that the system does not expose an individual's personal information may be tested by implementing test cases that search for sensitive data in network traffic, text files or other media that result from operating the entire system. The tester may discover network traffic that contains unencrypted, sensitive information and attempt to trace this issue back to the set of system components responsible for this failure. System testing may feature attempts to "break" the system by using it in unanticipated ways or by trying to defeat controls.

Unlike unit, integration and system testing, which **verify** that the privacy requirements were implemented correctly, acceptance testing **validates** that the system reflects the correct privacy requirements. Thus, acceptance testing involves the users of the system or those charged with representing those users. Systems may have multiple distinct types of users, and each of these types should be represented. Moreover, even if the system does not interact directly with the individuals to whom its information will pertain, those individuals are still stakeholders in the system. During acceptance testing, it is important to review data subject expectations and the extent to which the behavior of the system is compatible with those expectations. If, on the other hand, data subjects will directly interact with the system (e.g., a social networking platform), then it is preferable to concretely incorporate their perspective. This can be done via a variety of mechanisms, such as alpha and beta testing, focus groups or having employees independent of the development team stand in for external users. However, employees can be biased by the company culture and may make assumptions about what is acceptable that do not generalize to the target user population.

As changes are made to the system in response to bugs and other defects, the tester may need to repeat existing tests to ensure that these changes have not created new defects. This may occur when a bug fix to a function that supports a business value, such as delivering a web feature to a client browser, leads to disabling a privacy feature that interacts with the bug fix. By establishing test cases for privacy features, changes that break the privacy feature may be detected using regression testing. The scope and nature of the change will determine which tests should be repeated. To the extent that system components exhibit high cohesion and low coupling (i.e., minimal interdependence) with other components, the potential impact of changes can be contained and regression testing reduced.

2.6.2 Testing with Data

Testing requires data that is representative of the range of operations the system is expected to experience. Privacy requirements that apply to the runtime system should also apply to a testing environment. In a healthcare context, for example, if a tester is testing a function that assigns a wellness score derived from the health data of a real person, then this data must be protected to the same degree that it would be in a deployed system. However, because the testing environment differs significantly from the real environment (e.g., the complete system may not be available, or the tester may use rough, quickly assembled scaffolding to simulate missing pieces of the system), these privacy requirements may not be met. To address this and related issues, the tester should complete a test plan that includes privacy requirements for protecting test data. In addition, the tester may avoid these problems by using synthetic data, public data, transformed data or purchased data, discussed next.

2.6.2.1 Synthetic Data

Synthetic data is data generated for the purposes of testing when access to real-world data is difficult or restricted. Synthetic data aims to mimic the desired attributes of the real data.[57] The level of sophistication involved in the data-generation process may vary based on the test being conducted. For example, consider a tester who is testing a function that populates a table in a database within a specified time period. Synthetic data may be used if the values in the data do not influence the outcome of the test. Whether a database entry is populated with "John Smith" or "First and last name" is not a significant difference, assuming the second string reasonably represents the first string with respect to the length of average strings in the real dataset. If the tester wants to test the function's ability to handle non-English characters in the test data (e.g., the character æ), he or she could use synthetic data that accounts for this variation. If the tester has access to a real dataset, he or she could derive a statistical profile from the data that is used to generate a synthetic dataset that contains strings with the proper distribution of characters and string lengths as represented by the real dataset. The benefit of using synthetic data is that testers and other developers do not need special privacy training to prevent privacy harms when handling this data.

2.6.2.2 Public Data

Using publicly available datasets, such as U.S. census data, can be extremely valuable.[58] Census data is comprised of real data about specific individuals that is protected as personally identifiable information (PII). Furthermore, statistical disclosure controls are applied to this raw data so as to enable the public release of aggregated information that has very low risk of revealing PII. In the case of anonymized data, which has key identifiers removed, correlations with other public datasets raise the possibility that connections may be developed that violate privacy requirements (see Chapter 4 for more discussion on identifiability). In 2006, the online video rental company Netflix released millions of records that it believed comprised anonymized data about subscriber video viewing tastes in a contest to discover a better recommender system. Although the data had been stripped of personal identifiers, researchers were able to predict the identity of certain reviewers by cross-linking that data with publicly available reviews on the online movie database IMDb.[59] Thus, data that is publicly available may introduce or be vulnerable to re-identification and other privacy risks.

2.6.2.3 Transformed Data

In light of the risks that can be incurred by using real datasets, some organizations turn to data transformation as a means to avoid privacy risks. Data transformation—also known as data masking, data scrubbing and data anonymization—takes real data as its starting point and applies various kinds of manipulation to reduce the risk represented by the original data while preserving desired properties. Note that this is different from statistically representative synthetic data, which is new fabricated data generated from a statistical model of the real data. Transformation techniques include removal of particular fields, suppression of particular values, shuffling of values across records, encryption or hashing of values and generalization of values to render the data less precise. A variety of commercial products aim to support this process, either as standalone tools or as special-purpose add-ons to larger data management tools.

While transformed data can be effective, it is easy to underestimate the difficulty of creating it. Particularly for large database schemas with many interdependent tables, the act of designing and executing transformations that produce usable data with the needed reduction in privacy risk is not straightforward and can be very labor intensive. There is no simple approach that allows a developer or tester to press a single button and yield perfectly de-identified data. However, if the tester anticipates that the transformed data will be used across multiple IT development efforts, then the cost and time needed to implement this approach may be worthwhile.

2.6.2.4 Purchased Data

An organization may acquire testing data from another source. This has numerous benefits, as the data is often immediately available in a format convenient for testing. However, it is possible that the data provider will not legally be allowed to divulge that data—and consequently, the organization that receives the purchased data may not be allowed to use it. Notably, this occurred in 2002 when Torch Concepts, a U.S. Department of Defense contractor, acquired passenger data from the airline JetBlue in order to test an algorithm that was developed for the purpose of identifying suspected terrorists. This violated JetBlue's privacy policy and may have violated national privacy laws.[60]

2.6.3 Testing with Live Users

Testing with live users provides developers the opportunity to put their system in front of the actual users for whom the system has been designed. Doing so can provide extremely valuable information during the development process, as live users may use a system in unintended ways and attempt actions that have not been anticipated by the designers. Such attempts can then be addressed and accounted for in the system, especially if they lead to failures. However, live user testing comes with privacy risks because the users populate the system with their personal information or reveal their personal behaviors in ways that the system collects as data. In this section, we discuss some of the attributes of different types of live user testing and address concerns associated with alpha and beta testing, in particular.

While alpha and beta tests share similarities, we believe their differences can be specified along the following attributes, which also are strong determinants of the privacy precautions that should be taken:

- *Feature Completeness:* The number of a system's features that are made available to users during the test. This ranges from a small subset (e.g., only user registration and account confirmation) to the entire gamut of features the system is intended to deliver.

- *Scale:* The number of users who test the software. This can range from small groups of users to the public.

- *Goal:* The intent of the test, with different intents requiring different measurements and evaluations. For example, testing the system's ability to handle peak user load, which is the greatest number of users on the system at any one time, requires access to a large pool of users; testing the average time it takes a user to complete a specific task in the system may be performed with a smaller sample.

- *Location:* The place where testing is performed, which could include an on-site lab, an outsourcing agency overseas or individual users' PCs or smartphones.

- *Officiator:* Who is conducting the test. Is it the organization developing the software, or another agency performing testing as a service? This could also include the organization for which the software is developed.

- *Test Data Acquisition:* The means by which data is collected and stored for analysis.

2.6.3.1 Alpha Testing

Alpha testing occurs early in the implementation process when a system is not considered feature complete.[61] Alpha testing is seldom open to the public and is frequently conducted with small groups of in-house users. Often, this is the first time a significant portion of the system is exposed to users, or to professional testers acting as users. Thus, alpha testing can serve to both identify prominent issues early in development and offer an opportunity for requirements validation based on user input in a manner similar to acceptance testing. Based on the previously specified attributes, alpha testing:

- Is performed on feature-incomplete systems

- Occurs on a small scale, with tens to hundreds of users, rather than thousands or tens of thousands

- Is seldom open to the public

- Is intended to determine major bugs and offer early requirements validation

- Is conducted in-house or through a third-party testing service that will also conduct tests "behind closed doors"

- Will feature extensive means of data collection, given the low number of users involved in the test

Privacy concerns during alpha testing are driven largely by the incomplete and knowingly underdeveloped nature of the system in question. While the absence of some expected functionality might be obvious to users, the absence of proper data handling and security measures may not be transparent to the users who volunteer to test early versions of the system. Thus, any data the user provides to the system may not be fully protected, as it would be in later versions. Consider, for example, a user who volunteers to be an alpha tester for a new social networking site. Logging in, the user populates his or her profile with personal data and then begins exploring various features made accessible to him or her. Because this is an alpha test, however, developers focused primarily on implementing that functionality for the user that aligns with core business value, and did not address the additional privacy and security requirements. The user may be able to access information about others that has not been adequately protected, and could also be at risk of exposing personal information to unintended parties; for example, if the site has not yet been configured to use a secure (encrypted) connection and the user accesses the site using an unencrypted public wireless network.

When developers aim to alpha-test new features, they must ensure that each increment of the system is vetted by a privacy and security analyst. In a fast-paced, highly competitive environment, this analysis may be overlooked. Integrating privacy early in requirements and design will improve the likelihood that privacy concerns are identified and incorporated early, rather than later, at which point alpha tests are at risk of causing privacy harms. Because data gathered from alpha tests may also contain personal information (e.g., recording the screen of a user while he or she goes through the registration process and profile creation screens), the organization must make sure that the data is marked as being personally identifiable and treat this data as it would the same data in a fully operational system. Before using a third-party service for testing, the hiring organization should conduct appropriate due diligence and determine that the testing service has levels of privacy and security protection at least as strict as those in the hiring organization. In Chapter 7, we discuss governance, risk and compliance practices that may be used to assess a third-party testing service.

2.6.3.2 Beta Testing

Many of the concerns that arise during alpha testing apply to beta testing as well, which is usually performed on feature-complete systems with a much larger testing population. Beta tests are often open to the broader public, although they may be capped at a maximum number of participants, and often conclude the last tests that are conducted prior to live deployment of a system. Regarding the testing attributes, beta tests:

- Are performed on feature-complete systems

- Occur on a large scale, perhaps being open to the public

- Are intended to identify bugs and issues that may interfere with live deployment of the system

- Are often conducted on users' personal or employer-owned machines, which may feature a variety of configurations and states

- Are officiated by the organization developing the system

- Rely on user issue reporting and other means of data collection that may continue to be available once the system goes live

Privacy concerns during beta testing largely relate to the *scale* and *openness* with which the test is conducted. As this is the first time the system is made available to the public, any privacy violations or oversights could have drastic implications, and should be addressed immediately. Failure to identify and address these issues can result in a significant negative impact to user adoption. In 2010, Google deployed Google Buzz, a social networking platform, for all existing users of its Gmail electronic mail platform.[62] Google Buzz was deployed with a number of privacy issues, such as exposing a list of the user's most e-mailed contacts to other users by default; this exposure resulted in heavy criticism for these practices.[63] Alpha testing can be used to identify concerns early, similar to the use of focus groups in requirements engineering. Unlike alpha testing, user accounts and associated personal information that are created in beta testing may be retained for the live version of the system.[64] Changes in privacy policies or other privacy mechanisms for the live system should be introduced to beta users to transition these users to the live system.

2.6.4 Testing After Deployment

Testing is an ongoing process that continues after systems have been deployed. Post-deployment testing is similar to runtime monitoring, or analyzing usage and performance data collected from a running system. In addition, some unique testing-related concerns occur after a system is live, including privacy-sensitive bug handling and API testing.

2.6.4.1 Log Analysis

Systems can collect or log a large amount of data regarding user activity, and these logs themselves can become an unintentional source of personal information.[65] In 2006, AOL released the search terms of over 650,000 of its users; these terms and identifying personal information had been collected while these users interacted with the AOL search service.[66] The search queries, though not directly attributable to the users, contained sufficient personal information that users could be identified. Because it is difficult to anticipate how runtime data may be used, strict policies should be put in place to limit repurposing of the data. During design, developers may plan for secondary uses as they consider the various ways that data may be sanitized or summarized and the periods for which data may be retained. Once these data sources have been identified, they can be protected or otherwise isolated from the rest of the system as well as regularly sanitized, summarized or destroyed to comply with any applicable data retention policies.

2.6.4.2 Bug Tracking

Bug tracking involves the collection and organization of bugs (errors) in a system. When users encounter bugs, they may be guided to a bug tracker, or a piece of software explicitly designed for collecting bug-reporting data.[67] To report a bug, users are asked to provide sufficient detail regarding the context in which the error occurred as well as the effect of the bug itself, such as the system becoming unresponsive, or the user being unable to save data. Systems may be designed with an automated means of collecting and reporting runtime failures to a bug tracker, and the automated report may contain data leading up to the failure, including personal information.

To address these concerns, bug trackers should make explicit any personal information that is collected and present the bug report to the user for review before submitting the report. Systems that are transparent about what information is contained in an automated bug report can improve the likelihood that users will enable submissions. In the event that personal information must be collected and reported, that information should be encrypted or otherwise protected and appropriately handled during transmission and after receipt.

2.6.4.3 API Testing

Many systems implement application programming interfaces, or APIs, which allow other services to connect to the system in innovative ways.[68] For example, Google Maps provides users with the means to integrate Google Maps into their websites, generating driving directions, obtaining elevation profiles and enabling other interactive activities. Although an API may be active alongside system deployment, many are released after the system has seen extensive use. When a developer uses an API, they may unknowingly expose personal information under their own control through the API. If the data pertaining to an API remote procedure call is logged, this data may become a potentially unacknowledged repository of personal information or other sensitive data. In this situation, API developers should be careful to extend privacy protections to this data and work with developers who use the API to notify their users about how personal information is used through this API.

2.7 Chapter Summary

This chapter presents an overview of the software development lifecycle and risk management as these topics relate to developing IT systems that preserve, enhance and enable privacy. From requirements and design, to implementation and testing, privacy is a ~~cross-cutting concern~~ for IT professionals. Armed with the knowledge in this chapter, IT professionals can aim to incorporate privacy into IT system development and engage in deeper discussions to ensure that privacy requirements trace throughout the software development lifecycle. For example, in Chapter 7 we illustrate the critical role of appointing a permanent privacy area specialist, also called a privacy champion, who bridges the technical gap between software engineering and privacy and who consults across multiple IT projects within an organization to share privacy knowledge and reach a higher standard of care. In addition, we introduce and review several privacy risk models and illustrate how these models can be used to drive privacy requirements elicitation that may contribute to addressing privacy risk. Finally, we show by example how many modern software engineering practices can be applied to address privacy requirements in design, implementation and testing.

Endnotes

1 The predecessor to Facebook was first developed by Mark Zuckerberg as a local tool to search student profiles at Harvard University: Alan J. Tabak, "Hundreds Register for New Facebook Website," *Harvard Crimson*, Feb. 9, 2004. The online auction site eBay was single-handedly created by Pierre Omidyar over a single weekend: Adam Cohen, *The Perfect Store: Inside eBay* (Boston: Back Bay Books, 2003).

2 David G. Messerschmitt and Clemens Szyperski, Software Ecosystem: Understanding an Indispensable Technology and Industry (Boston: MIT Press, 2003).

3 Alan Westin, *Privacy and Freedom* (New York: Atheneum, 1967); Julie E. Cohen, "Examined Lives: Informational Privacy and the Subject as Object," *Stanford Law Review* 52, no. 5 (2000): 1373–1478.

4 Messerschmitt and Szyperski, Software Ecosystem.

5 Etienne Wenger, *Communities of Practice: Learning, Meaning, and Identity* (New York: Cambridge University Press, 1998).

6 Peter Naur and Brian Randell, eds., "Software Engineering: Report on a Conference Sponsored by the NATO Science Committee" (Garmisch, Germany, October 7–11, 1968).

7 Winston W. Royce, "Managing the Development of Large Software Systems," *Proceedings*, IEEE WESCON, 1970, 1–9; Barry W. Boehm, "A Spiral Model of Software Development and Enhancement," *ACM SIGSOFT Software Engineering Notes*, August 1986, 14–24; Kent Beck and Cynthia Andres, *Extreme Programming Explained: Embrace Change*, 2nd ed. (Boston: Addison-Wesley, 2004); Mike Cohn, *Succeeding with Agile: Software Development Using Scrum* (Boston: Pearson Education, 2009).

8 Watts S. Humphrey, *Introduction to the Team Software Process* (Boston: Addison-Wesley Professional, 1999).

9 Barry Boehm and Richard Turner, *Balancing Agility and Discipline: A Guide for the Perplexed* (Boston: Addison-Wesley/Pearson Education, 2003).

10 IEEE Standard 610.12-1990, *IEEE Standard Glossary of Software Engineering Terminology*.

11 M. Ryan Calo, "The Boundaries of Privacy Harm," *Indiana Law Journal* 86, no. 3 (2011): 1131–1162.

12 Daniel J. Solove, "A Taxonomy of Privacy," *University of Pennsylvania Law Review* 154, no. 3 (2006): 477–564.

13 Calo, "The Boundaries of Privacy Harm."

14 Westin, *Privacy and Freedom*; Cohen, "Examined Lives."

15 Solove, "A Taxonomy of Privacy."

16 Helen Nissenbaum, *Privacy in Context: Technology, Policy, and the Integrity of Social Life* (Stanford, CA: Stanford Law Books, 2009).

17 Frank Armour and Granville Miller, *Advanced Use Case Modeling: Software Systems* (Boston: Addison-Wesley Professional, 2001).

18 http://nvlpubs.nist.gov/nistpubs/SpecialPublications/NIST.SP.800-53r4.pdf.

19 Pamela Zave and Michael Jackson, "Four Dark Corners of Requirements Engineering," *ACM Transactions on Software Engineering and Methodology* 6, no. 1 (1997): 1–30.

20 Barry Boehm and Victor R. Basili, "Software Defect Reduction Top 10 List," *Computer* 34, no. 1 (2001): 135–137.

21 Joy Beatty and Anthony Chen, *Visual Models of Software Requirements* (Redmond, WA: Microsoft Press, 2012).

22 Don A. Dillman, Jolene D. Smyth and Leah Melani Christian, *Internet, Mail, and Mixed-Mode Surveys: The Tailored Design Method*, 3rd ed. (Hoboken, NJ: Wiley, 2008); Roger Tourangeau, Lance J. Rips and Kenneth Rasinski, The Psychology of Survey Response (Cambridge: Cambridge University Press, 2000); Richard A. Krueger and Mary Anne Casey, *Focus Groups: A Practical Guide for Applied Research*, 4th ed. (Thousand Oaks, CA: SAGE Publications, 2008).

23 The Privacy Act defines the term "system of records" as a group of records under the control of any U.S. government agency "from which information is retrieved by the name of the individual or by some identifying number, symbol, or other identifying particular assigned to the individual." 5 U.S.C. § 552a(a)(5).

24 There are other kinds of standards, which are predictable or functional. Industry standards, for example, may be functional or nonfunctional, depending on their scope and level of detail.

25 COPPA, 16 CFR Part 312.

26 Travis D. Breaux and Annie I. Antón, "Analyzing Regulatory Rules for Privacy and Security Requirements," *IEEE Transactions on Software Engineering* 34, no. 1 (2008): 5–20.

27 Travis D. Breaux and David L. Baumer, "Legally 'Reasonable' Security Requirements: A 10-Year FTC Retrospective," *Computers & Security* 30, no. 4 (2011): 178–193.

28 Ibid.

29 Julia B. Earp, Annie I. Antón and Ryan A. Carter, "Precluding Incongruous Behavior by Aligning Software Requirements with Security and Privacy Policies," *Information and Software Technology* 45, no. 14 (2003): 967–977.

30 www.google.com/policies/privacy/.

31 Julia Angwin and Jennifer Valentino-Devries, "Apple, Google Collect User Data," *Wall Street Journal*, April 22, 2011.

32 Travis D. Breaux, Annie I. Antón, Kent Boucher and Merlin Dorfman, "Legal Requirements, Compliance and Practice: An Industry Case Study in Accessibility," in *Proceedings of the 16th IEEE International Requirements Engineering Conference*, Barcelona, Spain, 2008, 43–52.

33 NRS 603A.200.

34 Va. Code Ann. §18.2-186.6(A).

35 *National Taxpayer Advocate: 2008 Annual Report to Congress*, Department of the Treasury, Internal Revenue Service, Volume 1, 2008, 213–226.

36 Axel van Lamsweerde, "Elaborating Security Requirements by Construction of Intentional Anti-models," in *Proceedings of the 26th IEEE International Conference on Software Engineering*, 2004, 148–157; Guttorm Sindre and Andreas L. Opdahl, "Eliciting Security Requirements with Misuse Cases," *Requirements Engineering Journal* 10, no. 1 (2005): 34–44; John McDermott and Chris Fox, "Using Abuse Case Models for Security Requirements Analysis," in *Proceedings of the 15th Annual Computer Security Applications Conference*, 1999, 55–64.

37 van Lamsweerde, "Elaborating Security Requirements by Construction of Intentional Anti-models."

38 In 2004, a nurse became the first criminal defendant convicted under the HIPAA Privacy Rule. The nurse stole a cancer patient's name, birthdate and Social Security number and used that information to obtain several credit cards: Mike Scott, "HIPAA Gavel Drops—A Message to Healthcare," *Radiology Today* 5, no. 24 (2004): 38.

39 John McDermott and Chris Fox, "Using Abuse Case Models for Security Requirements Analysis."

40 Grady Booch, James Rumbaugh and Ivar Jacobson, *The Unified Modeling Language User Guide*, 2nd ed. (Boston: Addison-Wesley Professional, 2005).

41 Paul Clements et al., *Documenting Software Architectures: Views and Beyond*, 2nd ed. (Boston: Addison-Wesley Professional, 2010).

42 In the Matter of FACEBOOK, INC., a corporation, U.S. FTC Decision and Order, FTC File No. 0923184, Docket No. C-4365, Commissioners: Jon Leibowitz, J. Thomas Rosch, Edith Ramirez, Julie Brill, Maureen K. Ohlhausen, July 27, 2012.

43 NIST Cloud Computing Program, www.nist.gov/itl/cloud/.

44 Erich Gamma, Richard Helm, Ralph Johnson and John Vlissides, *Design Patterns: Elements of Reusable Object-Oriented Software* (Reading, MA: Addison-Wesley Professional, 1994).

45 Sasha Romanowsky et al. "Privacy Patterns for Online Interactions," in *Proceedings of the 2006 Conference on Pattern Languages of Programs*, Article 12, 2006.

46 Sarah Spiekermann and Lorrie Faith Cranor, "Engineering Privacy," IEEE *Transactions on Software Engineering* 35, no. 1 (2009): 67–82.

47 Latanya Sweeney, "k-Anonymity: A Model for Protecting Privacy," *International Journal on Uncertainty, Fuzziness and Knowledge-based Systems* 10, no. 5 (2002): 557–570.

48 Peter Eckersley and Electronic Frontier Foundation, "How Unique Is Your Web Browser?" in *Proceedings of the 10th International Conference on Privacy Enhancing Technologies*, 2010, 1–18.

49 Spiekermann and Cranor, "Engineering Privacy."

50 John McCormick, "Records 'Full of Inaccuracies,'" *Baseline*, June 16, 2005, www.baselinemag.com/c/a/Projects-Security/ChoicePoint-Blur/5/.

51 Darlene Storm, "Nissan Leaf Secretly Leaks Driver Location, Speed to Websites," *Security Is Sexy* (blog), *ComputerWorld*, June 14, 2011, http://blogs.computerworld .com/18461/nissan_leaf_secretly_leaks_driver_location_speed_to_websites.

52 In 1996, a critical flaw was discovered in the MD5 cryptographic hash function that led security experts to downgrade the use of MD5 in applications where a collision-resistant function was needed, such as signing digital certificates: Hans Dobbertin, "The Status of MD5 After a Recent Attack," RSA Laboratories' CryptoBytes 2, no. 2 (1996): 1, 3–6.

53 IEEE Standard 610.12-1990, *IEEE Standard Glossary of Software Engineering Terminology*.

54 Stephen J. Andriole, ed., *Software Validation, Verification, Testing, and Documentation* (Princeton, NJ: Petrocelli Books, 1986).

55 William C. Hetzel, *The Complete Guide to Software Testing*, 2nd ed. (Wellesley, MA: Wiley, 1988).

56 Privacy Rights Clearinghouse, "Online Data Vendors: How Consumers Can Opt Out of Directory Services and Other Information Brokers," https://www.privacyrights .org/online-information-brokers-list (last updated March 2013).

57 Joseph E. Hoag, *Synthetic Data Generation: Theory, Techniques and Applications* (Ann Arbor, MI: ProQuest, UMI Dissertation Publishing, 2011).

58 Agency Datasets, Data.gov, www.data.gov/list/agency/1/16/catalog/raw/page/1/ count/50.

59 Arvind Narayanan and Vitaly Shmatikov, "Robust De-anonymization of Large Sparse Datasets," in *Proceedings of the 2008 IEEE Symposium on Security and Privacy*, 2008, 111–125.

60 Annie I. Antón, Qingfeng He and David L. Baumer, "Inside JetBlue's Privacy Policy Violations," *IEEE Security and Privacy* 2, no. 6 (2004): 12–18.

61 Carlos Delano Buskey, "A Software Metrics Based Approach to Enterprise Software Beta Testing Design," *ETD Collection for Pace University*, Paper AAI3191871, January 1, 2005.

62 Miguel Helft and Brad Stone, "With Buzz, Google Plunges into Social Networking," *New York Times*, February 9, 2010.

63 Ryan Paul, "EPIC Fail: Google Faces FTC Complaint Over Buzz Privacy," *Ars Technica*, February 17, 2010, http://arstechnica.com/security/2010/02/epic-fail-google-faces-complaint-over-buzz-privacy-issues/.

64 Juliet Lapidos, "Why Did It Take So Long to Get Gmail Out of 'Beta'?" *Slate*, July 7, 2009.

65 Bernard Jansen, Amanda Spink and Isak Taksa, *Handbook of Research on Web Log Analysis* (Hershey, PA: IGI Global, 2009).

66 Michael Barbaro and Tom Zeller, Jr., "A Face Is Exposed for AOL Searcher No. 4417749," *New York Times*, August 9, 2006.

67 Sascha Just, Rahul Premraj and Thomas Zimmermann, "Towards the Next Generation of Bug Tracking Systems," in *Proceeding of the 2008 IEEE Symposium on Visual Languages and Human-Centric Computing*, 2008, 82–85.

68 Josh Poley, "Best Practices: API Testing," Microsoft Corporation, February 2008, http://msdn.microsoft.com/en-us/library/cc300143.aspx.

CHAPTER 3

Encryption and Other Technologies

Simson L. Garfinkel

ncryption is the fundamental technology that is used to protect privacy in today's digital world. With encryption, large amounts of data can be rapidly scrambled so that it cannot be deciphered or understood by unauthorized entities. Encryption can protect information so that it can be sent over the Internet or stored on a laptop without fear of having its privacy compromised. Encryption can also be used to certify documents with *digital signatures*, making it possible for an unaffiliated third party to determine who signed the document as well as verify that the document has not been modified since signing.

This chapter introduces the fundamental concepts of encryption. It explains the difference between so-called *secret key* and *public key* algorithms, also known as *symmetric* and *asymmetric*. These algorithms are different from each other but have similar goals and limitations. The chapter presents a variety of applications for encryption in the modern information economy—some of which may be surprising, and some of which really do no good at all. Both kinds of encryption algorithms rely on a small number, string or password called a *key* to perform the encryption and decryption. To that end, the second half of the chapter focuses on the key distribution problem, and how public key infrastructure (PKI) attempts to solve it. Finally, the chapter explains how malware and other common security problems can render even the best encryption worthless.

3.1 Encryption, the Mathematics of Privacy Protection

Data encryption is a widely used tool that protects information belonging to individuals, businesses and governments. It is often said that sending information over the Internet is like sending a postcard—any person or computer along the path can read it. If the information is encrypted, interlopers can still read the postcard but they cannot decipher the postcard's meaning. A laptop that's left at a restaurant or the backseat of a taxi can be a disaster for privacy—anyone who has the laptop can access all of its information, unless the data on the hard drive is encrypted. Encryption can even restrict what someone can do with your data *after* you give it to them— preventing someone from printing an Adobe Acrobat PDF file, for example, even if they can read the text on their computer's screen. Finally, encryption can help verify that a document hasn't been modified since it was created.

3.1.1 Vocabulary

Encryption can do all of these things and more because encryption changes the way that data is stored inside a computer (*data at rest*) and the way it is sent over a network (*data in motion*). Instead of storing data in a form that can be easily understood and used, encryption scrambles (*encrypts*) data so that it cannot be understood or otherwise used without first being *decrypted*. Encrypting and decrypting are thus inverse operations. Encryption protects data by rendering it unusable; decryption takes that encrypted data and makes it usable, leaving it unprotected in the process.

(In recent years a new kind of encryption called *homomorphic encryption* has been invented that allows encrypted information to be manipulated without decrypting it first. Today homomorphic encryption is a research curiosity. Although the technique is potentially powerful, it is currently far too slow to be of practical use. As a result, homomorphic encryption is beyond the scope of this chapter and will not be further discussed.)

In today's world the words *encrypt*, *encipher* and *encode* are often used interchangeably to describe the process of locking up information so that it's unusable to unauthorized users. The word *scramble* serves a similar purpose. Likewise, the words *decrypt*, *decipher* and *decode* are frequently used to describe the reverse process. In fact, each of these words has slightly different meanings. Knowing those meanings is important if you want to avoid embarrassing usage mistakes.

According to the *New Oxford American Dictionary*, the word *encrypt* and its derivative *encryption* means to "convert (information or data) into a cipher or code, especially to prevent unauthorized access."[1] As the definition states, there are two ways to encrypt information— through the use of a cipher ("enciphering" the data) or a code ("encoding" the data). Ciphers are typically mathematical transformations of data, in which data is scrambled according to some kind of function. Codes are transformations that typically involve a one-to-one replacement of a word, letter, figure or symbol with another word, letter, figure or symbol. Interestingly, the word **encrypt** dates only to the 1950s, according to the *New Oxford American*, but the terms **cipher** and **code** have been around for hundreds of years.

Cryptographers—people who study the science of encryption—use the word **plaintext** to denote data before it is encrypted, and the word **ciphertext** to denote the encrypted message. Encryption was originally developed to secure messages that were sent from one location to another—especially diplomatic and military messages. Locks and guards could protect the endpoints, but a message carried by a courier between two protected endpoints was vulnerable—hence the need for encryption. Encryption can also be used to secure messages that are sent to the future: Charles Wesley, the cofounder of the Methodist movement, wrote his eighteenth-century diary in code to protect the document and its salacious secrets from other people's prying eyes, although presumably Wesley himself could still read those messages.[2] More than two centuries later, Professor Kenneth Newport of Liverpool Hope University successfully cracked Wesley's code.

Both ciphers and codes can be used in a *secure* manner, meaning that the plaintext can't be readily extracted from the ciphertext, but they can also be used in a manner that is not secure, allowing the messages to be deciphered by an adversary. The security, or strength, of a cipher or code is usually phrased in terms of a work factor—that is, the amount of effort that an adversary needs to expend to decrypt the message. In the case of the Wesley messages, the work factor was apparently nine years for a respected English professor.

It's both easy and common to overestimate the strength of an encryption scheme—that is, the amount of effort to decrypt a message. It's also both easy and common to underestimate the effort that an adversary is willing to spend to decrypt a message or find a flaw in an entire encryption scheme. It's also common to inadvertently damage the strength of an encryption scheme by using it incorrectly; such mistakes can be devastating. The German Third Reich possessed what should have been an unbreakable encryption system during the Second World War, but the Germans used the system in a way that made it susceptible to attack. The Germans also put unrealistic trust in their system—they never realized that the messages they were sending by radio were being systematically intercepted and decrypted by the Allied Powers. Historians believe that the ability to crack the Enigma family of ciphers shortened the war by roughly two years.[3]

It's easy to see how mistakes can compromise message privacy. But encryption ~~errors can also prevent~~ data ~~that's encrypted from ever being decrypted again, compromising both availability and integrity.~~ Many organizations are so frightened by the possibility of losing access to their encrypted data that they leave unencrypted copies locked away in presumably secure locations—sometimes suffering disastrous consequences when those copies are themselves compromised.

Even though it can't be used to prevent a document from being erased or altered, encryption technology can be used to detect unauthorized changes to the document. Here, the techniques used are known as *cryptographic hash functions* and *digital signatures.* Hash algorithms are fast mathematical functions that take an input file of any length and produce a typically shorter output that looks to be random, but which is in fact completely determined by the input. Good hash functions have the properties that the output cannot be readily predicted from the input without running the algorithm, and that changing any bit in the input will change, on average, half of the bits in the output.

Hash functions are sometimes erroneously referred to as *digital fingerprints,* because in practice every digital document has a distinctive cryptographic hash the same way that every person has a unique set of fingerprints. But the term is erroneous for a variety of important reasons. First, different hash functions will produce different outputs for the same document, so in addition to knowing a document's hash, it is important to know the algorithm that was used to produce the hash. Second, even though no two people have been found to have the same fingerprints, it is possible for many different documents to have the same hash value— such occurrences are called *hash collisions* and are the mark of a hash that is no longer secure. Because each set of latent prints is slightly different, fingerprints must be matched with a comparison function that allows for slight variations: Hashes, by contrast, are precisely matched bit for bit. Last, files don't have fingers, so they can't have fingerprints.

Table 3-1 provides a comparison of the popular hash functions currently in use.

Digital signatures combine hash functions with public key cryptography in a way that makes it possible to certify that a document has not been changed since it was digitally signed.

All of this cryptographic technology exists for one purpose—to frustrate the will of the *adversary.* This adversary is assumed to be a constant presence in security engineering. It is the outsider trying to gain access to an organization's private data, or the insider attempting to make unauthorized changes. Sometimes the adversary is a natural force, such as

Figure 3-1: A Hash Function Applied to a Variety of Inputs

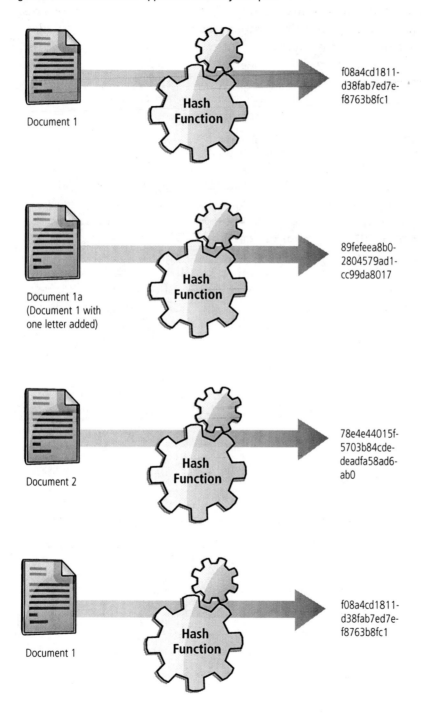

bad weather or a fire. No matter whether you are attempting to design a new data protection system or trying to understand a system that someone else has created, it is important to understand the adversary that the system has been designed to protect against. After all, if there is no adversary, there is no need for any protection.

A ~~cryptographic system~~ is the collection of cryptographic algorithms, protocols, software and other items that allow people to use cryptography to achieve their information security goals. Experience has shown that it is very difficult to take even the best encryption algorithms and create cryptographic systems that have even a modicum of security or privacy. Many of cryptography's goals of confidentiality, availability and integrity are frequently in conflict: Designing systems that deliver all of the required properties is not just a mathematical challenge, but an engineering challenge as well. ~~Even systems that are mathematically sound frequently contain implementation~~ flaws that ~~frustrate the systems'~~ ~~underlying purp~~ose.

Finally, it is important to remember that all cryptographic systems are designed to protect data against specific kinds of adversaries that have specific technical abilities and limitations. Clearly, there is no need to design against an all-powerful adversary; such an effort would be futile by definition.

Table 3-1: Comparison of Hash Algorithms

Hash Algorithm	Bits	Year Published	Status in 2013
MD5	128	1992	Widely used, but no longer secure.
SHA-1	160	1995	Slower and less widely used than MD5. Secure.
SHA-256	256	2001	Slower and less widely used than MD5; increasingly used to replace SHA-1.
SHA-3	Unknown	2013	Chosen by NIST through an academic competition in 2013. Significantly slower than SHA-256. Based on a different mathematical principle.

3.1.2 Encryption Algorithms and Keys

Digital computers perform encryption by applying a mathematical *algorithm* to a block of data. In addition to the algorithm, encryption requires a *key*, which is a small piece of data that controls the algorithm's execution. The same plaintext encrypted with two different keys will produce two different ciphertexts. Likewise, most ciphertexts can be decrypted by one and only one key to produce the original plaintext.

Figure 3-2: plaintext + key1 = ciphertext1; plaintext + key2 = ciphertext2

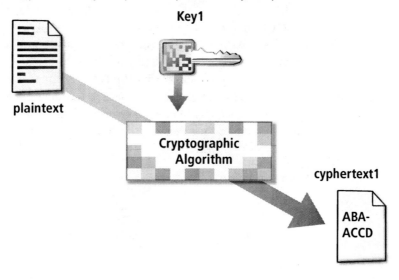

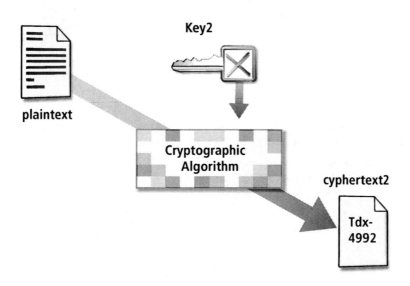

Broadly, there are two kinds of encryption algorithms. Secret key algorithms, also called *symmetric* algorithms (Section 3.2), use the same key to encrypt and decrypt. Public key algorithms, also called *asymmetric* algorithms (Section 3.3), use one key to encrypt and a second key to decrypt. A common metaphor for encryption is a combination lock on a box: The plaintext is the message inside the box, the lock is the algorithm and the combination is the key. With this metaphor, a secret key algorithm would use the same combination to lock and unlock the box, while public key algorithms use one combination to lock and a second combination to unlock.

A variety of asymmetric algorithms have been proposed. Most are based on some kind of deep mathematical or algorithmic property. One of the most common algorithms is RSA, named after its inventors—Rivest, Shamir and Adleman. RSA has the property that the two asymmetric keys can be used interchangeably. That is, either can serve as an encryption key or a decryption key, such that anything encrypted with the first can be decrypted with the second and vice versa. Other public key algorithms need not have this property, however.

Figure 3-3: A Box with a Combination Lock

My Box

locked

open box when combination is good

Modern encryption systems use keys that are very large numbers. The most common algorithm in use today, the Advanced Encryption Standard (AES), is typically used with keys that are either 128 bits or 256 bits in size. Each bit can be either a 0 or a 1. A 128-bit key therefore has $2^{128} = 340,282, 366,920,938,463,463,374,607,431,768,211,456 \approx 3 \times 10^{40}$ possible keys. This is an astoundingly large number!

One way to forcibly decrypt an encrypted message without knowing the key is to try every possible key, because the correct key, when tried, **will** decrypt the message. Such an attack is called a **brute force attack** or a **key search attack** and is infeasible with 128-bit AES. To understand why, imagine that an organization had a billion computers (10^9) and each computer could try a billion 128-bit AES keys (10^9) every second, for a total of a billion-billion (10^{18}) keys per second. Even with such impressive computing machinery, which is many times the computing power available today, it would still take $3x10^{40} \div 10^{18} = 3x10^{22}$ seconds or 258 trillion years to try every possible combination. That's approximately 13,000 times older than the age of the universe.

Another way to understand the impossibility of a key search attack on 128-bit AES is by comparing the difficulty of the problem to the mass of the earth. The mass of the earth is approximately $6x10^{24}$ Kg, while the mass of an Intel core i7 processor and heat sink is roughly 100 grams. If we pretend for a moment that the entire earth could be transmuted into Intel core i7 processors with heat sinks, and that those processors could crack a million AES keys per second (which they cannot), and that somehow all of those processors could run without power, memory or other hardware, then we would have $6x10^{25}$ processors each trying 10^6 keys/sec, for a total of $6x10^{31}$ keys/sec. Even this Earth-shattering computer would still require $5x10^{14}$ seconds to try all possible 128-bit AES keys, or roughly 16 million years. Clearly, no one is going to seriously attempt cracking an AES-encrypted message by trying all possible 128-bit encryption keys.

There are ways other than a brute force key search to decipher an encrypted message, however.

The security of an encrypted message depends primarily on the encryption algorithm and the key. Modern design principles hold that encryption algorithms should be publicly designed and vetted but that the key should remain secret. This is a hard concept for many people to accept—it certainly *seems* that since both the algorithm and the key are needed to decrypt a message, an encrypted message is probably more secure if both the algorithm and the key are kept secret. The flaw with this thinking is the assumption that secret algorithms are more secure than public ones. It is dramatically more complicated to design a strong encryption algorithm than to come up with a strong key. Any randomly chosen number is a strong key—modern computers can make hundreds of these keys *every second*. But to create a good algorithm takes years of careful design, analysis and testing. If the algorithm is flawed, it may be possible to rapidly decrypt the ciphertext without knowing the key at all, no matter how long the key is. If the strength of secret algorithms and public algorithms were equal, it would indeed be more secure to use a secret algorithm than a public one. However, secret algorithms are usually far weaker than public ones. It is invariably better to use a strong public algorithm with a randomly chosen key than a weak secret algorithm with a random key.

A **cryptosystem** is the entire collection of materials necessary to encrypt and decrypt information. Cryptographers take this term to mean the algorithms that are necessary to perform encryption or decryption. Security engineers have traditionally expanded this definition to include the collection of hardware, software, equipment and procedures needed to encrypt, decrypt, transmit and otherwise manipulate information that is being protected—that is, the cryptosystem is anything that will jeopardize the security of encrypted communications if it does not perform as expected. Research over the past decade in usable security makes it clear that this traditional definition needs to be expanded to include training, the human context in which the equipment is used and even the psychological state of the human operators.[4]

It is the strength of the overall system that determines the security of encrypted data, not the strength of any single part. For example, a system could have a secure key, but that key could be transmitted in the clear along with the encrypted message. This would be akin to securing a vault with a $1,500 combination lock, but then affixing the lock combination to the vault door with a sticky note.

One of the primary goals of a security or privacy professional is to minimize the amount of risk faced by users and customers—and to understand the risk that remains. This is another reason why it's better to use a well-known algorithm than a secret one. With algorithms that are well known and vetted, the security of the message lies with the key: Keep the key secret and the message is indecipherable; release the key and it's open. But with an algorithm that's secret, the message security requires that both the key be kept secret *and* the algorithm be strong. A weak algorithm can compromise a message just as effectively as a weak key. Minimizing risk means minimizing the number of things that can compromise security, which means using algorithms that are widely understood, vetted and accepted.

3.1.3 Cryptographic Keys vs. Passwords

Cryptographic keys are similar to passwords in that both are secrets that can be used to control access to information. But keys and passwords are different in important ways:

- With a cryptographic key, access to the controlled information requires that the information first be mathematically transformed from the ciphertext back into the plaintext. When information is encrypted, there is no program or agent that "decides" whether or not to grant access—the correct key can decrypt the data, and incorrect keys can't. Similarly, there is no way to "reset" the encrypted information and grant access to a new key if the first key is lost. Keys can be changed, but it requires that the information first be decrypted with the correct key and then re-encrypted with a second.

- With a password, access to the controlled information is mediated by a program running on some computer. The program compares the password provided by the user with a password that's on file; the program grants access if the two passwords match.[5] Because the program is making a *decision* as to whether or not access is granted, the decision can be manipulated by factors other than the correctness of the provided password—for example, the program could be modified by malware so that access is always granted on Tuesdays at 5 p.m. local time. Note also that the access-granting software has access to confidential parts of the system even when a password is not being provided. Thus, password-protected information can usually be accessed by a system administrator or a sufficiently skilled attacker even if the password remains secret.

These are important differences. As a result, cryptographic approaches typically provide more data privacy than password-only approaches—but cryptography is more susceptible to catastrophic data loss. In practice, cryptographic approaches offer less flexibility, because access control policies need to be implemented in the rather restrictive language of cryptography. For example, a password system can rather trivially be programmed with time-based access controls, so that even authorized individuals don't have access to data when they are on vacation. It may not be possible to implement such a restriction solely with cryptography in a manner that cannot be readily subverted.

3.1.4 Encryption in the 1990s

The principles of digital cryptography have been understood since the 1960s, and in 1977 the U.S. government published Federal Information Processing Standard (FIPS) Publication 46, entitled the Data Encryption Standard (DES), as a private key algorithm that U.S. businesses could use to protect digital information. DES was a surprisingly strong encryption algorithm—it was not until 1997 that there was a public demonstration of the forcible decryption of a message encrypted with DES, and the weakness that the attackers exploited can be easily overcome by encrypting a message with DES three times over, each time with a different key (a technique called "triple DES" or "3DES").

Despite the widespread availability of both cryptographic knowledge and DES implementations, cryptography was not widely used in computing until the late 1990s. This delay was primarily the result of three factors: the lack of electronic commerce, export controls and central processing unit (CPU) speed.

- **Lack of Electronic Commerce:** Before the widespread adoption of the Internet in the 1990s, few businesses or individuals had the need to send encrypted messages. Promoters of e-commerce in the 1990s said that cryptography was needed to allow consumers to send credit card numbers and other kinds of sensitive information over the Internet without the risk of interception and misuse by unauthorized parties. Cryptography was also sold to consumers as a way to verify the legitimacy of an organization's operating websites. In fact, many of the claims made by e-commerce promoters in the 1990s were incorrect, irrelevant or inconsequential for reasons we will see at the end of this chapter. Nevertheless, the belief that encryption was a key requirement for Internet commerce was a powerful catalyst for its widespread use.

- **Export Controls:** Cryptography's long association with diplomatic and military communications resulted in its legal regulation as a dual-use military technology for most of the twentieth century. In the 1980s, for example, the U.S. government restricted the exportation of computer hardware and software that could perform any kind of cryptography. The government even restricted software systems that allowed so-called *cryptography with a hole*—that is, systems that did not implement cryptography directly but allowed end users to add their own. In the early 1990s, the U.S. government modified its stance on cryptography, allowing the export of cryptosystems that used specific algorithms (RC2 and RC4) at a key length of 40 bits. In 2000, restrictions were eased further, such that today most cryptographic systems can now be freely exported provided that the software is available as open source software.

- **CPU Speed:** One of the first uses of digital cryptography outside of government sectors was to protect automatic teller machine (ATM) networks, but this was done by special-purpose hardware. Over the past 30 years, encryption algorithms have generally become faster and more secure. Computers have also become dramatically faster during the same time period. The result is that the percentage of CPU power that needs to be expended on cryptography has dropped precipitously. Whereas the impact of software cryptography was crippling on computers in the 1980s and merely significant in the 1990s, today's computers can encrypt and decrypt data with hardly any perceptible impact. Indeed, Apple's iPhone automatically encrypts data as it moves from the CPU to flash storage and decrypts data when it moves back: Encryption on these devices is essentially free.

The real breakthrough promoting the widespread use of cryptography came in 1995 with the release of Netscape Navigator, the first web browser to incorporate transparent cryptography. Netscape Navigator, and practically every web browser since, allows information that's sent over the Internet to be automatically encrypted as it travels between the web server and the web browser. Netscape Navigator did this with an encryption protocol called the secure sockets layer (SSL). This protocol was revised several times, renamed transport layer security (TLS) and adopted as an Internet standard in 1999.[6] Today TLS (sometimes called SSL/TLS) is probably the most widely used form of encryption in the world. TLS protects all kinds of information sent over the Internet, from Google searches and Facebook status updates to stock purchases worth hundreds of millions of dollars. Both these low- and high-value transactions use exactly the same protocol.

TLS is generally regarded as a strong protocol. However, TLS has had a few vulnerabilities disclosed over the years. One of the most recent vulnerabilities was reported in the National Vulnerability Database under the identifier CVE-2011-3389.[7] This vulnerability allows a man-in-the-middle attacker to obtain the plaintext of HTTP headers in an HTTPS session due to an error in the way that the TLS cipher-block chaining (CBC) mode was implemented. Fundamental cytological attacks such as this are infrequent but reoccurring, which is why it is important for all software to be kept up-to-date and properly patched.

3.1.5 Encryption Today: Data in Flight vs. Data at Rest

Because TLS encrypts data before it is sent over the Internet and decrypts the data when it is received at the other end, TLS is said to protect data in flight. TLS provides no security for data once it arrives at the other end.

TLS can protect all of the information that the web browser and server exchange, including the uniform resource locator (URL) requested by the client, the data in forms sent to the server, usernames, passwords and uploaded files. TLS also protects information sent from the server to the client, including the content of the web pages and any downloaded files. TLS can also be used to identify the web users to the remote server. However, to have these protections, it is necessary for all of the communications between the server and the browser to be secured with TLS. If a website contains a mix of content, some encrypted and some not, it is possible for an attacker to manipulate the unencrypted content and take control of a user's web browser. Even the encrypted content can then be vulnerable.

There are many things that TLS encryption does not protect, such as information about the amount of the data exchanged, the location of the endpoints, or the very fact that data is being exchanged at all. Analyzing this kind of information, called traffic analysis, can be very easy because TLS provides neither anonymity nor stealth.

TLS is just one of several Internet protocols for protecting data in flight. Some Internet telephony protocols use encryption at the application layer. Encryption is also built into the 802.11 WPA and WPA2 wireless network protocols. Nearly all virtual private network (VPN) systems use encryption to ensure that the encapsulated network traffic cannot be decoded by the networks that it passes over. Finally, IPv6, the next-generation Internet protocol, has built-in support for IPsec, an encryption protocol that operates on individual Internet protocol packets.

Encryption can also be used to protect information that is stored for an extended period of time on a computer system—what's called "data at rest." Two approaches are commonly used for data at rest encryption:

- *Application-level encryption*, also known as file-level or document-based encryption. This approach encrypts data on a file-by-file basis or record-by-record basis. The technology for performing the encryption is usually built into the application program itself. For example, Microsoft Word and Adobe Acrobat both support application-level encryption when the user saves a file with "password to open."[8] Encryption can also be applied to a file after it is created with add-on file encryption programs.

- *Disk-level encryption* is built into the computer's storage subsystem and performs encryption on a block-by-block basis. Disk-level encryption is typically done by the computer's operating system, by a special device driver or inside the hard drive. Examples of disk-level encryption include Microsoft's BitLocker, Apple's FileVault and Seagate's Momentus FDE (full-disk encryption) line of hard and solid-state drives (HDs and SSDs).

Encryption can also be used to certify that a document has not been modified since some time in the past, a technique that is frequently called *digital signatures* and will be described in Section 3.3.2.

3.2 Secret Key (Symmetric) Encryption for Data Privacy

In the last section, we learned that there are fundamentally two kinds of encryption used by digital computers today: secret key (symmetric) encryption, where the same key is used to encrypt and decrypt data, and public key (asymmetric) encryption, where one key encrypts and a second key decrypts. In this section, we'll dig deeper into the specifics of secret key cryptography.

3.2.1 Algorithms and Key Sizes

There are two kinds of secret key algorithms:

- **Stream ciphers** are encryption algorithms that transform one byte of data at a time. The RC4 algorithm was widely used in the 1990s with the Netscape SSL protocol and is still somewhat used today, although its popularity is waning.

- **Block ciphers** transform a small block of data at one time, typically 16, 32 or 64 bytes. Both DES and AES are block ciphers.

Many stream ciphers have the property that encryption and decryption is performed with the same cipher and the same key: These algorithms encrypt if provided with plaintext, and they decrypt if provided with ciphertext. For example, the stream cipher produces a pseudorandom bitstream and the encryption and decryption algorithms are simply the Boolean XOR function applied to the bitstream and the plaintext or ciphertext. Block ciphers, in contrast, typically require that decryption be performed by running the algorithm in reverse: Running it twice in the forward direction results in doubly encrypted data.

Ciphers are based on two mathematical operations: substitution, which substitutes one pattern for another according to a code book, and transposition, which scrambles the bits within a set of bytes. Traditionally stream ciphers used only substitution, whereas block ciphers could use both operations, making them somewhat more secure but also somewhat slower. Today's computers are fast enough to allow stream ciphers to be used as block ciphers and vice versa without any perceptible performance impact in the vast majority of applications, and the differences between the two kinds of cipher are no longer as relevant as they once were for most users.

The most common encryption algorithm today is the AES. This algorithm was developed in 1998 by two Belgian cryptographers, Joan Daemen and Vincent Rijmen, and adopted as a U.S. government standard in 2001.[9] After more than a decade of exhaustive analysis, AES is widely regarded as unbreakable. What's meant by "unbreakable" is that AES contains no significant algorithmic weaknesses: The only way to forcibly decrypt a message that has been encrypted with AES is to try all possible keys, one by one, until the correct decryption key is found. (Although some theoretical attacks on AES have been published, none of them can be performed in practice—at least, not yet.)

AES is actually a family of algorithms. The basic version of AES uses a 128-bit key and is called (not surprisingly) AES-128. The AES algorithm can also be run with a 192-bit or 256-bit key, and is correspondingly named AES-192 and AES-256. The AES algorithm itself consists of an inner mathematical operation that is repeated. AES-128 repeats this function 10 times and is therefore said to have 10 "rounds." AES-192 has 12 rounds and AES-256 has 14 rounds. Additional rounds make messages encrypted with AES harder to decrypt without knowing the key.[10]

Because AES-256 has both a longer encryption key than AES-128 and more rounds, the algorithm is widely regarded as being more secure than AES-128. But how much more secure is it? There is really no way to know. Block mode encryption algorithms can't be proven secure; they can only be shown to resist specific attacks. It's possible that in the future some new attack will be discovered that makes AES less secure than it is today. If the past provides any guidance, such attacks are likely. The only thing we don't know is when they will be discovered. If or when such an attack is discovered, it may be possible for an attacker to decrypt some AES-128 messages but not any AES-256 messages. For this reason, some organizations prefer AES-256 over AES-128—doing so protects against unknown attacks that may emerge in the future.

AES-256 has a real cost: Those additional rounds mean that it takes more computer time (and thus more electricity) to encrypt a message with AES-256 than with AES-128. What's more, that cost may be unnecessary. Recall that AES-128 has 2^{128} different keys and AES-256 has 2^{256} different keys. While 2^{256} is certainly a much larger number than 2^{128}, it is not meaningfully larger if the only threat is a brute force attack. Recall that it would take 258 trillion years for a billion computers, each trying a billion keys every second, to try all possible 128-bit keys—that's 2.58×10^{14} years. Those same billion computers would take 1.1×10^{59} years to try all possible 256-bit keys. The difference between these two times is not significant, since the sun is predicted to become a red giant and destroy Earth in roughly 5×10^{9} years.[11]

This brief math excursion shows that a key search attack will always be infeasible against both AES-128 and AES-256. So the only way that AES-128 could be less secure than AES-256 is if there is an attack that works against AES-128 but not against AES-256—some kind other than a key search attack. Currently, no such attack exists, so both algorithms are equally secure. On the other hand, while the U.S. National Security Agency (NSA) has approved certain AES-256 implementations for encrypting top secret data, no such approval has been given for AES-128.[12]

While there are other symmetric encryption algorithms, they are increasingly falling out of favor. AES replaced the DES, an algorithm developed by the International Business Machines (IBM) Corporation and the NSA in the 1970s. DES has a 56-bit key, which was deemed secure in 1977 when it was first published but was found to not be secure at all in July 1998, when a special-purpose computer built by the Electronic Frontier Foundation called "Deep Crack" brute-forced a 56-bit DES key in 56 hours.[13] Six months later, Deep Crack working in collaboration with a distributed network of computers broke a 56-bit key in 22 hours and 15 minutes.

3.2.2 Crypto Attacks and Threats

An attacker that tries to decrypt a single message by systematically trying all possible keys is just one of many possible threats and attacks that modern crypto systems must withstand. It is important to understand this kind of key search attack because there is fundamentally no way to protect against it—an attacker that gets an encrypted message can *always* try to decrypt it by trying all possible keys. That's why strong encryption algorithms use keys of at least 128 bits. With 2^{128} possible keys, it will always be infeasible to try them all.

(Some people believe that the way to protect against a brute force key search attack is to prevent the attacker from ever acquiring a copy of the encrypted message. However, if it is possible to prevent the attacker from acquiring a message, then the message doesn't need to be encrypted in the first place.)

However, the brute force key search attack is just one of many attacks that modern encryption algorithms need to be able to withstand. The other attacks all rely on *cryptanalysis,* a process that typically involves understanding the individual mathematical operations that create the encryption algorithm, and correlating many applications of the algorithm over a large set of data. Cryptanalysis frequently makes it possible for an attacker to break an encryption system with far less work than trying every possible key.

There are many ways that an encryption algorithm might be broken, and many different kinds of cryptanalytic attacks that an attacker can use. Here are some examples.

An encryption algorithm can be considered broken if:

- Given a ciphertext C, the attacker can determine the plaintext P. (This is called a **known ciphertext** attack.)

- Given a plaintext P and a ciphertext C, the attacker can determine the encryption key K. (This is called a **known plaintext** attack.)

- Given a plaintext P of the attacker's choosing and the encrypted ciphertext C of that message, the attacker can determine the encryption key K. (This is called a **chosen plaintext** attack.)

- Given a number of similar plaintext messages P_1 through P_N and the corresponding ciphertext messages C_1 through C_N, the attacker can determine encryption key K. (This kind of attack uses a technique known as **differential cryptanalysis**.)

- Given a number of related keys and a collection of ciphertext encrypted with each key, it is possible to learn some or all of the keys, and therefore decrypt some or all of the ciphertext. (This is called a **related key** attack.)

While these attacks may not seem particularly realistic, they are all well within the realm of possibility. Consider the chosen plaintext attack. This attack might have been performed in the past by giving a document to the ambassador of a country during the course of diplomatic negotiations. The ambassador would then provide the document to the embassy cryptographers, who would dutifully encrypt the document and send it back to the home country. The opposing country's analysts would intercept the encrypted message and would now have both a message of their choosing and the encryption of that message using the target country's diplomatic cipher. Similar attacks can be accomplished on modern cryptographic systems.

Cryptanalysis means that some encryption algorithms are far weaker than might be assumed based on their key size. For example, the DES algorithm was based on an algorithm developed earlier by IBM called Lucifer. IBM had submitted Lucifer to the National Bureau of Standards (NBS, the precursor of today's National Institute of Standards and Technology) as a candidate for the national standard. Lucifer had a 128-bit key; the algorithm that NBS eventually adopted had 56 bits. At the time, many people thought that the NSA had put pressure on IBM and NBS to purposely weaken Lucifer so that the U.S. government would be able to crack messages encrypted with DES.

In the 1980s, cryptographers Eli Biham and Adi Shamir developed an elaborate variant on the chosen plaintext attack, which they called **differential cryptanalysis**. Instead of sending just a few messages to be encrypted, the attacker would have millions or even billions of messages encrypted and then analyze all of the results to determine a secret key. Reportedly, the two would have published their technique several years earlier if they had not spent most of their time analyzing DES, which was surprisingly resistant to differential analysis. But Lucifer was not—Lucifer could be cracked if the same keys were used to encrypt just 2^{36} chosen plaintext messages—roughly 68 billion messages, well within the capabilities of a large corporation or a national government by the late 1980s.[14]

As it turns out, conspiracy theorists who had blamed the NSA for weakening the DES had been wrong. The original Lucifer, even with its longer key, was in fact weaker than the 56-bit DES. The change to the substitution boxes that NSA had applied to the original DES algorithm submitted by IBM had made the algorithm stronger, but it had strengthened the algorithm against an attack that was secret at the time.[15]

By the mid-1990s, it didn't matter much that the DES was resistant to differential cryptanalysis, because the algorithm's 56-bit key was no longer sufficiently long: It could be brute-forced by the Electronic Frontier Foundation.

When DES was shown to be not secure, parts of the U.S. government were attempting to get industry to standardize on a new 80-bit encryption algorithm embedded in the so-called Clipper chip. Despite the apparent closeness of the numbers 56 and 80, an 80-bit encryption algorithm has $2^{80-56}=2^{24}=16,777,216$ times more keys than a 56-bit algorithm. This means that if it previously required 22 hours to crack a 56-bit key, it would take 369 million minutes to crack an 80-bit key, or approximately 701 years. The Clipper chip was never adopted by U.S. industry, however, because the chip featured a mandatory key escrow that would have let the U.S. government decode Clipper-encoded messages with a valid court order. Instead, those who cared about cryptographic security went with an approach called triple DES or 3DES, which involves using the existing DES algorithm three times in a row, creating an encryption system with an effective key length of $56+56+56=168$ bits.

It is likely that vulnerabilities in the AES-128 and AES-256 algorithms will be discovered in the future. When such vulnerabilities are discovered, it's possible that AES-128 will be more vulnerable than its longer key length cousin, if for no other reason than it has longer keys and more rounds. But those attacks almost certainly won't be based on brute force key searches.

Because encryption algorithms come and go, modern encryption protocols like TLS allow the algorithms to be specified at runtime. In this way it is possible to migrate from old algorithms to new ones when vulnerabilities are discovered with minimal software change.

Table 3-2: Comparison of Encryption Algorithms

Symmetric Algorithms				
Algorithm	Type	Key Size	Block Size	Status
DES	Block Cipher	56 bits	64 bits	Not secure
3DES (Triple DES)	Block Cipher	168 bits	64 bits	Secure but slow; not widely used
RC4	Stream Cipher	40-2048 bits	8 bits (1 byte)	Was widely used in SSL and WEP; increasingly deprecated
AES	Block Cipher	128, 192 or 256 bits	128 bits	Widely used; generally thought to be secure

3.2.3 Modes of Operation

Block encryption algorithms, such as AES, DES and 3DES, all operate on relatively small blocks of data (see Table 3-2), but most data that needs to be encrypted is much longer. Cryptographic *modes of operation* are techniques for combining repeated invocations of block algorithm so that it can be used on more data.[16] Understanding modes of operation is important for people who are developing or evaluating cryptographic software, because the mode of operation can impact the security and flexibility of the system.

While many modes of operation have been devised, only a few are widely used:

- **Electronic codebook** (ECB) is the simplest mode of operation to implement, but it's also the least secure. This mode uses the same key to encrypt each block of data. The problem with this mode is that blocks that have the same content will encrypt to yield the same output. In practice, this makes it possible for an attacker to learn a great deal of information about the plaintext merely by observing the repeated portions of ciphertext. For most applications, this mode should not be used.

- **Cipher-block chaining** (CBC) overcomes the problem of ECB by encrypting each block as a function of the block's plaintext and the previous block's ciphertext. As a result of this chaining, the same block of plaintext will be encrypted differently each time. Because the first block of the message doesn't have a previous block, it is encrypted by combining the plaintext and a randomly generated block of data called the *initialization vector (IV)*. The IV does not need to be kept secret, but it does need to be different for every message that is encrypted. Because the IV is needed to decrypt the message, it is usually attached to the ciphertext. Disclosing the IV does not jeopardize the security of the ciphertext.

- *Counter mode* (CTR) is similar to CBC, except that the IV is replaced with a counter. This mode shares the advantage with CBC mode that long blocks of data that repeat are encrypted differently. CTR has the further advantage that it is possible to start decrypting at any point in the encrypted data, making this mode a popular choice for disk encryption algorithms. This is in contrast to the CBC mode, which must begin decrypting from the first block in the sequence. Moreover, counter mode has the advantages that errors in the ciphertext do not propagate and CTR encryption and decryption can be parallelized. Despite these advantages, counter mode is not widely used.

One of the problems with the three modes discussed above is that there is no way to validate the authenticity of encrypted data: Any ciphertext can be decrypted with any key. There is no way, in principle, to look at decrypted information and determine whether that information is correct or not—that is, there is no way to tell if the encrypted data was modified or corrupted after it was encrypted. Usually, this isn't a problem, because most data files have internal structure, and this structure is not correct if the encryption does not succeed. However, it is inappropriate to rely on a chance property, such as being able to display a JPEG or open a file in Microsoft Word, to determine whether or not data is intact, because this property can sometimes be exploited by an attacker.

For this reason, there is another family of modes:

- *Authenticated encryption* is a family of modes that provide for both confidentiality and authentication. These modes rely on additional information that is injected into the ciphertext so that the decrypting program can verify that decryption was performed using the correct key and that the decrypted plaintext was not modified after it was encrypted. Unfortunately, some of the authenticated encryption modes have been patented and, as a result, they are not widely used.

3.2.4 Making a Key from a Passphrase with a Hash Function

The security of an encrypted document depends on ~~both~~ the algorithm and the encryption key. Until now, this chapter has focused mostly on technical matters having to do with the algorithm: making sure that the algorithm itself is strong and correctly implemented, for example. However, other than discussing the key's length, this chapter has been silent on the characteristics of a good key or how to make a key.

In general, there are only two hard-and-fast rules for strong encryption keys. The first is that the key should be truly random. The second is that the key should be used as infrequently as possible—ideally just to protect a single message.

Creating a key that's random is surprisingly difficult. People are notoriously bad at picking random numbers. Surprisingly, so are computers. Computers are designed to be deterministic machines. Given the same input, different computers are supposed to generate the same output. But the same output is precisely wrong when it comes to generating encryption keys. We want every key to be different, even if the keys were generated in the same way.

Because encryption keys are both so important and so common, modern computers have ~~special-purpose~~ hardware and software that exist solely for the purpose of creating random numbers appropriate for use in cryptography. Most systems collect randomness from many different sources and use that randomness to scramble the bits in a mathematical structure called an ~~entropy pool~~. Most entropy pools are implemented as a collection of several thousand bits. Every time another random bit is collected, that bit is used to flip half of the bits in the pool. The half that's picked depends on the new random bit and all of the existing bits in the pool—essentially, the pool is a giant cryptographic hash function. When random numbers are needed for generating keys, those numbers are extracted from the pool with additional processing.

There are many ~~sources~~ of randomness that can be used for the entropy pool. For example, a computer can generate a few bits of randomness every time the user strikes the keyboard or moves the mouse—the random bits might be related to the number of nanoseconds since the previous keystroke or mouse movement. Digital cameras, microphones and even network activity are other potential sources of randomness. The best sources, though, derive their randomness from quantum mechanics. For example, many microprocessors have a hardware random number generator that gets entropy from thermal noise. The precise amount of energy required to spin a hard drive is another source of randomness, since that energy depends on micro wind vortices between the drive's spinning surface and the surrounding air.[17]

Encryption keys are typically displayed as hexadecimal strings. For example, a 128-bit key could be written as fb6cecc85a100197ae3ad68d1f9f2886. Such keys are hard to type and even harder to remember. One approach to working with long keys like this is to store them in a text file and then copy and paste them into whatever program needs the encryption key. The danger with this approach is that the security of the encrypted messages now depends on the security of that text file—which might not be all that secure, given that it's not encrypted. Of course the text file can be encrypted, but then there needs to be a way of remembering that key, which re-creates the original problem.

The standard approach for solving this seemly irreducible problem is to create highly random keys for the actual encryption, but to encrypt those keys with a secondary encryption key that is easier to remember—typically an encryption key generated by hashing a password or passphrase. Here's how it works:

1. Modern encryption systems use randomly generated keys to encrypt data. Let's call such a key K_1:

$$K_1 = \text{fb6cecc85a100197ae3ad68d1f9f2886}$$

   This key is then encrypted with a passphrase that the user supplies. The term *passphrase* is similar to the term *password*, except the use of the word *phrase* instead of *word* is meant to encourage users to supply something longer than a word. In this case, let's assume that the user provides the following passphrase:

   Passphrase: "This passphrase is long!"

2. To encrypt the key with the passphrase, we calculate a cryptographic hash. Here, we will use the SHA256 hash function:

$$H_1 = \text{SHA256}(\text{"This passphrase is long!"}) =$$
$$\text{62c994bf0431ea8f87c21de52703d2bd4d9c68c2ed37244d7e6fc3f75e22f93c}$$

3. The original K_1 key is now encrypted using H_1. This creates an encrypted value of E_1:

$$E_1 = \text{AES256}(K_1, H_1)$$

The original encryption key, K_1, can now be used to encrypt a document. The encrypted encryption key, E_1, may be stored with the document or stored separately.

To decrypt the document, E_1 must be recovered. If E_1 is stored with the document, an attacker only needs to try all possible passphrases in order to decrypt E_1 to get K_1. The security that's provided by this approach depends on the length of the passphrase. If the passphrase is short—fewer than eight characters—then the attacker can try all possible passphrases within a few days (or even a few hours). But if the passphrase is long and hard to guess, the security offered by this approach is quite adequate for most applications.

Alternatively, E_1 can be stored in a database. For example, many DRM systems are essentially databases of decryption keys combined with business logic that determines whether or not a specific user should have access to a specific decryption key. When all access to the document needs to be terminated, the encryption key is deleted.

3.2.5 Typical Uses

Throughout this section we've seen a few uses of secret-key encryption. Here they are again, each with a bit more explanation:

- *Documents with Passwords:* One of the most common uses of symmetric encryption is to encrypt documents. Both Microsoft Office and Adobe Acrobat use symmetric encryption when a document is given a "password to open." Typically these systems are implemented with a two-step encryption, where the document is encrypted with a randomly generated 128-bit or 256-bit encryption key and then the key itself is encrypted with a hash of the user's passphrase. The encrypted passphrase can be stored with the document or separately from the document for added security. Document encryption systems can also make multiple copies of the encryption key and encrypt each with a different passphrase, allowing multiple passphrases to unlock the document. This is how some systems implement a "master password."

- *Block-Level Disk Encryption:* Instead of encrypting at the document level, this approach applies encryption at the driver layer, separately encrypting each disk sector. Block-level disk encryption transparently encrypts every file stored on the disk: It can encrypt nonfile data as well, such as virtual memory and hibernation data (e.g., the contents of physical memory stored on disk during hibernation). Disk encryption schemes typically use a variant of counter mode so that any disk block can be decrypted without decrypting the adjacent blocks.

- *Persistent Virtual Private Networks (VPNs):* If two networks are going to be connected for a long period of time using a virtual private network, it may be advantageous to connect them with a static encryption key. In this case, the system administrator would create a random encryption key and program it into all systems that require access to the VPN.

- *Wireless Networks:* Symmetric encryption can also be used on wireless networks. For example, the typical use of the WPA2 encryption system requires that all units be programmed with the same passphrase or key. This passphrase or key is then used to derive a specific symmetric encryption key used to secure data sent over the wireless network.

Here are some additional uses of applied secret key encryption that have not been discussed so far:

- *Encrypted Databases:* Instead of storing encrypted data in a file, the data can be stored in a database. There are many strategies for database encryption. The entire database file can be encrypted with a single key; individual rows or columns can be encrypted; rows, columns or cells can be encrypted with keys stored in other rows, columns or cells; the database can be encrypted but the index left unencrypted to allow for rapid searching; and so on. Each strategy has different trade-offs regarding security, performance and recoverability. There is no one right way to encrypt databases, as different schemes are designed to address different threats and satisfy different performance requirements.

- *Cryptographic Erasure and Retention Rules:* Taking advantage of the fact that encrypted data cannot be decrypted without the key, there are a number of schemes for ensuring complete erasure of a storage media by simply erasing the key. For example, it typically takes two to three hours to overwrite all the sectors of a hard drive, and another two to three hours to verify that they have been overwritten. If the drive is encrypted with a key, the entire contents of the hard drive can be rendered indecipherable by erasing the key. At a law firm, each case file could have its records encrypted with a case file-specific key. Then, if all of the records having to do with a case file need to be erased, this specific key could be wiped. This approach would even make inaccessible document backups stored on tape, optical media or in the cloud. Many digital rights management systems use cryptographic erasure to block access to a document after a time period has expired: The software does this by automatically wiping a key at a predetermined time.

- *Secret Sharing and Secret Splitting:* A single document can be encrypted with multiple keys, requiring that all of the keys be present in order to decrypt the document. This concept can be taken a step further to create a document that can be decrypted by any two of three keys, or any two of four keys. For example, suppose there are four people, A, B, C and D, each with their own key (K_A, K_B, K_C and K_D), and it is desired to encrypt message M so that it can be decrypted by any two. One approach is to create six encrypted documents, encrypted with keys K_{AB}, K_{AC}, K_{AD}, K_{BC}, K_{BD} and K_{CD}, where each key K_{XY} is a mathematical function of K_X and K_Y. There are many variations on such schemes, collectively called *secret sharing* and *secret splitting*.

3.3 Public Key (Asymmetric) Encryption for Data Privacy

Asymmetric encryption algorithms use one key to encrypt data and a second key to decrypt the data. These keys are typically called the *public* and *private* keys, and as a result asymmetric cryptography is frequently called "public key cryptography" because one key is made publicly available and the other key is kept private.[18] The terms *public* and *private* can be misleading, however, since the e-mail encryption schemes perform encryption with the public key, while digital signature schemes perform decryption with the public key. To avoid confusion, this chapter will mostly use the phrases *encrypting key* and *decrypting key*.

3.3.1 Algorithms and Key Sizes

Most asymmetric algorithms are based on mathematical properties that arise through the manipulation of prime numbers. Asymmetric algorithms, also called public key algorithms, are typically much slower than their symmetric counterparts. Because of their reliance on certain mathematical properties, they have been harder to discover; it is also harder to establish their security. Whereas symmetric cryptography is thousands of years old and has been well understood since the 1950s, the basic concepts of asymmetric cryptography were not publicly disclosed until the 1970s. This novelty has resulted in many asymmetric algorithms being patented by their inventors.

It is far easier to crack an asymmetric encryption key than a symmetric key of the same key length. First, asymmetric cryptography takes advantage of mathematical principles and formulas. As a result, it is never necessary to perform a key search in order to crack an asymmetric key. The second reason it is easier to crack asymmetric algorithms is that asymmetric systems are used in applications in which the public key is widely distributed. As a result, an attacker who is targeting a public key system can create any number of chosen plaintext/ciphertext pairs.

There are several public key systems currently in use:

- *RSA*, named after its inventors Rivest, Shamir and Adleman, relies on the fact that it is easy to multiply two prime numbers together to create a composite, but it is relatively difficult to take a composite number and decompose it into its prime factors. RSA has the property that the private and public keys are interchangeable, that is, messages encrypted with the RSA public key can be decrypted with the private key, and messages encrypted with the private key can be decrypted with the public key. In this way RSA keys can be used both for message secrecy and for digital signatures. This leads to occasional confusion, as some RSA implementations use a single key for both operations, while other implementations use keys that are specifically created and used for privacy and authentication. RSA was covered under U.S. Patent 4,405,829 (itself a prime number), issued on September 20, 1983; exclusive rights to the patent expired on September 20, 2000.

- *The Digital Signature Algorithm (DSA)* (FIPS 186) is a public key algorithm created by the U.S. government in the 1990s and effective on December 1, 1994, as an alternative to RSA.[19] Compared with RSA, the DSA had three distinguishing features: (1) The algorithm was not covered under the RSA patent; (2) when it was created, the algorithm could be used for digital signatures but not for encryption, and as a result the algorithm did not fall under export control regulations at the time; and (3) the DSA required significantly more computational effort to verify signatures than did RSA. The algorithm itself is described in U.S. Patent 5,231,668, filed on July 26, 1991, by David W. Kravitz, a former NSA employee; the U.S. government made the patent available for use worldwide and royalty-free. (This patent right was disputed by Dr. Claus P. Schnorr, who claimed that DSA was actually a variant of the digital signature algorithm described in his patent, U.S. 4,995,082, which has now expired.)[20]

- *Elliptic curve cryptography* was recommended in 1999 by the National Institute of Standards and Technology, which sets security standards for the U.S. government.[21] Both the RSA and DSA algorithms make use of mathematical properties that arise from performing mathematics in a restricted range of numbers called a *number field*. It is possible to perform the same kinds of operations in a different kind of mathematical range called an *elliptic curve*. Performing the math in an elliptic curve has the advantage of making it dramatically harder to factor numbers and, thus, to crack a public key. The result is that public key cryptography performed in elliptic curves can achieve the ~~same security with much smaller keys, making the resulting cryptography faster and more energy efficient.~~ Elliptic curve public key cryptography is increasingly being used in mobile computing applications.

There are several other public key algorithms, but in general these other algorithms are only of academic curiosity and should not be used in production systems. Even though they work, they do not provide compelling advantages compared to existing standards, and their lack of widespread adoption means that any ~~implementations~~ are more likely to have significant security vulnerabilities.

3.3.2 Digital Signatures

Digital signatures are similar to other kinds of signatures in many ways:

- Like a human signature, a digital signature is a kind of mark that can be affixed to a digital document to identify the signer.

- Just as a person can sign his or her name in many different ways, so too can a person have more than one digital signature.

- Just as corporations and governments can have their own "signatures," such as the Great Seal of the United States, so too can corporations and governments have their own digital signatures.

- Signatures can be used to authenticate other signatures. For example, in the physical world, a driver's license typically displays a photo and signature of the driver, and on the sealed plastic is a seal of the certifying state. So too can digital signatures be used to certify one another: This process is performed with *digital signature certificates,* which typically contain a name, address and other kinds of digital identifiers, signed by some kind of certifying authority called a *certificate authority.*

But digital signatures are far more powerful than physical signatures.

- Unlike physical signatures, digital signatures certify that a document hasn't been modified since it was signed. This property is called *integrity.*

- To verify a physical signature, it is necessary to have a copy of the signature. Thus, any organization that can verify a physical signature can forge it as well. Digital signatures, in contrast, are created with a private key but verified with a public key. As a result, the only way to dispute the authenticity of a digital signature is make a claim that the private key was compromised or assert that the digital signature scheme itself was mathematically broken. This property is called **nonrepudiation**.

- As a result of **integrity** and **nonrepudiation**, a valid digital signature cannot be "lifted" from one document and fraudulently used to certify another.

- Although a physical signature must necessarily be affixed to the document that it certifies, this is not true of digital signatures. Thus, a signature can be distributed without a document, and then the document distributed at a later time. Such signatures are called **commitments** because they commit the signer to a statement that might itself be revealed at a later time. Commitments can be used to implement closed-bid auctions in such a manner that not even the auctioneer knows the identities of the bidders. In this application, the "bids" consist of a bid value and a digital signature. The winning bid is published on the Internet. At this point, the winner reveals the document that matches the signature. The document contains the bidder's bid and name.

Digital signatures combine two mathematical techniques discussed earlier in this chapter, cryptographic hash functions and public key cryptography:

- To **sign** a document, a program first computes the hash value of that document. Next, the program encrypts the hash value with an encrypting asymmetric key. The result is an encrypted hash value that can only be decrypted with a matching decrypting key.

- To **verify** the signature, the signature is decrypted with the matching key. This produces the claimed hash value of the document. Finally, the document is re-hashed to see if the two hash values match.

- If the two hashes match, the verifier knows two things: (1) The document has not been modified since it was signed and (2) the document was signed by the encrypting key that matches the decrypting key.

Because of the way that digital signatures are used in practice, the encrypting key is called the **private key** and is kept confidential; the decrypting key is called the **public key** and is typically made freely available. You can think of a private key like a signature stamp in the physical world—it can stamp a signature on a document or on a piece of paper that is affixed to the document. And just like the theft of a signature stamp, if a person's private key is stolen, the thief can forge the victim's signature without anyone being able to tell the difference.

3.3.3 Hybrid Systems: TLS and S/MIME

Another property resulting from the mathematical basis is that asymmetric systems typically encrypt only a relatively small amount of information—often no more than 1024 bits, and typically only 128 or 256 bits. This is not nearly enough bits to encrypt an entire message, but this is just right for encrypting an encryption key. As a result, asymmetric cryptography is typically used in hybrid systems that combine both symmetric and asymmetric cryptography. Two of the most widespread hybrid systems are TLS and S/MIME.

- *Transport Layer Security (TLS)*: TLS is a protocol that is used to encrypt data as it is sent over the Internet. The most common use of TLS is to encrypt web pages. When a web browser attempts to access a web page that begins with the letters "https," the browser attempts to download the page using TLS encryption. (As mentioned in the introduction, TLS was originally called the secure sockets layer and is still occasionally called SSL or SSL/TLS.)

- *Secure/Multipurpose Internet Mail Extensions (S/MIME) E-mail Security*: The S/MIME protocol allows e-mail messages to be digitally signed to verify the sender and encrypted so that they can be understood only by their intended recipient. The digital signature is a pure use of asymmetric cryptography, but the encryption is a hybrid system that relies on both asymmetric and symmetric cryptography.

TLS and S/MIME are both complex protocols that are the result of many years of engineering and analysis. In both cases the original protocols appeared to be secure, but additional analysis found important flaws. This is yet another example of why it is better to use existing encryption protocols than attempt to create your own: When you use an existing protocol, you can benefit from the work, including testing, that other people have done. But if you create your own, you will almost certainly have design and implementation flaws, and in most cases those flaws will not be detected until long after the software is deployed.

Although the details of TLS and S/MIME are beyond the scope of this chapter, the remainder of this section presents a skeletal description of both so that you can understand the role played by both asymmetric and symmetric cryptography as well as the need for a functioning public key infrastructure (PKI), which will be described in the following section.

When a user types the URL "https://www.company.com/" into a web browser, the following typically happens (see Figure 3-4):

1. The web browser issues a domain name system (DNS) request to convert the name www.company.com into an Internet protocol (IP) address.

2. The web browser opens a TLS connection to the web server at the specified IP address. The browser sends a *ClientHello* message containing information about the TLS protocols that the client supports, a set of ciphers it supports and a random number.

3. The server responds with a *ServerHello* message that contains information about the server, including the ciphers it will support, a random number, its TLS certificate and a *ServerHelloDone*. The TLS certificate contains a variety of information, including name of the web server (in this case www.company.com), the server's public key and a set of dates specifying the key's validity period (at what date and time the key started being valid, and when it expires).

4. The web browser creates a randomly generated number called a *PreMasterSecret*. Typically, this key will be 128 or 256 bits in size. Call this $K_{Session}$.

5. The web browser encrypts the *PreMasterSecret* with the server's public key and sends this to the server.

6. The server decrypts the *PreMasterSecret*.

7. Both the server and the client use the same algorithm to convert the *PreMasterSecret* into an encryption key, which they now use to encrypt the data for all of their subsequent communications.

The security of this scheme depends on two things. First, it requires that the web browser be able to make a truly random *PreMasterSecret*. If that value is not random and can be guessed by an attacker, then an attacker can decrypt the SSL session. The first web browsers in the 1990s did not have a good source of randomness and used the time of day to initialize their random number generators. This *seemed* random to the programmers at the time, as the resulting keys were always different. But "always different" does not mean unpredictable. Academics were able to demonstrate in the lab that it was relatively easy to guess the random number with only a few thousand attempts. As a result, it was quite easy to render these early cryptographic systems useless.

Figure 3-4: Normal Client-Server SSL Communications

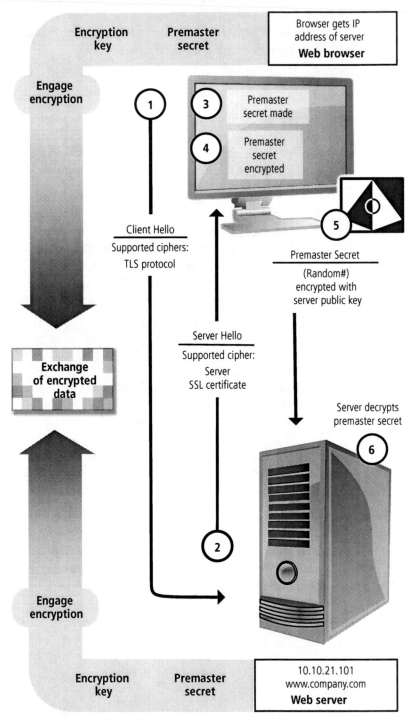

The second security requirement is that the web browser must positively have the public key belonging to the authentic server and not some interloper. Imagine what could go wrong if, instead of reaching the legitimate web server of company.com, the web browser instead placed a connection to evil.org (the evil changes are presented in bold):

1. The web browser issues a domain name system (DNS) request to convert the name www.company.com into an Internet protocol (IP) address.

2. The web browser opens a TLS connection to the web server—but the communication is intercepted and instead of going to company.com, it goes to evil.org. Now, instead of receiving the authentic server's TLS certificate, it receives a fraudulent certificate that has the legitimate company's name but the public key belonging to the interloper.

3. The interloper opens a TLS connection to the legitimate company's web server.

4. The web browser creates a randomly generated *PreMasterSecret*, encrypts it with the interloper's public key and sends it to the interloper.

5. The interloper receives the encrypted *PreMasterSecret*, decrypts it with the interloper's private key and re-encrypts it with the legitimate server's public key. The re-encrypted *PreMasterSecret* is now sent to the legitimate web server, where it is decrypted with the web server's private key.

6. All three computers—the client, the interloper and the legitimate web server—now have the same encryption key. Messages from the browser are encrypted with the encryption key and sent to the interloper, where they are decrypted, recorded for evil purposes, and then re-encrypted and sent to the legitimate server. Now the web browser and company.com can communicate with encryption. Both sides think that the communications are secure, but they are in fact being systematically decrypted and recorded.

The attack described above is known as a **man-in-the-middle** attack (see Figure 3-5). The attack is possible in the crypto system described here because the web browser has no way of knowing that the certificate that was downloaded was not legitimate. That's because by themselves, the simple certificates described above do not contain enough information to allow the browser to verify their authenticity. Because verification is not possible, there is no way for the browser to distinguish the legitimate certificate in the first example from the fraudulent certificate in the second.

Figure 3-5: Man-in-the-Middle Attack

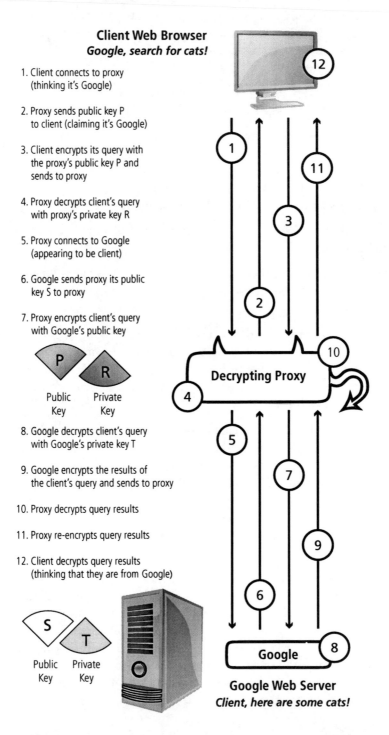

Client Web Browser
Google, search for cats!

1. Client connects to proxy
(thinking it's Google)

2. Proxy sends public key P
to client (claiming it's Google)

3. Client encrypts its query with
the proxy's public key P and
sends to proxy

4. Proxy decrypts client's query
with proxy's private key R

5. Proxy connects to Google
(appearing to be client)

6. Google sends proxy its public
key S to proxy

7. Proxy encrypts client's query
with Google's public key

P   R

Public   Private
Key   Key

8. Google decrypts client's query
with Google's private key T

9. Google encrypts the results of
the client's query and sends to proxy

10. Proxy decrypts query results

11. Proxy re-encrypts query results

12. Client decrypts query results
(thinking that they are from Google)

S   T

Public   Private
Key   Key

Decrypting Proxy

Google

Google Web Server
Client, here are some cats!

Figure 3-6: Signing and Verifying a Digital Signature

Making a Signature

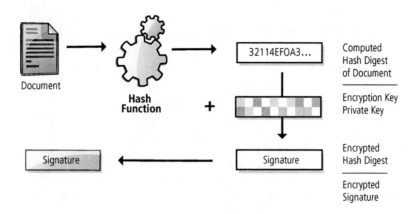

Verifying a Signature

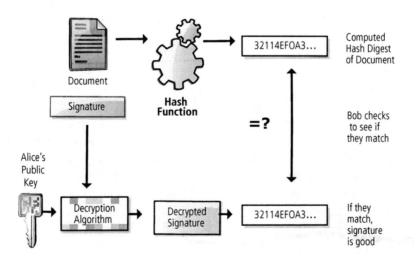

This is not a hard attack to execute. In fact, there is a free program called "Burp Suite," which performs the attack more or less automatically.[22]

The inventors of public key cryptography didn't realize the danger of man-in-the-middle attacks back in the 1970s. In their seminal paper "New Directions in Cryptography," Whitfield Diffie and Martin E. Hellman suggested this scenario:

> Each user of the network can, therefore, place his enciphering key in a public directory. This enables any user of the system to send a message to any other user enciphered in such a way that only the intended receiver is able to decipher it. . . . The enciphering key E can be made public by placing it in a public directory along with the user's name and address. Anyone can then encrypt messages and send them to the user, but no one can decipher messages intended for him.[23]

That is, Diffie and Hellman envisioned some kind of public directory containing every person's enciphering key—a directory that would be implicitly trusted by all users of the system. As it turns out, this early vision wasn't all that different from the way things turned out. The major difference between Diffie and Hellman's original vision of a public key directory and the system that we are using today is a matter of scale. A printed or simple electronic directory as imagined by Diffie and Hellman would have been sufficient to serve a few hundred users. The problem is that today, public key cryptography is used by billions of users and computers. If such a directory were actually made and distributed, it would invariably be out-of-date.

3.4 Public Key Infrastructure (PKI)

Public key infrastructure (PKI) is the name that has been adopted to describe the modern system that makes public key cryptography workable. Properly implemented, PKI provides tools for obtaining and verifying public keys that belong to individuals, web servers, organizations and most other kinds of entities that require some form of digital identification. PKI also contains schemes for revoking keys after they have been abandoned or in the event that they are compromised.

PKI is based on the principle of certification. An entity called a certificate authority asserts that a particular public key belongs to a particular entity. These assertions are stored in small documents called certificates.

Figure 3-7: www.google.com Certificate as Shown by Google Chrome on MacOS

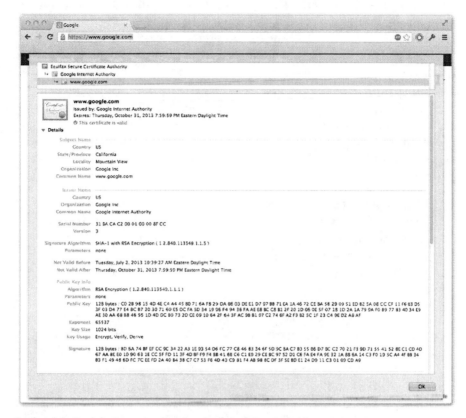

Google and the Google logo are registered trademarks of Google Inc., used with permission.

Figure 3-7 shows a portion of a digital certificate as displayed by the Google Chrome web browser for the www.google.com domain name. The certificate says that it was issued by the Google Internet Authority and that the authority's certificate was itself certified by the Equifax Security Certificate Authority. The Equifax authority is built into the computer on which the browser is running, which is why it has a different icon. The certificate is valid from July 2, 2013, through October 31, 2013.

The portion of the certificate display that says "Public Key Info" shows the technical information about the key that is being certified. In this case it is an RSA encryption key that is 128 bytes (1024 bits long). The first byte is C and the last byte is AF. RSA keys require something called an **exponent**; in this case, the exponent is 65537. The key is certified to be used for encryption, verification and deriving.

This certificate was provided to a web browser when a TLS connection was initiated to the server www.google.com. The certificate says that the browser should use the key C0...AF when connecting to the server. Having received this certificate, the browser would create a randomly generated session key, encrypt the key and send it back to the server—the very steps that are described in Section 3.3.2.

Recall from above that the primary vulnerability of TLS is a man-in-the-middle attack. Digital certificates protect against such an attack. The digital certificate represents a promise made by a third party, in this case an organization called Thawte SGC CA, that the public key on the certificate really does belong to a company called Google which operates a web server at www.google.com. Here's how:

1. The digital certificate contains not only the server's public key, but also the server's DNS name and the name of the company that runs the web server. The browser uses the DNS name to verify that it has the certificate for the correct server; the browser shows the company name to the user, allowing the user to verify the corporate name.

2. Google got the certificate sometime before October 25, 2011. To get the certificate, Google gave Thawte SGC CA a document called a *certificate signing request* (CSR), which consisted of Google's public key, its corporate name (Google Inc.), its domain name (www.google.com) and various legal documents that establish that the people who were presenting the information to Thawte actually had permission to act on behalf of Google. Thawte verified this information, put it on a digital certificate, signed the certificate with the Thawte private key and then gave the signed certificate back to Google. At this point Google took the signed certificate and put it on its web server.

3. The browser can verify the information on the certificate by verifying the digital signature. To verify the signature, the browser computes the cryptographic hash of all the information on the certificate *other than the signature*. Let's call this hash H1. Next, the browser takes the signature that's on the certificate and *decrypts the signature with the certificate authority's public key*. Let's call this decrypted value H2. Finally, the browser checks to see if H1=H2. If they are equal, the signature validates, and the information on the certificate is the same information that was there when the signature was signed.

The previous three steps rely on two presuppositions. First, that the browser has a copy of Thawte's public key; and second, that Thawte behaved in a trustworthy manner. Both of these presuppositions are the result of a deal between Thawte and the company that created the web user's web browser. The companies that make web browsers, including Microsoft, Apple, Google, the Mozilla Foundation and others, have all evaluated Thawte and concluded that the company is a trustworthy certificate authority (CA). That is, they trust Thawte's promises on certificates. As a result of this evaluation, the browser vendors have agreed to put a copy of Thawte's public key into their browsers.

3.4.1 PKI Limitations and EV Certificates

The PKI system works pretty well, but it is far from perfect. In fact, today's PKI system is badly frayed. Worse, the more it is used, the more problems are exposed.

Thawte is a widely trusted CA, but it is hardly the only one. Modern web browsers have more than 100 CAs built into their browsers, including well-known companies like AOL Time Warner and Wells Fargo, the national certificate authorities for Belgium and China, and companies with suspicious-sounding names like "AAA Certificate Services" (which is a name used by Comodo, a commercial certificate authority).

The current system of multiple certificate authorities was designed to allow different countries to have their own CAs, as well as to enable competition in the free market. The problem is that there is no practical means for users to distinguish between high-quality CAs and bargain-basement ones. As a result, all certificate authorities are equally trusted. This can create problems, as different CAs have different procedures and different security standards.

For example, in July 2011 the certificate authority DigiNotar, a Dutch certificate authority owned by VASCO Data Security International, apparently issued a certificate for the domain name ".google.com." The problem is that DigiNotar didn't issue the certificate to Google—it appears that it was issued to the government of Iran, which allegedly used the certificate to spy on Iranian citizens accessing Gmail and Google docs.[24]

Extended validation (EV) certificates are an attempt to create a high-quality certificate. EV certificates look different in the web browser, and certificate authorities are supposed to demand higher levels of assurance that they are dealing with the actual entity requesting the certificate. Unlike traditional TLS certificates, EV certificates also contain more information about the provider. And not surprisingly, EV certificates are more expensive.

Figures 3-8 and 3-9 illustrate the differences in how a site without an EV certificate and a site with an EV certificate display in a web browser.

Some security professionals dispute the effectiveness of EV certificates. They argue against their very premise, saying that the rigorous checking of identity and liability protection was supposed to be part of the original certificates and should not be reserved only for EV certificates. They further argue that the price of EV certificates has dropped and, as a result, CAs will eventually be unable to perform the identity checking and certification that the EV brand requires. Moreover, EV certificates still cannot protect end users against corrupt or compromised certificate authorities. For example, DigiNotar was able to issue EV certificates. What ultimately protected users against the DigiNotar certificates was the software vendors that make browsers, most of whom issued software updates that removed the malicious DigiNotar CA certificates from their browsers shortly after the fraudulently issued certificates were discovered.[25]

Figure 3-8: Website Without an EV Certificate

Google and the Google logo are registered trademarks of Google Inc., used with permission.

Figure 3-9: Website with an EV Certificate

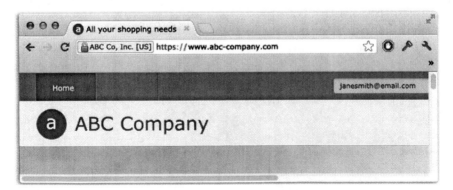

3.4.2 Client-Side PKI

In addition to verifying the identity of websites, PKI can also verify the identity of users. This process is similar to the way that websites are validated, except the certificate is issued to an individual, not to an organization.

Client-side PKI systems require a means for individuals to securely maintain their private key and to use it to prove their identity when this proof is required. Currently, there are two ways that individuals can maintain their private keys:

1. The private key can be stored inside a smart card or another kind of physical token. This is the most secure means for an individual to maintain a private key. The private key never leaves the smart card. Instead, when the individual needs to sign something, the cryptographic hash is provided to the smart card. Most smart cards also require that the individual have a personal identification number (PIN), which is typically four to eight digits long. The user inserts his smart card into a reader, provides the PIN and the identity is proven. Most smart cards will lock if the wrong PIN is provided three times in a row.[26]

2. The private key can be stored in an encrypted file on the user's computer. To use the private key, the user provides a password that is used to decrypt the key.

Smart cards are significantly more secure than storing the private key in an encrypted file for two reasons. First, the private key does not leave the smart card under normal circumstances. This makes the key more resistant to malware, since malware cannot directly access the key and copy it to another system. Second, the user normally removes his or her smart card from the reader when the smart card is not in use. This significantly reduces the chances that the key can be used without the user's knowledge.

Currently, there are four common uses for client-side PKI:

1. Using a web browser, users can provide their identity to a remote website. Here, PKI is a useful alternative to a system of usernames and passwords.

2. With client-side PKI, a user can add a signed name to a digital document. Adobe Acrobat provides this functionality.

3. Client-side PKI, can also be used to certify the contents of the digital document. Both Microsoft Word and Adobe Acrobat provide this functionality.

4. Users can digitally sign software, asserting that they are the author and that it has not been modified since it was created. Digital signatures on software are available on Microsoft Windows, Mac OS, iOS and Android. Sometimes the signatures are created on behalf of organizations, rather than individuals, but even these signatures are created with client-side PKI.

3.4.3 Certificate Revocation

Although PKI certificates have expiration dates, sometimes it is necessary to invalidate a certificate before it expires. For example, a user's private key may be inadvertently compromised. In these cases, the certificate authority responds by revoking the user's certificate.

There are two approaches to handling certificate revocation: through the use of revocation lists that are downloaded by a relying party, and through the use of the online certificate status protocol (OCSP). In the first case, a certificate revocation list (CRL) is downloaded from a URL that is published by the CA. In the second case, each time the certificate is used, a URL can be checked on the Internet to verify that the certificate is still good.

While it is possible to revoke individual certificates, it is not possible to revoke a CA. For example, when DigiNotar's certificates were compromised, vendors had to distribute patches for web browsers and operating systems to remove the DigiNotar CA certificates.

3.5 The Threat of Malware

This chapter has presented the way that encryption can be used to improve privacy and data security. But the security provided by encryption can be readily defeated if there are errors in the underlying design of the software or defects in the implementation. Indeed, much of the past two decades' worth of research in computer security has been the slow and methodical identification and correction of such flaws and errors.

Malware poses another threat to the privacy offered by encryption and cryptographic technology. Unlike design errors and implementation defects, some kinds of malware will intentionally circumvent security mechanisms in the most damaging way possible. Malware can do this because, unlike design errors and defects, malware is created for the purpose of doing bad things to unsuspecting users.

3.5.1 What Is Malware?

Malware is a term that has evolved since the early 2000s to cover a broad class of software that was written with malicious intent. The category includes viruses, worms, Trojan horses, fake antivirus programs and more. We use the term *malware* to avoid arguing about the fine minutiae of malicious program taxonomy: For most users it matters little whether the culprit is actually a worm or a virus.

Although most malware is written by people or organizations with malicious intent, it is not written solely by criminals. One of the most unfortunate incidents of malware involved a piece of copy protection software that was placed on audio discs by the Sony Corporation. The program covertly installed itself on Windows-based machines whenever an audio CD was played on one of these systems. Sony wrote the program with the intention of preventing unauthorized copying of its music, and antivirus vendors specifically modified their programs so that the Sony software would not be detected and removed. Unfortunately, the Sony program was more powerful than it needed to be. The software contained bugs that could be exploited by others and used to compromise a computer's security. Ultimately, Sony was caught, resulting in much embarrassment to the company.[27]

3.5.2 How Malware Can Impact Cryptography

Different kinds of malware have different capabilities, and not all of them are relevant to encryption. Not all malware will target encryption software, and malware that targets encryption is not always successful in its attempts. However, if malware is running on a computer, then there is no way to trust any encryption that the computer performs. There is no way to trust that the computer's keys are secure or that passphrases are not captured and provided to others. There is no way to trust that information digitally signed was not modified before it was signed, and no way to trust that failed signatures will be properly reported. Malware makes computers untrustworthy.

For example, malware on an end-user machine equipped with a smart card can detect when the smart card has been inserted and capture the user's PIN. At this point, the malware can sign literally hundreds of documents and gain access to thousands of websites, being forced to stop only when the user removes the smart card from the machine.

3.5.3 Anti-Malware Approaches and Malware Countermeasures

While malware is certainly powerful, it is not all-powerful. Indeed, one of the emerging uses of cryptography on modern computers is to detect malware so that it can be removed.

Digital signatures are a very powerful tool in the anti-malware arsenal. The theory is that software from legitimate vendors will be digitally signed. The signatures will allow virus scanners to detect programs that are infected with viruses, because an infected program's signature will no longer be valid. The signatures will also make it possible to find malware, since malware is typically not signed. In rare occasions a malware author might actually sign his malware with the author's own key. This actually happened in August 2012, when a digital certificate that was used to sign a piece of telephone spyware was also used to identify the spyware's author.[28]

Of course, as the case of DigiNotar demonstrates, there are many ways that malefactors could arrange to have malware signed even without using their own name on the certificate. For example, the malware authors could simply obtain a certificate in a fake name, or they could steal a certificate belonging to a legitimate company. Alternatively, the malware authors could break into the certificate authority and create fake certificates that supposedly belonged to other companies. While digital signatures can allow us to identify signed code, such signatures should not be used as evidence that the code is trustworthy.

3.6 Chapter Summary

As this chapter has shown, encryption and digital signatures are two of the fundamental technologies for assuring privacy and providing security in the digital domain. They are not all-powerful—any technology running on a computer system can be circumvented. But unlike passwords and other technologies, encryption and digital signatures offer the promise of mathematically sound security. For this reason encryption and digital signatures are likely to play an increasingly important role in preserving privacy and assuring accountability in the digital world.

Endnotes

1 *New Oxford American Dictionary*, 3rd ed., s.v. "encrypt."
2 Alex Hudson, "The Secret Code of Diaries," BBC Radio 4, *Today*, August 29, 2008, http://news.bbc.co.uk/today/hi/today/newsid_7586000/7586683.stm.
3 Andrew Lycett, "Breaking Germany's Enigma Code," *BBC History*, www.bbc.co.uk/history/worldwars/wwtwo/enigma_01.shtml (last updated February 17, 2011).
4 Lorrie Faith Cranor and Simson Garfinkel, *Security and Usability: Designing Secure Systems That People Can Use* (Sebastopol, CA: O'Reilly Media, 2005).
5 Modern password systems don't actually store the user's password. Instead, they process the password with a one-way function. The password provided by the user is processed by the same one-way function: If the two processed passwords match, then they must have been the same. More discussion about password hashing can be found in the classic paper by Robert Morris and Ken Thompson, "Password Security: A Case History," *Communications of the ACM* 22, no. 11 (1979): 594–597.

6 T. Dierks and C. Allen, "The TLS Protocol Version 1.0," Network Working Group Request for Comments: 2246, January 1999.

7 National Institute of Standards and Technology, "Vulnerability Summary for CVE-2011-3389," National Vulnerability Database, http://web.nvd.nist.gov/view/vuln/detail?vulnId=CVE-2011-3389 (last revised July 23, 2013).

8 These programs also use encryption when a file is saved with a "password to print" or "password to edit." However, in these cases, the decryption password is stored in the document itself. The restrictions against printing or editing provided by these programs are implemented in code, not with cryptography.

9 Joan Daemen and Vincent Rijmen, *The Design of Rijndael: AES—The Advanced Encryption Standard* (Berlin: Springer-Verlag, 2002).

10 When attempting to break an encryption algorithm, it is common for cryptographers to first attempt their attacks against "weakened" versions of the algorithm that use fewer rounds. Variants of AES-128 with 9 rounds and AES-256 with 12 rounds have been shown to be susceptible to attack. See Alex Biryukov et al., "Key Recovery Attacks of Practical Complexity on AES Variants with Up to 10 Rounds," in *Proceedings of the 29th Annual International Conference on Theory and Applications of Cryptographic Techniques*, 2010, 299–319.

11 Jeremy Hsu, "Can Life on Earth Escape the Swelling Sun?" Space.com, August 3, 2009, www.space.com/7084-life-earth-escape-swelling-sun.html.

12 National Security Agency, *Suite B Cryptography / Cryptographic Interoperability*, www.nsa.gov/ia/programs/suiteb_cryptography/index.shtml (posted January 15, 2009; last modified May 22, 2013; last reviewed May 22, 2013).

13 Electronic Frontier Foundation, "Cracking DES: Secrets of Encryption Research, Wiretap Politics & Chip Design," 1999, http://w2.eff.org/Privacy/Crypto/Crypto_misc/DESCracker/.

14 Eli Biham and Adi Shamir, "Differential Cryptanalysis of Snefru, Khafre, REDOC-II, LOKI and Lucifer," in *Proceedings of Advances in Cryptology—CRYPTO '91, Lecture Notes in Computer Science*, 576 (1992): 156–171.

15 D. Coppersmith, "The Data Encryption Standard (DES) and Its Strength Against Attacks," IBM *Journal of Research and Development* 38, no. 3 (1994): 243–250.

16 "Block Cipher Modes," Computer Security Resource Center, Computer Security Division, Information Technology Laboratory, National Institute of Standards and Technology, http://csrc.nist.gov/groups/ST/toolkit/BCM/index.html (last updated January 2, 2013).

17 D. Eastlake III, S. Crocker and J. Schiller, "Randomness Recommendations for Security," Network Working Group Request for Comments: 1750, December 1994.

18 Many people think that public keys are invariably used for encryption and that private keys are used for decryption, but this is not necessarily the case. Further complicating matters, the most widely used public key algorithm (RSA) has the property that either key can be used for either encryption or decryption—a message encrypted with one key can be decrypted with the other—but this is not necessarily true of other public key algorithms. To add to the confusion, e-mail encryption schemes typically use the recipient's "public" key to encrypt the message (which the receiver decrypts with its "private" key), but use the sender's "private" key to sign a message (which the receiver verifies with the sender's "public" key).

19 Approval of Federal Information Processing Standards Publication 186, Digital Signature Standard (DSS), 59 *Fed. Reg.* 26208-01 (May 19, 1994).

20 *1994 Annual Report of the National Institute of Standards and Technology Information Security and Advisory Board*, http://csrc.nist.gov/groups/SMA/ispab/documents/94-rpt.txt.

21 National Institute of Standards and Technology, "Recommended Elliptic Curves for Federal Government Use," July 1999, http://csrc.nist.gov/groups/ST/toolkit/documents/dss/NISTReCur.pdf.

22 "Burp Suite," PortSwigger Web Security, www.portswigger.net/burp/ (accessed October 17, 2013).

23 Whitfield Diffie and Martin E. Hellman, "New Directions in Cryptography," IEEE *Transactions on Information Theory* 22, no. 6 (November 1976): 644–654.

24 "DigiNotar Hacked by Black.Spook and Iranian Hackers," News from the Lab, F-Secure, August 30, 2011, www.f-secure.com/weblog/archives/00002228.html.

25 See, e.g., Johnathan Nightingale, "Fraudulent *.google.com Certificate," *Mozilla Security Blog*, August 29, 2011, http://blog.mozilla.org/security/2011/08/29/fraudulent-google-com-certificate/.

26 Although 3 times in a row is standard for smart cards, usability is dramatically increased when this number is increased to 5 or even 10, and increasing the limit does not significantly impact security. See Sacha Brostoff and M. Angela Sasse, "'Ten Strikes and You're Out': Increasing the Number of Login Attempts Can Improve Password Usability," in *Proceedings of CHI 2003 Workshop on HCI and Security Systems*, 2003.

27 Bruce Schneier, "Real Story of the Rogue Rootkit," Commentary, *Wired*, November 17, 2005, www.wired.com/politics/security/commentary/securitymatters/2005/11/69601.

28 Nicole Perlroth, "How Two Amateur Sleuths Looked for FinSpy Software," Bits (blog), *New York Times*, August 31, 2012, http://bits.blogs.nytimes.com/2012/08/31/how-two-amateur-sleuths-looked-for-finspy-software/.

CHAPTER 4

Identity and Anonymity

Chris Clifton

IT poses new challenges and new opportunities for managing identity and the resulting impact on privacy. These are nicely summed up in the now famous cartoon that appeared in the *New Yorker* magazine in 1993, with the caption "On the Internet, nobody knows you're a dog."[1] Information technology enables us to remain anonymous—conducting transactions without revealing who (or what) we are. But it also poses challenges—we may (wrongly) assume that we know who (or what) someone is.

Furthermore, advances in IT make it easier to defeat anonymization measures. Perhaps nobody knows we're a dog, but based on purchases of dog food, visits to veterinary medicine websites and so on, someone with access to all this information can make a pretty good guess. This poses real risks to personal privacy and the desire to remain anonymous during the course of everyday activities.

This chapter starts by categorizing types of digital identity, describing the different types of identity, how these can be used and how they are typically represented in information systems. This is followed by authentication, giving an understanding of methods of validating identity, and the strengths and weaknesses of each. We then look at privacy issues that arise with digital identity, particularly how types of identity map to privacy law and regulation. Finally, we discuss anonymization techniques and challenges, including the basic principles and techniques that are available to de-identify data and the challenges in adequately anonymizing data with respect to privacy legislation.

4.1 What Is Identity?

Information systems don't contain people, only data about people. So when we refer to identity, we really mean the link between a piece of information and the individual (or individuals) associated with that data. For example, a data item can be about an individual, created by an individual or sent to an individual. Identity captures what we know about who that individual is.

The clearest case of identity is when we know exactly who the individual is—we can link the data to a single person. This gives us an *identified individual*—the strongest form of identity.

A weaker form of identity is a *pseudonym*. With a pseudonym, we can link different data items about the same individual, but we don't know the actual person the data is about. The ability to create and use pseudonyms is a big privacy advantage of digital identity—we can detach online presence from the actual person. However, this kind of privacy can be illusory, as it is often possible to identify the actual person behind the pseudonym—this will be discussed in Section 4.4.1.

The weakest form of identity is *anonymity*. With truly anonymous data, we not only do not know the individual the data is about, we cannot even tell if two data items are about the same individual.

The differences can easily be seen using a formal definition. Assume we have a set of data items $D = \{d_1, \ldots, d_n\}$, and an identity function $I(d)$ that gives us information on whom the data item d is about. If we can say that for a known individual i, $I(d) = i$, then $I(d)$ is an identified individual. If we can say that $I(d_j) = I(d_k)$ (the two data items are about the same individual), but we do not know who that individual is, then $I(d_k)$ is a pseudonym. If we cannot make either statement (identified individual or pseudonym), then the data is anonymous.

A related concept is that of a *role*. Often, it is not important who an individual is, only that the person is authorized to perform an action. For example, a credit card account may have several authorized users, and the merchant only needs to know that one of the authorized users is making a purchase (a role), not which one (an identity). While this can be hard to do in person, electronic systems have capabilities that allow us to quickly distinguish between the role and the identity.

Another issue that arises is who can make the determination of identity. Say that Alice sent an e-mail to Bob. We normally think of the e-mail as being identified if Bob knows that it came from Alice and he knows the actual person corresponding to the name Alice. However, an alternative exists when Bob doesn't know who Alice actually is, but the real person (Alice) is able to prove she wrote the message. This provides pseudonymity and privacy for Alice, and the option of revealing identity resides with the individual to whom the identity belongs. Keyed hash functions, which are discussed in Chapter 3, provide an easy way to accomplish this. A third alternative is when an independent third party is able to validate that the message came from Alice.

4.1.1 How Is Identity Used?

There are a variety of reasons why an information system may need to know the identity of an individual, or of the individual associated with a piece of data. The most obvious is access control: Should a given individual see a given piece of data? While this seems to be a clear case for having an identified individual, this is often not necessary and, from a privacy point of view, may be inappropriate. For example, access to a subscription-based patent search system needs to be limited to subscribers, but companies may be reluctant to use a system requiring individual identification because of fears of revealing corporate intentions and plans. Information technology provides ways to support identification based on roles without requiring individual identification—providing the ability to significantly improve privacy.

A second reason for obtaining identity is attribution: the ability to prove who performed an action or generated a piece of data. For example, in a credit card transaction, the merchant needs to be able to show that a purchase is legitimate. Again, while systems are set up to require an identified individual for this purpose, all that is really needed is a role (an authorized user). Though this distinction may be difficult for face-to-face transactions, IT provides new opportunities to protect identity while ensuring correctness of information.

Identity is also used in information systems to enhance the user experience—particularly personalization. For example, web searches by an identified individual can be customized based on expressed desires or previous history of that individual. In this case all that is needed is a pseudonym—knowing that a set of searches all come from the same individual, including preferences provided by that individual, is equally effective even if I do not actually know the identity of that individual.

4.1.2 Representing Identity

There are a variety of ways to represent identity, each with advantages and drawbacks. The most basic means is to rely on external, easy-to-remember identifiers, such as an individual's name. Unfortunately, names are rarely unique—leading to the possibility of misidentification. This is why hospitals and health insurance companies typically require name and date of birth, and online credit card transactions ask for name and address. The combination of multiple factors is often unique, or the nonunique cases are sufficiently rare that they can be addressed after the fact. Such combinations typically result in an identified individual.

A second representation of identity is to allow a user to specify the identifier for a given system—typically referred to as userids or login names. This gives certain advantages—the system can guarantee uniqueness by forbidding creation of an "already taken" ID, and it provides for pseudonymity if the individual is allowed to choose the ID, which is an additional measure of privacy. The disadvantages are that users may want the same userid—for example, my use of the userid "clifton" at some websites results in my being locked out due to authentication failures. Other individuals who have the same last name and who don't remember their userid can try the ID "clifton" and fail to give the correct password. After a number of failures, the system locks out future attempts, blocking the legitimate user from obtaining access. Some systems try to prevent this by requiring userids of a certain length, or requiring combinations of numbers and letters. This is a usability trade-off—while such userids are hard to remember, they reduce the chance of conflict.

An alternative is a system-generated userid or unique number. This provides the same opportunity for pseudonymity, and if properly created, can ensure a degree of privacy—for example, by not using people's names as part of the userid. While user-generated userids can provide privacy, a system-generated, unique userid ensures privacy for all users, even those who do not realize the associated privacy risks of identifiability. To truly provide privacy, system-generated userids must not be based on other identifying data—for example, U.S. Social Security numbers, which are unique nine-digit numbers, are generated using location and date information that can help to link individuals to their number.[2]

An increasingly popular approach is to use externally created and managed unique identifiers. This has advantages and disadvantages. Externally created identifiers are often a user-friendly option, because the user can reuse another identifier, and this approach reduces the number of identifiers that a user must remember. Externally created identifiers also "outsource" the burden of ensuring uniqueness. Finally, these identifiers make it easier to link information across multiple systems. However, linkability also creates a privacy risk—linking information across multiple systems makes it easier to conduct fraud or other misuse of identity. In the United States, the Social Security number was once widely used as a unique identifier, but this eased identity theft and fraud—knowing an individual's Social Security number provided too much access to the individual's information. A better approach is to allow the user to choose the external identifier. E-mail addresses are a good example—the structure of the Internet guarantees that e-mail addresses are unique, but it is possible for a user to have multiple e-mail addresses, including addresses that were created without revealing identity, providing the option of pseudonymity for users who desire it.

Finally, identity can be represented using systems created for that purpose. The X.500 standard provides a flexible framework for storing and maintaining identifying information, as do commercial systems such as Microsoft Passport or Google Wallet. Cryptographic certificates and public-key infrastructure (see Chapter 3) also provide mechanisms to verify identity. These systems generally combine representations of identity with other identity-related information (name, address) and can provide authentication mechanisms as well, which we discuss in the next section.

To summarize, identity can come in a variety of manners: identified individual, pseudonymous or truly anonymous, providing progressively greater levels of privacy. It may be sufficient to know a role rather than an identity, and it is important to understand what identity is used in order to ensure that an appropriate level of identity is used. Given these concerns, we can choose appropriate mechanisms to represent identity, providing appropriate trade-offs between level of identification, ease of use and privacy.

4.2 Authentication

Authentication is closely tied to identity. While identity links information to an individual, authentication is used to ensure that an individual performing an action matches the expected identity. Authentication can be accomplished by a variety of mechanisms, each with advantages and drawbacks. These mechanisms fall into four main categories:

1. What you know: secret knowledge held only by the individual corresponding to the identity

2. What you have: authentication requires an object possessed by the individual

3. Where you are: the location matches the expected location

4. What you are: biometric data from the individual

These mechanisms vary in terms of their ability to be defeated, ease of use, cost and privacy implications. In addition to the trade-offs in using authentication mechanisms, any decision to use one should consider the challenges of both creating and revoking credentials. For a particular mechanism, establishing or changing the credentials used to authenticate an individual can be much more expensive and prone to misuse than for other mechanisms. For example, a personal identification number (PIN, such as a four-digit number used for a bank card) that is sent by postal mail can be compromised through theft or picking through trash, where the PIN may have been discarded. Requiring an individual to appear in person to select a PIN protects against these attacks, but may result in a PIN that can be guessed by someone knowing the individual, because the PIN was not randomized. A recent study of PINs shows that many people choose four- and six-digit PINs according to specific patterns that increase the predictability of PINs.[3] Revocation, which is the repealing and reissuing of compromised credentials, poses similar issues—in particular, revoking biometric data is generally impossible, so systems using biometric data for authentication must be constructed using strong cryptographic techniques to ensure that such data is never compromised.

4.2.1 Passwords

One of the most common approaches to authenticating a user is through passwords or PINs. This is an example of *what you know* authentication: It is assumed that only the proper individual knows the password. Passwords can provide a high level of assurance that the correct individual is being identified, but when used improperly can easily be broken.

Attacks on password-based authentication fall into two categories: attacks on the password itself and password attacks performed directly through the system. One approach, which is most useful with short passwords, such as four-digit PINs, is guessing passwords. This can be prevented by disabling access after too many failed attempts—but this also places a burden on legitimate users who incorrectly enter the password. Setting an appropriate number of failed authentication attempts should balance the need for correct identification against the cost of resetting a password; if an easy and secure mechanism exists to reset passwords, then locking out is not a big problem. But if a reset requires, for example, a trip to the bank, the system quickly becomes unusable.

The dictionary attack is an example of password guessing. Given a choice, users tend to choose easy-to-remember passwords—typically normal words. There are other forms of authorization, such as *what you have*, that are harder to obtain using social engineering without exposing the attacker to increased risks of detection.

A simple example of a password attack performed directly through the system is the man-in-the-middle attack, in which a computer program intercepts traffic and reads the password contained in the intercept. To combat this attack, passwords are typically encrypted. Instead of presenting the password to a system, the system uses a one-way hash of the password, and the system stores only the hash. As it is extremely difficult to discover the password from the hash, this prevents the man in the middle, or an intruder who has gained access to the system, from obtaining a user's password.

While the man in the middle may not know the password, he only needs to replay the hash of the password to gain access; this is called a *replay attack*. This kind of attack is easily combated through system design. *Challenge response* authentication issues a unique challenge for each authentication: The response must be correct for each challenge. With a hashed password, the challenge is an encryption key sent by the system. The user application uses the key to encrypt the hash of the password; this is compared with the system's encryption of the stored value of the hashed password. Each authentication uses a different key, and thus a replay attack fails because the replayed password (response) is not encrypted with the current key (challenge).

The proper design and implementation of password systems are important concerns for information security experts. Due to the risk of stealing an individual's identity through a weak password system, however, there is a growing need for IT professionals who are responsible for privacy to be engaged in this discussion. In addition to passwords, systems will ask security questions (e.g., what was the name of your high school, or in what city were you born?). These questions are often used as a secondary form of authentication; for example, during a password reset mechanism. To reduce the risk of a stolen identity, these questions must target information that is unlikely to be known by an attacker, and is therefore likely to be private information. Consequently, the answers must be protected (e.g., through a hash mechanism similar to that used for passwords) to ensure that this data is not disclosed.

4.2.2 Devices

The *what you have* approach to authentication typically uses computing devices. Identification badges or smart cards can be used; these require that the computing terminal have the ability to read the computing device. A convenient approach is to embed a radio frequency identification (RFID) chip in the device; this does require a reader, but the user doesn't actually have to swipe the card. This particular technology introduces a privacy risk in that a malicious actor with a remote RFID reader can detect when the user is nearby, even though he or she is not actually trying to authenticate. If the actor can read the RFID card, then he may be able to "become" that individual through a replay attack.

Devices also exist that don't require special hardware at the client's terminal. These are typically in the form of small devices that display a changing PIN; the timing and sequence of PINs are known to the system. The user can type the PIN being displayed by the device just like a password, and the system checks to see if the given PIN matches what the device should be displaying.

Lastly, the computing device may be the computer that the user uses to access the system (e.g., a home computer, laptop, or smartphone). The system stores the IP address of the device or uses browser cookies to store a unique key on the machine; this allows the system to check whether the attempt to authenticate comes from a device previously used. Since the user already has the device, this requires no additional hardware.

Device-based authentication becomes problematic when devices are lost or stolen—until the loss is recognized and reported, access to the system may be compromised. As a result, these systems are typically combined with passwords or some other form of authentication so that the lost device alone cannot be used to gain access.

4.2.3 Location

Location-based authentication is typically used in corporate networks. Access to corporate resources is limited to computers physically located in the company. This requires an attacker to gain physical access as well as defeat other authentication (such as passwords), making unauthorized access far more difficult. Of course, this also prevents legitimate use from outside the network, requiring the use of virtual private networks (VPNs). A VPN provides an encrypted link to the corporate network, and typically requires a high standard of authentication to make up for the loss of location-based authentication.

Note that location-based authentication can be used in other ways as well. Credit card issuers may reject transactions at unfamiliar locations, unless the customer has provided advance notice of travel. While this may seem invasive from a privacy point of view, such location information will likely be made available anyway—for example, from the credit card use, or the IP address used to connect to the system, so little additional information is disclosed when providing a list of authorized locations, such as a travel itinerary.

While location is useful, it should almost always be viewed as a secondary form of authentication, used to provide stronger evidence that the primary form of authentication is correct.

4.2.4 Biometrics

What you are as a form of authentication is growing increasingly popular. Notebook computers are available with fingerprint readers, and cameras and microphones are becoming standard equipment on many devices. Fingerprints, face and voice recognition and other biometric methods for authentication are becoming increasingly available. This brings advantages, but also raises privacy issues.

First, systems using biometric data must protect that data. If a user's password is compromised, the user can change it—but cannot be asked to change his or her face or fingerprint. As with passwords, careful system design is needed to ensure that an attacker cannot obtain or spoof the biometric data. In 2009, Duc Nguyen demonstrated how the face recognition software in three different laptop models, manufactured by Asus, Lenovo and Toshiba, could be tricked into believing that a photo of the laptop owner's face was the physical owner, thus bypassing the face recognition software.[4] The attack scenarios include obtaining a person's face from his or her website, social networking site or online chat.

Second, use of biometric data raises inherent privacy concerns. While passwords can be associated with a pseudonym, a fingerprint is inherently identifying, and a pseudonymous account using a fingerprint for authentication should probably be considered individually identifiable. There may also be cultural issues; some users may be reluctant to have a photograph taken or to display their face for use in biometric authentication.

A second type of biometrics is based on behavior—for example, typing rate or patterns of mouse movement. While these give only a degree of assurance, they provide the opportunity for continuous authentication. Once a user authenticates to the system, the behavior in using the system can be used to ensure that the user hasn't walked away and someone else has stepped in to use the account.

4.2.5 Authentication Summary

Authentication is the means by which a system knows that the identity matches the individual who is actually using the system. There are several approaches to authentication. Often, these can be used in combination, significantly decreasing the risk of a successful attack or attempt at impersonating the user.

Authentication must balance assuring the accuracy of an individual's identity and the usability of the system. While authentication needs to be strong enough to protect private information, excessive use of technology to perform authentication can reduce the practical effectiveness of the system and create new privacy issues by collecting sensitive personal information needed to implement complex authentication mechanisms.

4.3 Identity Issues

How are privacy and identity related? The key is that privacy laws and regulations typically apply only to data that is *individually identifiable*. At first glance, this would suggest that pseudonymous or anonymous data is not subject to privacy law. The problem is that "individually identifiable" is a somewhat broader concept than "individually identified." From an identity point of view, data is individually identified if we know which individual the data is about. From a privacy point of view, however, we are also interested in the question of whether or not the data could be linked to a specific individual. The difficulty is in determining if pseudonymous or anonymous data could be linked to the individual the data is actually about. This continues to be a challenging and unsolved research problem, although there are several areas where legislation and regulation provide good guidelines.

4.3.1 Individually Identifiable Data

Almost all privacy regulations have some definition of the information to which they apply; for example, the EU Data Protection Directive 95/46/EC applies to "personal data," and the U.S. Healthcare Insurance Portability and Accountability Act (HIPAA) applies to "protected health information." What do these terms mean? Unfortunately, this is often not entirely clear. While data that is not about an individual is obviously not covered, and data that is individually identified clearly is, there is a large middle area of data that is not overtly identified, but may be identifiable. An obvious case pointed out by Latanya Sweeney is the use of home address and date of birth.[5] She showed that, given a person's postal code, date of birth and gender, which were contained in state-gathered hospital admission data presumed to be anonymous, she was able to identify numerous individuals by cross-referencing this data with publicly available voter registration data. In fact, she estimates that 87 percent of U.S. persons could be identified from date of birth, postal code and gender. As a result, this data is considered privacy-sensitive and not subject to disclosure under U.S. freedom of information rules.

Little guidance has been given as to exactly how much information is needed to cross the threshold into individually identifiable data. Is it okay if only 10 percent can be identified? Guidance from the European Community Article 29 Working Party formed under 95/46/EC suggests that no individuals should be identifiable. However, it is less clear on a related point—what if I am not certain about an individual, but I can identify the person with some degree of confidence? For example, suppose I know a data item is about a doctor in a town containing only two doctors. While the Article 29 Working Party suggests that if there is only one doctor in town, the record is individually identifiable, the question of how many doctors are needed to make the data nonidentifiable is not clearly answered.[6]

In some cases, the answers are clear. For example, most U.S. data breach notification laws are triggered if a last name, first initial and account number are disclosed. HIPAA provides a broader statement: It contains a "safe harbor" provision that specifies that data can be considered nonidentifiable after the removal or generalization of 18 specific types of potentially identifying information. For example, dates, such as birth date, must be no finer-grained than a year, and postal code can include only the first three digits, or an area encompassing at least 20,000 people. Furthermore, birth year can only be included for individuals under 85. Using this, we can conclude that on average, 67 people could potentially be tied to a record for a male in his lower 80s, suggesting that a confidence in identification under 1.5 percent would not be considered individually identifiable. While this guideline is only inferred from the rule, it does suggest that data can be sufficiently de-identified to prevent triggering privacy regulations.

HIPAA also provides a specific example of pseudonymity. A de-identified dataset may include "a code or other means of record identification to allow information de-identified under this section to be re-identified by the covered entity, provided that: (1) the code or other means of record identification is not derived from or related to information about the individual and is not otherwise capable of being translated so as to identify the individual; and (2) the covered entity does not use or disclose the code or other means of record identification for any other purpose, and does not disclose the mechanism for re-identification."[7] This is a somewhat convoluted, but precise, legal definition of pseudonymity. The challenge for IT professionals is identifying these various definitions and managing the definitions in a consistent and legally compliant manner across their systems.

4.3.2 Identity Through History

Pseudonymous data and anonymous data pose different privacy risks. Given a set of data items about an individual, such as user purchases, it may be possible to identify the individual even if no individual data item can be linked to that person. Pseudonymous data may be identifiable even if the same data made anonymous is not by itself identifiable. Perhaps the most famous example of this is from web search log data made publicly available by AOL. Reporters were able to identify an individual based on a collection of queries, including information such as names and locations.[8] Similar studies found risks with transaction data released under the Netflix challenge.[9]

The need to tread pseudonymous data collections with particular care is recognized in law. The U.S. HIPAA Privacy Rule does not apply to *anonymous* data. However, it makes a special provision for "limited data sets," which are not individually identified; individual identifiers must be replaced with a number. This gives a pseudonymous dataset. Limited datasets can be shared under a data use agreement, but they may not be publicly released.

There has been work on ensuring anonymity in such pseudonymous datasets.[10] However, this is still an open challenge, and extra care must be taken when releasing log files or transaction data. The IT professional may use encryption (see Chapter 3) or rely on contractual agreements with the receiving party (see Chapter 7) to ensure that privacy protections are afforded to potentially re-identifiable data.

4.3.3 Incidental or Unplanned Sources of Identity

There are many nonobvious sources of identifying information. For example, the IP address of a computer making a remote HTTP or HTTPS request is frequently logged. For some network providers, there is evidence that even dynamically assigned IP addresses do not change frequently, thus allowing a client computer to repeatedly be linked to the same IP address for long periods of time. Early implementations of IPv6 used addresses in which a unique 64-bit number derived from a computer's hardware address was used in every address regardless of which network the computer was on. The Article 29 Working Party suggested that IP addresses should be considered individually identifiable information; for many people, their computer hosts a website identifying them.[11] Thus, logs that contain IP addresses need to be treated as individually identifiable information, and protected appropriately.

Browser fingerprinting is another example. In an effort to personalize or customize the user experience, websites can track the user through the use of browser cookies or other techniques. Peter Eckersley demonstrates how advanced techniques can uniquely identify most browsers by using data reported to the web server, including the client operating system, browser plug-ins and system fonts.[12] While tracking can be beneficial to the individual, it also turns anonymous exchanges into pseudonymous exchanges—and as seen previously, this can make data individually identifiable. (In Chapter 5, we discuss surveillance and tracking technology and the associated privacy risks in more detail.) Finally, logs can include sensitive information that a user may assume is anonymous, resulting in serious privacy risk. Thus, any comprehensive collection of information must be carefully evaluated for privacy risk, and both the risk and cost of protecting the data must be weighed against the value obtained from collecting the data.

4.4 Anonymization

The least restrictive way to utilize data while ensuring that privacy is protected is through anonymization. If data is not individually identifiable, it does not pose a privacy risk. Anonymization techniques attempt to ensure that data is not identifiable. This is a challenging problem: For each anonymization technique, there are attacks showing conditions under which data can be re-identified. Though these attacks sometimes make very strong assumptions, it is clear that any attempt at anonymizing data faces risks. However, these risks are likely to be much smaller than the risk of misuse of identifiable data, through either insider misuse or external attackers gaining access to data.

4.4.1 Strong vs. Weak Identifiers and Individual Identifiability

Some information is clearly identifying—for example, identifying numbers such as a national identification, passport or credit card number. These are referred to as strong identifiers. Names can be strong identifiers, but common names may not be uniquely identifying. This is why names are typically used in combination with other information (birth date, address) to identify individuals. Identifiers that must be used in combination with other information to determine identity are referred to as weak identifiers. A related concept is quasi-identifiers: data that can be combined with external knowledge to link data to an individual.

A related issue is linkable data vs. linked data. Given an identifier—either a strong identifier or a collection of weak identifiers—can we determine an individual's identity? Given a bank account number and nothing else, most of us would not be able to determine who the individual is—the link from bank account number to the individual is generally protected. This raises an interesting issue: Is data individually identifiable if it requires substantial background knowledge to link the data to an individual? Laws on this issue are unclear, but state data breach notification laws provide some hints within the United States. Disclosure of a financial account number alone does not trigger these laws (even though this is typically a strong identifier): It is the financial account number and name in combination that trigger these laws. Generally, if a quasi-identifier can be linked to an individual using publicly available information, it should be considered individually identifiable.

Even if linking data is not public, it is a good idea to consider strong identifiers or a combination of weak identifiers as sufficient to make data identifiable. As an example, the Article 29 Working Party notes that an IP address should be considered identifiable data. While it is clear that an Internet service provider (ISP) is likely to be able to link an IP address to an individual, the Working Party also says that this should apply to search engines.[13] The reasoning is that third parties (e.g., through civil litigation) can obtain the data necessary to make the link.

A somewhat murky area is the distinction between identifying a record, which clearly triggers a privacy law, and identifying a sensitive value associated with an individual. While it is unclear whether the latter triggers privacy law, it pretty clearly poses a risk to privacy. This will be discussed further in Section 4.4.3, when we discuss the role of microdata.

4.4.2 Approaches to Anonymization

Anonymization techniques hide identity in a variety of ways. The simplest approach is *suppression*: removing identifying values from a record. Names and identifying numbers are typically handled through suppression.

Some types of data are amenable to *generalization*, which is performed by replacing a data element with a more general element, for example, by removing the day and month from a birth date or removing a street from a postal address and leaving only the city, state or province name. Replacing a date of birth by just the year of birth substantially reduces the risk that an individual can be identified, but still leaves valuable information for use in data analysis.

A third approach is *noise addition*. By replacing actual data values with other values that are selected from the same class of data, the risk of identification is lowered. The addition is often aimed at preserving statistical properties of the data, while disrupting future attempts to identify individuals from the data. In many ways, the protection obtained by noise addition is similar to generalization.

Generalization and noise addition not only reduce the risk of identification, they can also reduce the sensitivity of data. For example, birth date is frequently used as a form of authentication—"what you know." Generalizing birth date to year prevents this data from being used to support identity theft. Because generalized individually identifiable data is still individually identifiable, and thus probably covered by privacy law, it does reduce the risk of damage should data be inadvertently disclosed.

4.4.3 Anonymization of Microdata

The most obvious approach to anonymizing data is using what is commonly referred to as microdata sets. A microdata set contains the original records, but the data values have been suppressed or generalized, or noise has been added to protect privacy. The open question is how much suppression, generalization or noise is needed for data to no longer be considered individually identifiable.

Government publishers of data about individuals, such as census bureaus, have a long history of studying this problem, and numerous techniques have been developed. In addition to generalizing values to ranges (e.g., birth decade rather than birth year), values are often *top-* and *bottom-coded* (e.g., reporting all ages over 80 as ">80" as opposed to reporting decade). Rounding can also be used as a form of generalization (e.g., to the nearest integer, or nearest 10); *controlled rounding* ensures that rounding is done in a way that preserves column summations. Where data must be suppressed, *data imputation* can be used to replace the suppressed values with plausible data without risking privacy. Another technique includes *value swapping*, which means switching values between records in ways that preserve most statistics but no longer give correct information about individuals. Much of this work is summarized in a 2005 U.S. government report.[14]

One particularly valuable resource from this community is the "Checklist on Disclosure Potential of Proposed Data Releases."[15] While it does not contain hard-and-fast rules, the checklist provides several guidelines, such as generalizing geographic units to regions containing at least 100,000 individuals, and top-coding ages over 85. Furthermore, it provides a comprehensive list of questions that should be considered before releasing data. Though directed toward U.S. government agencies, the procedures and questions are worth considering for any release of microdata.

Perhaps the only clear legal answer to the question of what makes data individually identifiable is the HIPAA "safe harbor" rules. These specify the removal or generalization of 18 types of data. Name, identifying numbers (telephone number, insurance ID, etc.) and several other data types must be suppressed. Dates must be generalized to a year, and addresses to the first three digits of the postal code or more general if this does not yield a region containing at least 20,000 people. Furthermore, age must be "top-coded" as follows: All ages greater than 89 must simply be reported as ">89." If these steps have been taken, and there is no other reason to believe that the data is identifiable, then the data can be considered de-identified and no longer subject to the HIPAA Privacy Rule.

In addition to regulatory rules and guidelines, a formal definition was established in computer science. Perhaps the first definition was k-anonymity.[16] The k-anonymity requires that every record in the microdata set must be part of a group of at least k records having identical quasi-identifying information. To achieve this, records with similar identifying information are formed into groups of at least k in size, and the identifying information is generalized or suppressed so that all the records have identical quasi-identifiers. This ensures that no record can be individually identified; given identifying information for an individual, there are at least k records that are equally likely to belong to the individual. (Note that we are assuming there is only one record for each individual; extending to cases where there are multiple records about an individual is straightforward.)

The k-anonymity does not provide an absolute guarantee of privacy protection. For example, suppose we have a microdata set listing occupation. If we assume that occupation is not publicly known, but age and address are, then age and address are quasi-identifiers. Table 4-1 is an example of a 2-anonymous table: For any given age range and address, there are at least two records corresponding to that age/address. Suppose we know Patricia is 19 years old and lives in West Lafayette—we know she is one of the first two records, but we have no idea which one. However, since the occupation of both of these people is "student," we now know that Patricia is a student—even though the record is not individually identifiable.

Table 4-1: Sample 2-Anonymous Dataset

Age	Address	Occupation
[18-22]	West Lafayette	Student
[18-22]	West Lafayette	Student
[18-22]	Lafayette	Steamfitter
[18-22]	Lafayette	Student
[23-30]	West Lafayette	Teacher
[23-30]	West Lafayette	Farmer

This issue is addressed by l-diversity.[17] The l-diversity extends k-anonymity by further requiring that there be at least l distinct values in each group of k records. This prevents the privacy breach noted above; there are at least l possible occupations for an individual, even if we know which group of k people he or she belongs to.

Even l-diversity has issues. For example, suppose one of the occupations is "CEO." Even though we don't know which record belongs to Patricia, we know that CEOs are rare, and since she is one of k people, one of whom is a CEO, the probability that she is a CEO is much higher than we would think without having access to the microdata. This issue spawned a definition t-closeness, which ensures that the distribution of values in a group of k is sufficiently close to the overall distribution.[18]

While these definitions seem strong, given sufficient background knowledge it is almost always possible to learn private information from such a microdata set. This is even true of the HIPAA safe harbor rules, so it appears that some level of risk to privacy is deemed acceptable. However, there is not yet a generally legally accepted definition of what constitutes nonidentifiable data.

4.4.4 Aggregation-Based Approaches

Instead of publishing de-identified individual-level records, one can publish aggregate statistics derived from the data. On the face of it, this would eliminate privacy concerns. Unfortunately, it is often possible to determine individual values from such statistics. For example, publishing a table giving statistics on the number of individuals with given income levels broken down by age could reveal both age and income for certain well-known high-income individuals. More subtle attacks on privacy come from comparison of values across multiple cells; an example of such a problem, and a method to deal with it, can be found in a paper by Wang et al.[19] The official statistics community has led the way in techniques to safely publish so-called contingency tables. Many of the techniques are similar to microdata—top- and bottom-coding, suppression and noise addition, to name a few.

A key issue when releasing aggregates is to determine whether the data is *frequency* or *magnitude* data. The easiest way to distinguish these two types of data is to determine whether individuals contribute equally or unequally to the value released. For example, a count of the number of individuals at a given income and age is frequency data: Each individual contributes one to the cell he or she is in. A table giving average income by age is magnitude data: Someone with a high income will affect the average much more than an individual whose income is close to the average. For magnitude data, noise addition or entire suppression of the cell is typically needed to ensure privacy; for frequency data, rounding techniques may well be sufficient. The previously described microdata checklist includes a section with recommendations for disclosure of aggregates.[20]

Aggregation has led to formal definitions to measure when aggregation is sufficient to protect privacy. The most widely accepted definition at this time is **differential privacy.**[21] Differential privacy is a noise addition approach; the idea is to add sufficient noise to the aggregates to hide the impact of any one individual. The key idea is to compare the difference in the aggregate result between two databases that differ by one individual. Differential privacy requires that the added noise be large relative to that difference, for *any two databases and any individual.* Formally, the definition is as follows:

For $S \subseteq Range(f)$, an $\in$-differentially private mechanism M satisfies $\dfrac{Pr[M_f(D_1) \in S]}{Pr[M_f(D_2) \in S]} \leq e^{\in}$, where D_1 and D_2 differ on at most one element.

We can see that when $\in = 0$, the answers must be the same for the two databases—perfect privacy. As $\in$ increases, the quality of the answer improves, but the privacy provided decreases. Though perhaps not obvious from the definition, differential privacy is quite general—it can apply to a function f that returns a discrete value, a continuous value, or even a set of values (such as a contingency table). Furthermore, there is a general mechanism—adding noise from a Laplace distribution—that can be applied to provide differential privacy. A survey of mechanisms for achieving differential privacy is given in a paper by Cynthia Dwork.[22]

Differential privacy deals with a key challenge in the release of aggregates: Even though it may be safe to release two aggregate values (e.g., two tables) independently, given both, is it possible to re-identify individuals from these tables? The answer may be yes. A simple example would be releasing the total payroll of a company, and the total payroll of the company exclusive of the CEO. While neither datum by itself reveals individual salaries, given both of these numbers it is easy to determine the CEO's salary. If we use differential privacy to release two aggregates, one providing $\in_1$ privacy, and the other providing $\in_2$ privacy, the two in combination give at least $\in_1 + \in_2$ privacy.

One open question is the appropriate value of $\in$ for differential privacy. It turns out that the parameter $\in$ is really a measure of the quality of the aggregate rather than the risk to an individual. **Differential identifiability** is a reformulation of differential privacy that limits the confidence that any particular individual has contributed to the aggregate value:[23]

$$\forall D'=D-\{i\}, \forall i \in U-D', S \subseteq Range(f), \text{ a } \rho\text{-differentially identifiable}$$
$$\text{mechanism } M \text{ satisfies } Pr[I(i) \in D | M_f(D)=S,D'] \leq \rho.$$

We can compute an expected value for ρ for the HIPAA safe harbor rules. Assuming a geographic area of 20,000 individuals, we would expect to find 68 males of age 83, giving $\rho=1.7\%$. While the confidence in identifying younger individuals is likely to be lower, and in some cases the safe harbor rules may not provide this level of protection, we can assume that the goal of the rule is no stronger than this. Differential identifiability guarantees that we limit identification confidence to this level, providing a defensible argument of the sufficiency of the mechanism.

Though still evolving, releasing data aggregates rather than microdata often provides significantly better privacy protection and still meets the needs for data analysis.

4.4.5 Client-Side Control of Anonymization

While anonymization is typically viewed as something done by a data custodian, there are client-side techniques to enhance anonymity. For example, proxy servers can hide the IP address of a request by replacing it with that of the proxy server. Techniques such as onion routing and Crowds further extend this notion of proxies by hiding IP addresses even from the proxy server.[24] Tor is a practical example of such a system. Tor is a peer-to-peer network where each request is routed to another peer, which routes it to another peer, and so on until a final peer makes the actual request. Encryption is used to ensure that only the first peer knows where the request came from, and only the last peer knows the server to which the request is being routed.

This hides only the IP address. Most Internet traffic contains considerably more identifying information. For example, a typical HTTP request contains information on the browser, last page visited, type of machine and so on. This can make such a request identifiable even if the IP address is not known. Private Web Search is a browser plug-in that strips such information from the request.[25] This leaves only the search text itself, but as we have seen with the AOL query log disclosure, even this may be sufficient to identify an individual. Tools have been developed to generate "cover queries"—fake query traffic that disguises the actual request.[26] Supporting such client-side approaches by requesting only necessary information (e.g., requiring use of cookies only when necessary for a transaction) enables users who are concerned about privacy to provide their own protection. This can increase comfort level for privacy-sensitive users.

4.5 Chapter Summary

An important privacy concern for IT professionals is procedures for handling *individually identifiable* data. Data that cannot be linked to a specific individual is generally not constrained by privacy regulations. Unfortunately, it is not easy to determine if data can be linked to an individual. While *anonymous* data can be shared freely, it is difficult to ensure that data is truly anonymous. *Pseudonymous* data can also be safe to share, but re-identifying the individual associated with this data is easier than with anonymous data. As a result, all data about individuals should be treated with care. The level of protections afforded this data should be commensurate with the privacy risk, a topic discussed further in Chapter 2.

Access to data that is individually identified must be controlled, and should be limited to those with a clear need to access data about the individual for purposes that benefit the individual. Authentication should be appropriate to the privacy risk. The main issue is the trade-off between strength of authentication and convenience. Authentication methods that impose a high overhead on users can backfire. For example, requiring complex passwords often leads people to write passwords down, often posting them near their computer—resulting in little security from the password (*what you know*), and replacing it with physical location security (*where you are*). A better approach for authenticating employees is through multifactor authentication, which combines several factors into a single authentication process. Reading an RFID-tagged ID badge (*what you have*) or using a fingerprint reader (*what you are*) along with a simple password can provide better protection and more convenience.

Authenticating external access (e.g., to give people access to data about themselves) is more challenging, as techniques based on ID card readers or biometrics require special hardware that the public is not likely to have. This leads to a privacy trade-off: Imposing higher hurdles on access to data about oneself does provide greater protection against violations of privacy, but preventing individuals from seeing data about themselves is, itself, a violation of privacy. The risk of harm to an individual from disclosure of the data needs to be compared with the risk from use of incorrect data or use without the individual's knowledge to determine how easy or difficult individual access should be.

The less likely it is that data can be linked to an individual, the lower the privacy risk. Therefore, data should be stored and used in anonymized form whenever feasible. Even when data must be kept in identified form, creating de-identified data for analysis and data warehousing is a good idea. A good model is the use of limited datasets for healthcare research: While hospital records need to be identified for use in treating the patient, for use in research, the names, addresses and identifying numbers may be removed. Though many of the records in limited datasets are identifiable (e.g., birth date and postal code) and thus access must be restricted, the likelihood of a privacy breach is reduced (re-identification requires active effort, as opposed to accidentally spotting the health record of a friend or neighbor when analyzing the data). The same principle should be applied to any use of data; using anonymization techniques to give access only to the information needed for the task greatly reduces the risk of privacy violations, even if the data could potentially be re-identified.

Data anonymization is still an open research area; progress is being made in ways to both anonymize data and re-identify supposedly anonymous data. While there is often great value in publicly disclosing anonymous data, there is always some potential privacy risk from doing so. The principle of informed consent applies here as well; informing data subjects that their data may be disclosed as part of an anonymized dataset, and obtaining consent to do so, can go a long way to alleviating the fallout should the anonymization fail to protect against identifying individuals.

Endnotes

1 Peter Steiner, "On the Internet, Nobody Knows You're a Dog," New Yorker, July 5, 1993, 61.

2 Alessandro Acquisti and Ralph Gross, "Predicting Social Security Numbers from Public Data," Proceedings of the National Academy of Sciences 106, no. 27 (July 7, 2009): 10975–10980, www.pnas.org/content/106/27/10975.

3 Joseph Bonneau, Sören Preibusch and Ross Anderson, "A Birthday Present Every Eleven Wallets? The Security of Customer-Chosen Banking PINs," Financial Cryptography and Data Security: The 16th International Conference, 2012, 25–40.

4 Nguyen Minh Duc and Bui Quang Ming, "Your Face Is NOT Your Password," Washington, DC, 2009, www.blackhat.com/presentations/bh-dc-09/Nguyen/BlackHat-DC-09-Nguyen-Face-not-your-password.pdf.

5 Latanya Sweeney, "Computational Disclosure Control: A Primer on Data Privacy Protection" (PhD dissertation, Massachusetts Institute of Technology, 2001).

6 Article 29 Data Protection Working Party, "Opinion 4/2007 on the Concept of Personal Data," Directorate C (Civil Justice, Rights and Citizenship) of the European Commission, B-1049 Brussels, Belgium, Office No LX-46 01/43, Tech. Rep. 01248/07/EN WP 136, June 20, 2007, http://ec.europa.eu/justice/policies/privacy/docs/wpdocs/2007/wp136_en.pdf.

7 HIPAA, 45 CFR 164.514 (c).

8 Michael Barbaro and Tom Zeller, Jr., "A Face Is Exposed for AOL Searcher No. 4417749," New York Times, August 9, 2006, www.nytimes.com/2006/08/09/technology/09aol.html.

9 A. Narayanan and V. Shmatikov, "Robust De-anonymization of Large Datasets," in Proceedings of the IEEE Symposium of Security and Privacy, (2008): 111–125.

10 Bradley Malin, "Trail Re-identification and Unlinkability in Distributed Databases" (PhD thesis, Carnegie Mellon University, May 2006), http://reports-archive .adm.cs.cmu.edu/anon/isri2006/abstracts/06-105.html; Manolis Terrovitis, Nikos Mamoulis and Panos Kalnis, "Privacy-Preserving Anonymization of Set-Valued Data," *Proceedings of the VLDB Endowment* 1, no. 1 (2008): 115–125, http://doi .acm.org/10.1145/1453856.1453874.

11 Article 29 Data Protection Working Party, "Opinion 1/2008 on Data Protection Issues Related to Search Engines," Directorate C (Civil Justice, Rights and Citizenship) of the European Commission, B-1049 Brussels, Belgium, Office No. LX-46 01/43, Tech. Rep. 00737/EN WP 148, April 4, 2008, http://ec.europa.eu/ justice/policies/privacy/docs/wpdocs/2008/wp148_en.pdf.

12 Peter Eckersley, "How Unique Is Your Web Browser?" Electronic Frontier Foundation, 2010, https://panopticlick.eff.org/browser-uniqueness.pdf.

13 Article 29 Data Protection Working Party, "Opinion 1/2008 on Data Protection Issues Related to Search Engines."

14 Federal Committee on Statistical Methodology, "Statistical Policy Working Paper 22 (Revised 2005)—Report on Statistical Disclosure Limitation Methodology," Statistical and Science Policy, Office of Information and Regulatory Affairs, Office of Management and Budget, Tech. Rep., December 2005, www.fcsm.gov/working-papers/spwp22.html.

15 Interagency Confidentiality and Data Access Group: An Interest Group of the Federal Committee on Statistical Methodology, "Checklist on Disclosure Potential of Proposed Data Releases," Statistical Policy Office, Office of Information and Regulatory Affairs, Office of Management and Budget, Tech. Rep., July 1999, www.fcsm.gov/committees/cdac/.

16 Pierangela Samarati, "Protecting Respondent's Identities in Microdata Release," *IEEE Transactions on Knowledge and Data Engineering* 13, no. 6 (2001): 1010–1027, http://ieeexplore.ieee.org/xpl/articleDetails.jsp?arnumber=971193; Latanya Sweeney, "k-Anonymity: A Model for Protecting Privacy," *International Journal on Uncertainty, Fuzziness and Knowledge-based Systems* 10, no. 5 (2002): 557–570, www.worldscientific.com/doi/abs/10.1142/S0218488502001648.

17 Ashwin Machanavajjhala, Johannes Gehrke, Daniel Kifer and Muthuramakrishnan Venkitasubramaniam, "l-Diversity: Privacy Beyond k-Anonymity," in *Proceedings of the 22nd IEEE International Conference on Data Engineering* (ICDE 2006, Atlanta, Georgia, April 2006), http://ieeexplore.ieee.org/xpl/articleDetails .jsp?arnumber=1617392.

18 Ninghui Li, Tiancheng Li and Suresh Venkatasubramanian, "t-Closeness: Privacy Beyond k-Anonymity and l-Diversity," in *Proceedings of the IEEE 23rd International Conference on Data Engineering* (ICDE 2007, Istanbul, Turkey, April 15–20, 2007), http://ieeexplore.ieee.org/xpl/articleDetails.jsp?arnumber=4221659.

19 Lingyu Wang, Duminda Wijesekera and Sushil Jajodia, "Cardinality-Based Inference Control in Data Cubes," *Journal of Computer Security* 12, no. 5 (2004): 655–692.

20 Interagency Confidentiality and Data Access Group, "Checklist on Disclosure Potential of Proposed Data Releases."

21 Cynthia Dwork, "Differential Privacy," in *Proceedings of the 33rd International Colloquium on Automata, Languages and Programming* (ICALP 2006, Venice, Italy, July 9–16, 2006), 1–12, http://link.springer.com/chapter/10.1007%2F11787006_1.

22 Cynthia Dwork, "Differential Privacy: A Survey of Results," *Theory and Applications of Models of Computation*, April 2008, 1–19, http://link.springer.com/chapter/ 10.1007%2F978-3-540-79228-4_1.

23 Jaewoo Lee and Chris Clifton, "Differential Identifiability" (presentation at the 18th ACM SIGKDD Conference on Knowledge Discovery and Data Mining, Beijing, China, August 12–16, 2012).

24 David Goldschlag, Michael Reed and Paul Syverson, "Onion Routing," *Communications of the ACM* 42, no. 2 (1999): 39–41, http://dl.acm.org/citation .cfm?doid=293411.293443; Michael K. Reiter and Aviel D. Rubin, "Crowds: Anonymity for Web Transactions," *ACM Transactions on Information and System Security* 1, no. 1 (1998): 66–92, http://dl.acm.org/citation .cfm?doid=290163.290168.

25 Felipe Saint-Jean, Aaron Johnson, Dan Boneh and Joan Feigenbaum, "Private Web Search," in *Proceedings of the 6th Workshop on Privacy in the Electronic Society* (Alexandria, VA: ACM Press, October 29, 2007), 84–90, http://dl.acm.org/citation .cfm?doid=1314333.1314351.

26 Daniel C. Howe and Helen Nissenbaum, "TrackMeNot: Resisting Surveillance in Web Search," in Ian Kerr, Carole Lucock and Valerie Steeves, eds., *Lessons from the Identity Trail: Anonymity, Privacy and Identity in a Networked Society* (New York: Oxford University Press, 2009), 417–436, www.idtrail.org/content/view/799; Mummoorthy Murugesan and Chris Clifton, "Providing Privacy Through Plausibly Deniable Search," in *Proceedings of the SIAM International Conference on Data Mining*, Sparks, Nevada, April 30–May 2, 2009), 768–779, www.siam.org/ proceedings/datamining/2009/dm09_070_murugesanm.pdf.

CHAPTER 5

Tracking and Surveillance

Lorrie Faith Cranor, Manya Sleeper, Blase Ur

In today's digital world, our communications and our actions—both online and offline—have the potential to be tracked and surveilled. Reasons for tracking are manifold. On one level, advertising companies wish to profile users so that they can better target relevant ads. Other groups or individuals might wish to spy on a person for the purpose of blackmail, extortion, or causing embarrassment. On a grander scale, a government or other organization may hope to gather intelligence to thwart an act of terrorism, or perhaps to spy on a group or individual for more insidious purposes. These large-scale goals came into particular focus worldwide in 2013 with disclosures about the PRISM program in the United States one day after disclosures about government collection of telephone call metadata.[1] In the PRISM program, intelligence organizations in the United States and Great Britain established partnerships with major Internet companies to facilitate the handover of customers' communication upon request.[2] The primary oversight mechanism of this previously secret program was a secret court system. These revelations led to public outcry. Though some individuals responded to these revelations with the familiar "I have nothing to hide" argument, privacy scholars argue that the collection, processing and indefinite retention of data about an individual can increase the power imbalance between a government and citizens, have a chilling effect on free communication and leave individuals vulnerable.[3]

The goal of this chapter is to provide IT professionals with a broader understanding of the techniques that enable tracking and surveillance on a number of levels, alongside both an explanation of the countermeasures to these techniques and the limitations of these countermeasures. As the people responsible for developing IT within a company, government agency or other organization, IT professionals must be aware of the impact that surveillance technology has on individual privacy.

We start by looking at how Internet usage can be surveilled on a large scale. Following a brief overview of the main technologies underlying Internet communication, we will discuss how network traffic can be surveilled using techniques such as deep packet inspection. We will also look at more localized approaches for tracking all of a user's communications, such as eavesdropping on a Wi-Fi connection or monitoring a school or workplace network, before explaining how anonymizing systems can help defend against this sort of tracking.

Next, we will turn our attention to web tracking, in which companies work to profile the websites that a particular user visits, most prominently for advertising purposes. We will discuss how a combination of hypertext transfer protocol (HTTP) cookies and an ecosystem in which a handful of advertising companies serve advertisements on many popular websites enables this sort of tracking. We will also explain a number of additional mechanisms that enable tracking even when HTTP cookies are disabled or deleted. We will briefly survey how a user's web searches can be tracked, and how the sender of an e-mail can employ tricks to determine exactly when an e-mail recipient opens the message.

A number of web blocking tools have been designed to combat the myriad techniques through which a user's web browsing can be tracked. We will introduce a range of these tools, some of which work automatically or are as simple as clicking an obvious button in software that a user has already installed. However, many privacy tools must be installed separately and require time-consuming and potentially confusing configuration. Along with pointing out the features of the potpourri of tools available for privacy-conscious users, we will highlight the shortcomings and usability issues of each approach.

Tracking and surveillance aren't limited to interception of communications or logging of web browsing behaviors. We will show how the mere presence of a cell phone or radio frequency identification (RFID) chip in an individual's pocket can reveal his or her location, in addition to explaining the relationship between global positioning system (GPS) technologies and tracking. We will then discuss how the use and misuse of location-sharing features on social media sites can leak potentially private information. We will also explain how users might control the disclosure of location information at a finer-grained level. Finally, we will provide a brief overview of audio and video surveillance techniques.

It is essential that IT professionals understand the technologies that enable tracking and surveillance in order to prevent privacy violations.

From a corporate standpoint, it is critical to avoid privacy violations that could lead to negative press reports, a tarnished reputation or regulatory or legal consequences. It is also important to avoid making users feel that their privacy has been violated, since they may stop using products from companies they do not trust. In addition, knowledge of tools that limit tracking and surveillance is valuable both to illuminate possible opportunities for a company to compete on privacy and to understand steps that users can take to protect their own privacy.

5.1 Internet Monitoring

The Internet provides a variety of opportunities for tracking and surveillance. These include a range of activities from automated monitoring by network administrators to detect malicious software, to illegal monitoring by criminals who are trying to steal passwords and account information. Employers may monitor their employees' Internet connections to enforce company policies. Law enforcement may obtain warrants that allow them to monitor Internet traffic to investigate a crime. Internet service providers (ISPs) or e-mail providers may monitor web browsing behavior or e-mail to deliver targeted advertising. This section describes the basics of how data travels across the Internet and how such data can be, and is, picked up in transit. It also outlines several defenses against Internet monitoring and surveillance.

5.1.1 An Overview of Internet Communications

To travel from source to destination on the Internet, data must be directed across intermediate networking links and switches. Monitoring tools may be placed anywhere along the path that data travels.

5.1.1.1 Packets

When data is sent over the Internet, it is broken down into segments and encapsulated in packets. Packets are pieces of data combined with additional information that specifies how they should be directed over a network. In the Internet protocol (IP), which is the primary protocol used to transmit data on the Internet, data is put into IP packets before being directed over a series of intermediate links and routers to reach its final destination. The IP is primarily concerned with delivering the data in a packet from a source to a destination based on an address, known as an IP address.

An IP address is a numerical identifier given to Internet-connected devices. The network adapters on devices ranging from laptops to tablets (e.g., iPads) to smartphones (e.g., iPhones) have IP addresses when they are connected to the Internet. The Internet of Things (IoT) concept goes further and proposes assigning an IP address to most electronic devices, from temperature sensors to "smart" toasters, which would mean that these devices would be accessible over the Internet. As IP addresses are assigned hierarchically, they aid in the process of identifying how to route data to a particular device. A major transition is currently occurring from IPv4 addresses, which have effectively been exhausted, to much larger IPv6 addresses. An IPv4 address is 32 bits (232 possible values), while IPv6 addresses are 128 bits (2128 possible values).

Each IP packet consists of a header and the data payload. The exact format of the packet depends on the protocol being implemented, but includes the IP address of the data's source and the address of its destination. It also includes a checksum over the header for error checking, as well as information about how the packet should be routed and the protocol that the packet is using.

In the typical case, the information included in an IP packet allows it to be transmitted across networks using packet routing. Using the information included in the header of the IP packet, each router passes a packet on to the next router closer to its final destination. Once packets reach their final destination, the contents are reassembled into their original form, such as an image or other user-friendly file.

Two of the most popular protocols that sit on top of IP are the transmission control protocol (TCP) and user datagram protocol (UDP). Whereas TCP guarantees delivery of a packet and encompasses mechanisms for verifying delivery and resending packets that did not make their way to the destination, UDP makes no such guarantees. As a result, TCP is generally used when it is important that data be delivered in its entirety, even if it takes longer. For instance, TCP would normally be used when downloading a photograph from a website. In contrast, by not making guarantees about the eventual delivery of data, UDP can operate more quickly and with less overhead. In cases where speed trumps reliability, such as in a video stream of a live sports event, UDP is generally used. If the data for a few seconds of this live video stream were to be lost in transit, it would not be useful to invoke a retransmission procedure and receive this data at a later point since the moment would have passed.

5.1.1.2 E-mail

One of the myriad types of communications split into packets for transmission across the Internet is electronic mail, or e-mail. E-mails are structured in two parts: a header containing information about the message, and a body that contains the message itself.

A user creates an e-mail message using a mail user agent (MUA) at the application level of her computer. A desktop e-mail client like Microsoft

Outlook is an example of a MUA. The e-mail message is made up of a message header and a body. The body includes the e-mail message. The header includes a variety of addressing fields, such as the sender's and recipients' e-mail addresses, the subject and cc'd recipients.

The e-mail message is transmitted to the user's outgoing mail server and then sent across the Internet to its destination using the Simple Mail Transfer Protocol (SMTP). Once the e-mail reaches its destination mail server, it is available for access either directly or by using a mail server protocol, such as the Post Office Protocol (POP) or Internet Message Access Protocol (IMAP). In POP, the MUA removes the e-mails from the server after storing them locally. In POP3, the e-mail server can be configured to leave e-mails in the inbox. When using IMAP, the e-mails remain on the server for access later or for access by multiple clients (e.g., a MUA on a desktop computer or a smartphone).

5.1.1.3 Hypertext Transfer Protocols (HTTP and HTTPS)

Like e-mails, web pages are split into packets as they are sent across the Internet. However, while the SMTP specifies how e-mails are sent between servers, the HTTP specifies how web pages are transmitted to browsers.

Users typically visit web pages using web browsers, such as Microsoft Internet Explorer, Mozilla Firefox, Google Chrome or Apple Safari. The address that a user types into the browser is known as the URL, or uniform resource locator, and it contains four main parts. For instance, a user might send a request to the IAPP's website using the following URL:

https://www.privacyassociation.org/about_iapp
[____] [_____] [_____]
service   host   (:port)   resource

The *service* component of a URL specifies the protocol that will be used for the request. Most commonly, web pages use HTTP for communication between a web browser and the web server that hosts the page. Messages sent over HTTP are sent in plaintext, and thus are susceptible to monitoring and tampering by any of the intermediary nodes through which the HTTP packets are sent. To prevent monitoring or tampering of data traveling over the Internet, HTTPS (hypertext transfer protocol secure) can be used. This protocol is similar to HTTP except that data is encrypted using transport layer security (TLS), which improves upon its predecessor, secure sockets layer (SSL). An encrypted connection is specified by HTTPS in place of HTTP in the browser's URL.

The *host* portion of the URL specifies who will receive the request, most often a computer server owned or contracted by the group represented by the website. The host can also be referred to as the site's domain. Along with the host, a *port* can optionally be specified. Ports allow numerous programs and processes on one computer to communicate simultaneously with many other machines without accidentally jumbling the conversations, similar to the way mail can be correctly routed to a resident of a large apartment building that has a single street address by specifying an apartment number. Although a single computer has 65,535 ports for use by both TCP and UDP, there are default ports to which requests following particular protocols should be made. For instance, HTTP requests are sent to TCP port 80 by default, while HTTPS requests are sent to TCP port 443. Since no port was specified in the URL above, the default port for the HTTPS protocol will be used. Finally, the *resource* portion of the URL specifies exactly which page, image or other object should be returned.

An HTTP request for web content is first initiated by a user's web browser, which sends a request message to the host. First, the name of the host is converted to an IP address. For instance, the IAPP's hostname of **privacyassociation.org** is converted to the IPv4 address 50.116.48.191. Once the host's IP address is known, the request can be broken into packets and accurately routed to its recipient.

A browser can make one of several types of HTTP requests, of which GET and POST requests are most relevant for surveillance techniques. In the case of a GET request, the browser simply requests that a particular resource be returned. A POST request is similar to a GET request except that the body of a POST request can contain information sent from the browser to the server, such as the data that a user typed into an online form. A GET request can also send data to the server, though as part of the URL itself. For either type of request, the server replies with a short status code indicating the success of the request (e.g., the code 200 indicates a successful request, whereas 404 indicates that the resource was not found). For successful requests, the content is also included in the body of the response. In the HTTP protocol, a single request results in a single reply. Furthermore, the connection is stateless, which means that the server isn't required to recall anything about past requests to fulfill future requests.

Both HTTP requests and HTTP responses include headers, which are short messages containing additional information. For instance, HTTP requests include the verb *GET*, *POST* or *HEAD* along with the resource requested. They can include the date and time the request was sent in the *date* field, as well as identifiers and version numbers for the web browser and operating system. Other data can be included, too, depending on the request and the browser used. When a user clicks on a hyperlink on a page, an HTTP request for the new page is initiated. For these sorts of requests, a *referer* header is included to indicate to the new page the identity of the page on which the link was clicked. The HTTP response headers can include fields such as *content-language*, specifying the natural language in which the page is written.

5.1.2 Network-Scale Monitoring and Deep Packet Inspection

Only the IP header, the first part of a packet, is required for network hardware to accurately route a packet to its destination. It is possible for network hardware to examine header information for other protocols or the full body of the network packet for a variety of purposes. When nodes look at this additional data, it is called deep packet inspection.

Deep packet inspection serves multiple purposes. For example, the ability to examine additional information within packets before they pass into a local organizational network can help determine whether or not the packets contain malicious content, such as known viruses. Alternatively, examining packets before they leave a network can help prevent data leaks, assuming the organization can scan these packets to detect sensitive information that should not leave the organization.

Deep packet inspection is also used for a variety of nonorganizational purposes. It is used by advertisers to track users' online behavior to better target ads and by government entities to censor or track citizens' online behaviors; both of these activities raise privacy concerns.[4] In China, deep packet inspection is used as part of the "Great Firewall," which the government uses to perform large-scale censorship on potentially sensitive topics.[5]

Some opponents of deep packet inspection view it as violating net neutrality, because it allows network traffic and bandwidth shaping based on the content of a packet. In the United States, for example, the Federal Communications Commission (FCC) ordered Comcast to stop using deep packet inspection to limit the bandwidth of peer-to-peer connections, called rate-limiting.[6] Because deep packet inspection can be used to determine the type of content being sent from one host to another, Comcast was able to rate-limit its customer Internet use based on whether the use was for peer-to-peer networking applications or file sharing.

5.1.3 Wi-Fi Eavesdropping

Monitoring can also occur on wireless (Wi-Fi) networks. It is possible to eavesdrop on or capture data being sent over a wireless network at the packet level. Several systems for Wi-Fi eavesdropping, including packet sniffing and analysis tools, are freely available.

Unsecured communications sent over an open, or shared, wireless network can be intercepted easily by others. This risk is often present in Wi-Fi hotspots in public spaces, such as hotels or coffee shops, where many users share a common Wi-Fi network that is either unprotected by a password or protected through a password known to a large group of users.

Packet sniffing systems capture packets sent over such networks. If the data is unencrypted, these packets can be examined and reassembled. These reassembled packets can then provide information about all the network user's activities, including websites he or she visited, e-mails and files sent and the data included in session cookies, such as website authentication information. Wireshark is one example of a packet sniffing and network analysis tool.[7] It captures packet-level data on wired or wireless networks to which a user has access, allowing a user to examine and reassemble packet content. Other examples of packet sniffers include Kismet for Unix and Eavesdrop for Mac.[8]

There are also more specialized Wi-Fi eavesdropping systems. One such tool enables HTTP session hijacking, or "sidejacking," attacks. When a user logs in to an Internet site, the initial login process is usually encrypted. Sites often store a token on the user's computer, and this token is sent along with future HTTP requests as proof that the user has logged in. However, some popular sites use HTTP, rather than HTTPS, to send this token, which means the token is sent unencrypted. Firesheep is a Firefox extension that enables an adversary listening to this Wi-Fi connection to hijack these tokens and impersonate a user who is logged in.[9] It captures tokens it sees transmitted across the wireless network to which the user is connected. It then displays information about the captured accounts (e.g., the site, the username and the user's photo) and allows the adversary to send requests to the applicable website as if he had originally logged in as that user. At the time of its deployment, Firesheep was commonly used to allow users to log in to Facebook using other users' accounts.

Tools like Wireshark, Eavesdrop and Firesheep are intended to allow users to purposefully eavesdrop on network information included in the body of packets for benevolent or malicious purposes. However, companies can also run into trouble when they are careless about how much data they are recording. In the recent case involving Google's Street View cars, Google captured data from unencrypted Wi-Fi networks using packet sniffers that were installed on these cars. The discovery that the captured data included passwords, personal information and other network traffic that consumers never expected would be collected resulted in a public outcry and an investigation by the U.S. FCC, as well as actions by other governments across the world. In 2013, Google acknowledged that these actions were a privacy violation as part of a $7 million settlement in the United States.[10]

There are several potential defenses against Wi-Fi eavesdropping. First, Wi-Fi eavesdropping requires that the eavesdropper have access to the Wi-Fi network and be able to read the packets that are sent. Ensuring that Wi-Fi networks are encrypted using strong passwords can limit the danger of Wi-Fi eavesdropping by preventing some adversaries from reading the traffic passing across the network. However, one Wi-Fi encryption scheme that is still in use, Wired Equivalent Privacy (WEP), has significant vulnerabilities and can often be broken within seconds.[11] The Wi-Fi Protected Access (WPA) encryption scheme is also considered insecure and should not be used. Even more recent security schemes for Wi-Fi routers can sometimes be defeated, which means that strong Wi-Fi passwords are often not sufficient to protect this communication channel.[12] Virtual private networks (VPNs), which allow users to create secure, encrypted tunnels to send data through more trusted channels, offer a defense against interception on unsecured networks. Additionally, regardless of the security of the network itself, encrypting web requests using HTTPS can prevent eavesdroppers from intercepting sensitive or personally identifiable data.

5.1.4 Internet Monitoring for Employers, Schools and Parents

There are also systems that allow people in positions of authority to monitor local networks. Some of these systems are specifically designed for employers, schools and parents. Such monitoring may be used to ensure both security and appropriate behavior on the network, often by blacklisting, or blocking access to, websites considered inappropriate.

Employers in the United States are legally allowed to monitor their employees' Internet usage on their organization's network or company-owned machines.[13] Companies monitor e-mail and Internet usage for a variety of reasons, including tracking employee productivity, maintaining security within the corporate network, and ensuring appropriate behavior among employees. As of 2007, the American Management Association found that 66 percent of surveyed companies monitored Internet browsing and 65 percent blocked access to blacklisted websites. Forty-three percent of companies also monitored e-mail, both to limit security breaches and to prevent potential lawsuits.[14] For example, some companies decrypt SSL and TLS protocols for external websites accessed from within their internal networks by intercepting the website's digital certificate and replacing it with the company's own certificate that was previously installed on workplace computers. This is equivalent to a man-in-the-middle attack, which allows employers to read and intercept communications on their internal networks.

The U.S. Children's Internet Protection Act (CIPA) requires schools and public libraries to install filters to prevent children from viewing inappropriate content online.[15] Many schools also track students' Internet usage to prevent inappropriate behavior, such as illegal downloading.[16]

Parents too can monitor their children's Internet usage. A variety of tools allow parents to limit the types of sites their children are allowed to visit, typically using blacklists. Parents can also track the sites their children visit and view the e-mails and chat messages they send. These tools help protect children from online predators as well as allow parents to better supervise their children's online activities.

5.1.5 Spyware

Beyond monitoring the network connection, there is also potential for malicious software to surveil data before it even leaves the user's own computer. *Spyware* is malicious software that is covertly installed on a user's computer, often by tricking users through social engineering attacks. Spyware can then monitor the user's activities through a variety of methods. It can track online activity in several ways, including capturing cookie data to determine browsing history or directly monitoring and reporting on browsing behavior. Spyware can also directly monitor what a user is doing on his or her computer, either by performing screen capture and transmitting an image of the user's screen back to the attacker, or by performing keylogging. In keylogging, malware is installed that tracks all keystrokes performed by the user. This data is then sent back to the attacker, allowing him or her to capture sensitive information typed by the user, such as passwords.

Antivirus providers offer anti-spyware programs that can be used to protect against known spyware. These systems use anti-malware signatures that are created from components of the malware code to detect and remove spyware from installed software. However, these programs are often reactive, successfully detecting well-known malware, yet failing to detect new types of spyware. Additionally, it is possible for systems to track known spyware websites and block installations coming from those sites at the firewall level.[17]

5.1.6 Preventing Network-Level Surveillance

Even if packets are encrypted when a user accesses the Internet, it is often possible for an observer, such as an ISP or government, to learn what sites the user accesses by examining the headers of the packets. This type of tracking is problematic in a variety of circumstances, such as when citizens who live under a hostile regime wish to access political websites secretly.

To prevent such tracking, anonymizers can be used to mask the link between the source—the user—and the destination of the network traffic.

Two major types of anonymizers are anonymous proxies and onion routers like Tor.

Anonymous proxies allow users to anonymize their network traffic by forwarding the traffic through an intermediary. Thus, the user's traffic appears to come from the proxy server's IP address, rather than the original user's IP address. JonDonym is a service that anonymizes traffic by routing packets through a mix of multiple user-chosen anonymous proxies.[18] However, the use of an anonymous proxy requires that the user trust the anonymous proxy, and this approach runs the risk of presenting a single point of failure.

An alternative to anonymous proxies is the use of onion routing systems, the most popular of which is Tor. Similar to the layers of an onion, packets sent through an onion routing system are encrypted in layers and then sent through a series of relays in a way that is very difficult to trace. At each stage of the circuit, a node receives a packet from the previous node, strips off a layer of encryption and sends it on to the next node. Because there are multiple nodes within the circuit, each internal node does not know anything beyond the node it received the packet from and the node to which it needs to forward the packet. This configuration allows a layer of anonymity to be inserted into network traffic. However, encryption is still required to keep the data itself anonymous once it leaves the virtual circuit.[19] Tor is an implementation of the onion routing protocol that uses a network of volunteer-run relay nodes to enable a variety of anonymous services.[20]

A particular concern for users is who controls their data. For instance, even if a user has transmitted his or her data securely across a network using encryption, and even if the company follows industry best practices in storing this data securely, the user often still needs to worry whether personal data will be disclosed to a government or other organization through the cooperation of an Internet company, without the user's knowledge. The extent of this type of cooperation in supporting government surveillance was one of the major surprises of the 2013 PRISM revelations.[21] Users must also carefully evaluate promises made to them by companies, yet they often have no way to do so. For instance, even though Skype had asserted for years that it could not intercept users' communications, the PRISM revelations in 2013 showed this assertion to be patently false.[22]

5.1.7 Effective Practices

A variety of tools are available for Internet monitoring. There are several effective practices to keep in mind both when performing such monitoring and when trying to prevent such monitoring from occurring.

To minimize privacy impacts, Internet monitoring should have a stated and narrow goal. If it is necessary to monitor online activities—for example, within a corporate environment—it should be done in a manner that best protects the privacy of the monitored individuals while achieving the desired goals. Neglecting privacy in pursuit of a goal can result in negative consequences.

As was apparent in the Google Street View example, this often means determining what data is necessary to achieve the desired goal, and then capturing only this data. Additionally, whenever possible, this data should be captured in an aggregate or anonymized fashion (see Chapter 4 for more details on data aggregation, sanitization and anonymization). For example, if deep packet inspection is being performed for network statistics, data should be examined in aggregate; the contents of individual packets should not be examined. To further protect privacy and limit liability, data should not be retained or shared beyond a necessary level.

Conducting surveillance at a level that exceeds consumers' expectations can have direct financial implications for an organization, including regulatory fines and lost business. For instance, major companies including Google and Facebook have paid fines as part of settling privacy complaints with the Federal Trade Commission in recent years. In addition, in the wake of the PRISM revelations in 2013, 10 percent of survey respondents indicated that they had canceled a project to use a cloud provider based in the United States.[23]

There are several effective practices to prevent monitoring. First, HTTPS should always be used for transmitting sensitive information between clients and servers. Additionally, sensitive information should not be sent over unsecured Wi-Fi networks, nor should a user rely on a Wi-Fi network's security to provide confidentiality. VPNs provide some protection in such an environment, although they require that one trust the operator of the VPN. Finally, sensitive information, such as confidential e-mails, should also be encrypted to provide an additional layer of protection.

5.2 Web Tracking

Companies and websites have many reasons for wanting to track users on the Internet, ranging from analysis and personalization on an individual website to targeting advertisements to users based on their activities across multiple websites.

Many websites personalize their content or user experience for each visitor. For instance, if a user has changed his or her language settings for a website from English to Romanian, the website would want to identify that user when he or she returns and automatically show the page in the correct language. Furthermore, many websites like to calculate analytics about their own pages, such as understanding how users navigate the layout of the page. Websites also might want to show a particular user the stories or products that they believe are most relevant based on that person's past actions or purchases on that website.

Online advertising companies create detailed profiles about what websites a particular user visits so they can target advertisements and offers to that user. For instance, if a company tracks exactly what pages a user visits across the Internet over a long period of time, the company can infer information ranging from general categories of user interests to potentially detailed personal information.

On a technical level, the amount of information a determined company could collect about a particular user is nearly limitless. For instance, based on which articles a user views on health websites and the terms he or she enters into search engines, a company could likely infer the health status of a user, including what diseases he or she had. Furthermore, even seemingly anonymous data can sometimes be connected to a particular individual. For instance, in 2006 AOL publicly released supposedly anonymized search queries for research purposes, yet some of the users were identified in real life based on searches they had made about themselves or their neighborhoods.[24]

In practice, many companies on the Internet say that they collect far less information than is theoretically possible, usually outlining in a privacy policy what information they collect and how they will use it. However, it is not possible for an end user to verify what information is actually collected, and a user would need to expend hundreds of hours a year to read the privacy policies for every site he or she visits.[25] Furthermore, it is difficult for users to grasp how data from different online sources can be combined, or particularly how online data can be combined with data from offline sources (e.g., Wi-Fi hotspot data collected in the Google Street View incident).

To better understand what types of information can be collected and by whom, in the rest of this section we delve into common mechanisms for tracking Internet users. We begin by discussing how web pages remember settings for a particular user using HTTP cookies, and then show how these cookies can be used for tracking that user across the Internet. These techniques have applications that even privacy-sensitive users might consider benign, yet they can also be used for potentially privacy-invasive purposes.

5.2.1 HTTP Cookies and Web Tracking

The HTTP is the most common protocol through which web browsers communicate with web servers in order to access websites. Although the HTTP is stateless, which means it is not expected to remember past transactions, ~~it is useful for websites to be able to save state about a particular user~~. For instance, a website should be able to remember that a particular user is logged in. If a user were required to log in to a website anew each time he or she clicked on a link or navigated to a new page, that person would likely be quite annoyed. Similarly, if a user places an item in an online shopping cart or updates his or her preferences for how the site is displayed, it is useful for the website to be able to remember these changes not just for that particular visit, but for all future visits from the same user.

To remember state, ~~websites can request that the web browser save small text files, known as HTTP cookies, on the user's computer~~. In an HTTP response from a server, one possible header is *set-cookie*, which is followed by the value(s) that the site would like to store in the web browser. Along with the value(s) to be stored, a cookie will contain an expiration date, as well as the domain and path for which that cookie is valid. Taken together, the domain and path define the scope of the cookie, which specifies to which parts of a domain the cookie applies.

Every major web browser has a particular location on the hard drive of a user's computer where it stores these cookies. Users can examine their cookies, which contain plaintext. However, while some cookies may contain words indicating what has been saved, cookies more commonly contain codes that are intended to be understood ~~only by the website~~ that originally set each cookie.

When a particular website has set one or more cookies on the user's computer, the contents of those cookies may be included as part of the header in HTTP requests sent to that site if the resource being requested falls within the cookie's scope and if the same browser is being used. ~~Cookies are included regardless of the type of content being requested.~~ Therefore, requests for content ranging from the main page of a website to a single image from the web server will include the cookies.

Cookies can be set just for a particular visit to a website or for extended periods of time. ~~Session cookies~~ are those cookies that are stored only until the web browser is closed and thus contain information only for a ~~particular visit to a page~~. For instance, a token that can be used to prove to a website that a particular user has successfully logged in to his or her e-mail account would often be saved as a session cookie and thus sent along with every HTTP request to that site. In contrast, ~~persistent cookies~~ can be saved indefinitely and are often used to save website preferences or a unique identifier to correlate multiple visits over time.

Web domains can ~~only~~ read and write cookies that they themselves have set, a practice known generally as the *single-origin policy*. Thus, Facebook cannot directly read cookies set by Google, nor can Google directly read cookies placed by Facebook. However, it is often the case that visiting a single website will result in cookies from multiple companies being placed on a user's computer because websites that appear as a single entity to the user may actually be cobbled together transparently from many different sources. For instance, a news website might load articles from its own Internet domain (for instance, www.news-website.com). These sorts of cookies from the primary page that the user is visiting are known as first-party cookies. However, images on this page might be downloaded from another company (such as www.photojournalism-aggregator.com), while each advertisement on the page might be served by a different advertising network (such as www.xyz-advertising.com). Each of these domains can also set its own cookies. Cookies set from all companies other than the primary website whose URL is displayed in a browser are known as third-party cookies.

The content contributed by these different third-party companies need not even be visible to the user. Elements used for tracking that are not visible to the user in the rendered web page are known as beacons or web bugs. Beacons are loaded onto a page using elements of the HTML markup language, which is the most widely used language for specifying the layout of a web page. HTML allows text and multimedia from a variety of different sources to be brought together to form a web page. For instance, one HTML tag instructs a web browser to download an image from a remote web server and include it in the web page (the <img> tag), which is how images are most commonly displayed on the Internet. Similarly, another HTML tag specifies that an entire web page should be included inside another web page (the <iframe> tag), while another tag runs computer code written in certain other languages (the <script> tag), such as JavaScript. Since HTTP requests for all types of content include the cookie as a header, and since the cookie can contain an identifier unique to that user, beacons can enable tracking. The most canonical example of a beacon is a one-pixel image whose sole purpose is to generate an HTTP request. If a user visits website A and website A embeds third-party content, such as a beacon or an advertisement, the browser will visit the third-party site to get the content and will receive a cookie alongside the content. When the user visits a completely different site, website B, that site might also reference content from the same third party. If it does, the browser again visits the third party to fetch that content, and the cookie received on the visit to website A is sent back to the third party. The third party then knows that the user has visited both website A and website B.

Although a company can only track a user's visits to websites on which it serves content, widespread tracking is still possible since a small number of companies include their content and beacons on many popular websites across the Internet. For instance, a 2009 study identified ten domains that served content on 70 percent of 1,000 popular web pages examined.[26]

Much of this tracking across popular sites supports *online behavioral advertising*, the practice of targeting advertisements using a profile of a user based on the websites he or she visits. The canonical method of profiling involves having a list of interest categories, such as "home and garden." These interest categories are either selected or unselected for a particular user based on the websites he or she has visited. However, some companies may be collecting more detailed information. Online behavioral advertising has attracted substantial attention in the media and from regulators. For instance, in the United States, both the Federal Trade Commission and the White House released privacy reports in 2012 discussing concerns about online behavioral advertising.[27]

In recent years, social media sites have also begun to serve content on many different websites, allowing these social media companies to track a user's activities across a broad swath of the Internet. The content served by such companies often takes the form of social widgets. For instance, the social network Facebook places a "Like" button on many pages, allowing users to click a button and share that article on their Facebook profile. Whether or not a user clicks on the button, and whether or not the user is logged in to Facebook at the time, Facebook notices the user's visit to that page.[28] On one hand, these widgets provide a frictionless way for a user to share articles and information with his or her social circle. On the other hand, they raise privacy concerns since they allow the social networking companies to track a user's movement across many websites.

Websites can also track the links a user clicks on a web page. Using a technique known as *URL rewriting*, a website can be crafted to determine whether or not a user has clicked on an individual link. Understanding how a user has navigated a page can be useful for analytics, such as helping a search engine determine which of the links it presented to a user were actually clicked on. For example, if a user goes to Google and searches for "privacy organizations," the results would likely include a link to the IAPP. However, rather than presenting a direct link to the IAPP's website at *https://www.privacyassociation.org/*, Google might instead present a link of the form:

http://www.google.com/url?query=privacy_organization&user=2fE6
5Da&url=privacyassociation.org

Such a link would automatically redirect the user to the IAPP website. However, by first directing the user's browser to Google's own server, Google is able to learn which link a particular user clicked on from a particular set of results. The unique identifier for the user can be the same unique identifier contained in a cookie that Google stored on that user's computer, allowing that action to be associated with that particular user. Furthermore, by analyzing the time and IP address associated with this redirection request, Google can reconstruct the order in which the user clicked on links in search results as well as the geographic location and ISP from which the user is connecting to the Internet.

JavaScript, a programming language used to create dynamic and interactive websites, can be used to track how a user navigates a web page in even greater detail than simple URL rewriting. In order to enable web pages that dynamically change as a user interacts with the page, JavaScript has functions for determining where a user's mouse cursor is placed on the page, when a user has placed the mouse cursor over a particular element of the page, what the user has typed and in what sequence. Of course, these functions can be used to capture navigation information in great detail and then to send it to a remote web server for analysis.

5.2.2 Web Tracking Beyond HTTP Cookies

While third-party cookies are a primary means of tracking a user's web browsing, many additional technological mechanisms enable tracking. Some of these technologies have been used to respawn cookies that have been deleted by the user; others present entirely different tracking and surveillance paradigms.

Though a user's IP address might initially seem to be a promising mechanism for tracking, the potentially large number of users who share an IP address and the frequency with which users acquire new IP addresses as they move between locations makes the use of IP addresses for tracking less attractive. Currently, users are tracked using some of their computers' local storage mechanisms that are accessible to web browsers, as well as through techniques that subtly misuse features of web browsers to glean information about a user. As more devices transition to IPv6, some implementations of which use a device's permanent media access control (MAC) address, tracking using the IP address may become more viable.

Web browsers or their plug-ins can write data to the hard drive of the user's computer in a number of ways beyond simple HTTP cookies. Many of these mechanisms have been used for tracking purposes. For instance, the Adobe Flash plug-in that is used to display videos and other interactive content on a number of sites has its own means of storing information, commonly called either local shared objects (LSOs) or "Flash cookies." LSOs can store approximately 25 times as much information as a standard HTTP cookie. A particular plug-in will generally be configured to run in each web browser on a user's computer. As a result, a website that utilizes that plug-in can access the same cookies regardless of which web browser is being used. Furthermore, LSOs are stored in a location on the hard drive separate from HTTP cookies, which means that hitting the "clear cookies" button in a web browser may not clear LSOs. While LSOs can be used for purposes like remembering the volume setting for watching videos on a particular website, they can also be used for storing unique identifiers for users that may not be deleted when a user deletes his or her cookies.

A 2009 study examined the 100 most popular websites and found that more than 50 percent were using LSOs.[29] While some of these sites seemed to be using LSOs for caching data, many others, including U.S. government websites, were using them to store unique identifiers about the user. For many years, LSOs were not deleted when a user cleared the cookies in his or her web browser, during which time some of these sites used LSOs to respawn deleted HTTP cookies. These respawned cookies often contained the same unique identifier as before deletion and thus seemingly contradicted the wishes of a user to clear this information. Following controversy over the use of LSOs for tracking, the Flash plug-in and some browsers, including Firefox and Chrome, were updated so that choosing to clear the history in the browser would also delete LSOs.

There are a number of similar techniques for using a web browser to store tracking information on a user's computer. For instance, Silverlight isolated storage provides an analogous function to LSOs for Microsoft's Silverlight framework, which competes with Adobe Flash. In addition to these plug-ins, core features of many modern websites, including JavaScript and HTML5, can enable tracking. The JavaScript programming language can store data using a property called window.name, which was originally designed for web designers to assign each browser window a name that they could reference in computer code. This JavaScript property allows up to two megabytes of data to be stored during a particular web browsing session.[30] Unlike HTTP cookies, the window.name property is initially empty each time a new browser window or browser tab is opened, limiting the amount of time a unique identifier will persist. Of course, this method can be used in conjunction with other methods to retain data over a long period of time.

The Internet Explorer browser itself is also able to store information on the local hard drive using userData storage, which enables each domain to store up to one megabyte of data. Like the other alternatives to HTTP cookies, a user who deletes his or her cookies will not delete information stored in userData. A more subtle method is a *pixel hack*, in which a unique identifier is written into a minuscule image, generated on the fly, in the form of the color values for one or more pixels. Since images are often cached, or stored locally by the browser to avoid having to download the resource again in the future, these tracking values can often be retrieved later.

HTML5, an updated specification of the HTML markup language for web pages that enables the embedding of videos, audio and visual canvas elements in web pages, also specifies methods for storing information locally, which can lead to tracking. These storage methods, which have been separated from HTML5 for specification purposes and are currently known as either Document Object Model (DOM) Storage or Web Storage, are supported by all major web browsers as of 2012. The session storage method can save information for a particular web browsing window; other web browsing windows, even containing the same application or website, cannot access this information, which is removed when the window is closed. In contrast, the local storage method stores data semi-permanently. This stored information is available to all resources on the web domain that stored the data.

Additional methods for DOM Storage have been proposed and debated, yet are in flux at the time of press. For instance, Mozilla Firefox has previously supported a storage mechanism called Global Storage, but support for this feature was removed in version 13 of the browser.[31] Similarly, Database Storage using SQLite was considered as a possible W3C standard and was implemented in some browsers, but official efforts toward its standardization ended in 2010.[32]

Yet another mechanism for a browser to store information locally leverages the way web browsers cache data. Entity tags (ETags) are HTTP headers that allow a browser to permanently tag a previously viewed resource (a web page or an object contained in the page) with an identifier. They were originally designed to enhance performance when loading previously viewed websites. When a user views a website, browsers generally save a copy of objects viewed on the user's hard drive so that identical content does not need to be downloaded multiple times. A site can tag content with an HTTP ETag identifier, which changes each time the content is updated on the server. As a result, a browser can request a resource from a website while specifying that the resource should be returned only if it has changed, based on the ETag. If the resource has not changed, the site only needs to confirm this fact so that the browser can use the local copy. To enable tracking, a web server needs only change and track ETags during each transaction to re-identify a visitor across multiple transactions. ETags are generally not deleted when a user clears his or her cookies; rather, ETags may be deleted when a user clears the browser's cache of previously viewed pages. Thus, ETags enable tracking even if cookies are deleted.

In recent years, there have been rapid changes in tracking techniques. For instance, a 2011 study found a substantial decline in the proportion of popular websites using LSOs compared to the 2009 study that initially brought attention to the issue.[33] However, a separate 2011 study noted that HTML5 (DOM Storage) and ETags were being used for the same tracking purposes.[34] In 2010, a security researcher prototyped a tracking mechanism, the "Evercookie," designed to be extremely difficult to delete.[35] The Evercookie combined many of the above techniques, storing unique identifiers in over ten different locations on a user's computer. If data from one storage location was deleted, this data would be respawned from other locations.

Features of web browsers designed to enhance users' experience on the web can also be misused for tracking purposes. By default, web browsers show links on a page that have already been visited in one color, while links that have not yet been visited are displayed in a different color. Although it cannot directly access a user's browsing history, JavaScript can access the color of any element on a web page, including links. Therefore, in a technique known as browser history stealing or sniffing, an unscrupulous page can include thousands of invisible links to popular sites and then use JavaScript to query the color of those links and learn whether a particular page has been visited by the client browser.[36]

Another technique that misuses features of JavaScript and HTML for tracking purposes is browser fingerprinting. So that websites can adjust their pages to match the configuration of a particular user's computer, there are JavaScript functions that reveal the time zone and screen resolution, as well as fonts and plug-ins that have been installed on a particular computer. A 2010 study found that, even among a sample of potentially privacy-conscious users, 94.2 percent of browser configurations with Flash or Java installed could be uniquely fingerprinted.[37]

5.2.3 Tracking E-mail Recipients

Many of the mechanisms that can be used to track what websites are visited from a particular computer can also be used to determine whether or not an e-mail has been opened. Knowing when an e-mail has been opened or when a particular link in the e-mail has been clicked can be useful for advertising companies to evaluate the effectiveness of a campaign, but can also have more pernicious uses. Two common techniques for tracking e-mail recipients are variants of the beacon and URL rewriting techniques used for web tracking.

Popular e-mail programs, such as Microsoft Outlook and Gmail, can display e-mails containing HTML code, the markup language used to format many websites. HTML code enables e-mails to contain different colors, advanced formatting and images, just like websites. Images can be attached to the e-mail, or they can be downloaded automatically from a remote server. To determine whether a particular recipient has opened an e-mail, the HTML code sent in an e-mail to that user can request that content uniquely tied to that user be downloaded automatically from a remote server when the message is opened by the recipient.

For instance, when Bob opens an e-mail from ABC Advertising, the e-mail's HTML code can instruct the e-mail program to download a one-pixel image with a filename unique to Bob from ABCAdvertising.com. Since the advertising company controls the server, it can tell whether it has ever received a request for this image, which is unique to Bob. If it has, then it knows that Bob opened the e-mail, along with exactly when this occurred. If it has not received a request for the image, Bob may not have opened the e-mail, or he may have opened the e-mail using a mail client configured not to download images.

As on web pages, links to websites that are included in an e-mail can also be customized to track whether or not a user has clicked on them. An e-mail might contain a link that will eventually bring the e-mail recipient to a specific website, such as www.big-sale.com, if he or she clicks on the link. However, rather than containing a direct link to that page, the e-mail might contain a link to www.big-sale.com/174cx3a, where 174cx3a is an identifier sent only to Bob. Therefore, if big-sale.com receives a request for the page 174cx3a, it knows this request originated from the e-mail that it sent to Bob.

5.2.4 Effective Practices

In crafting a system that tracks the activities of users on the Internet for any purpose, it is essential to adhere to the core privacy principles of "notice" and "consent." Key goals include providing clear notice about any tracking that occurs, asking users to consent to the collection of data, and explaining what information is collected, how it is used and stored and with whom it may be shared.

Some jurisdictions have legal or regulatory requirements that mandate specific forms of notice or consent, or that restrict the use of trackers. For instance, amendments to the European e-Privacy Directive (Directive 2002/58/EC) that were written in 2009 (Directive 2009/136/EC) and went into effect in May 2012 specify how companies should handle storing or reading information from a user's computer. In particular, these activities are "only allowed on condition that the subscriber or user concerned has given his or her consent, having been provided with clear and comprehensive information" about the storage or access of information.[38] As a result of these changes, some websites have begun to provide opt-in boxes when visitors from the EU first visit their websites, setting cookies only if a user has clicked a button or performed a similar opt-in action.

Violating either the privacy expectations or the trust of users can lead to serious repercussions in both the legal and public relations domains. For instance, a series of class-action lawsuits was brought over the use of LSOs for surreptitious tracking, while privacy concerns about some of the tracking technologies discussed in this chapter led to front-page coverage in major media outlets.[39] On the other hand, communicating clearly with users can directly benefit companies and organizations. For instance, a 2012 study revealed that a confluence of privacy concerns and misconceptions that advertisers collect more personal information than they generally do leads users to oppose behaviorally targeted advertisements, suggesting that openly communicating about practices the average user would deem reasonable might lead to increased user acceptance of tracking.[40]

5.3 Blocking and Controlling Web Tracking

Users who wish to either block or limit web tracking have a number of options at their disposal. Unfortunately, there is no one silver bullet that protects a user against most tracking threats. Software that automatically protects users' privacy, such as an e-mail client that blocks images from being downloaded by default, is simplest from the perspective of a user. More commonly, users are able to control web tracking to some degree by taking action, either by adjusting default settings in software they're likely to already have, configuring settings using a web-based interface or downloading additional software designed primarily for privacy. Of course, for all but the automatic tools, the user must know to take certain steps, having learned to do so from the news media, from a software vendor or from a friend.

Tools for blocking or controlling web tracking are provided either by groups who would not benefit directly from the tracking that is being blocked, or by the companies or organizations that are conducting this tracking themselves. In the former case, some of the tools are provided by organizations or companies that focus on protecting consumer privacy either as a public service or as a business goal. Other tools are provided by companies with a broad mission, including the makers of web browsers. In the latter case, tools are provided by the same group that would be tracking the user. Although these groups sometimes offer privacy mechanisms in order to distinguish their organization in a competitive market or to enhance the end-user experience, it is often the case that suggestion or writ from legal and regulatory authorities leads companies to craft these tools.

In this section, we discuss ways that a user can block or limit web tracking by third parties, which include companies whose domains are not shown in the URL bar. Beyond a user choosing to cease doing business with a particular company, tracking by first parties is much more difficult to prevent. Tools that block all requests to trackers, including first parties, would break the functionality of most websites. Furthermore, in the United States, first parties are generally exempt from legal and regulatory frameworks concerning tracking. As a result, one of the few resources left to a user who chooses to engage with those sites is reading those sites' privacy policies to understand their practices. Unfortunately, past research has found that reading long privacy policies leads to unrealistic opportunity costs for the user, that these privacy policies are written at an advanced reading level, and that privacy policies sometimes are not translated into languages to which the rest of the site has been translated.[41] After focusing primarily on how a user can block third-party web tracking designed to profile behavior across many websites, we also discuss how a user can prevent his or her web searches from being tracked, as well as how a user can block e-mail tracking.

5.3.1 Blocking Web Tracking

Web browsers' cookie settings are the primary way for users to disable tracking based on HTTP cookies. In some browsers, privacy-protective processes are automatic; for instance, Apple Safari blocks third-party cookies by default, and Mozilla has announced that it will develop features making it easier to block third-party cookies selectively in future versions of Firefox. As part of this effort, Mozilla will work with Stanford's Center for Internet and Society to develop a Cookie Clearinghouse for differentiating between essential and nonessential cookies.[42] In addition, the default setting of Microsoft Internet Explorer blocks some third-party cookies, as detailed below. When third-party cookie blocking is not on by default, users hoping to block third-party cookies must change the browser's default setting, which many users never do.[43] Of course, at best, these methods only prevent tracking that uses cookies exclusively.

5.3.1.1 Privacy Settings in Browsers and Do Not Track

Browsers differ in the prominence and types of cookie settings that they provide. At a high level, most browsers enable users to allow all cookies, allow only first-party cookies or block all cookies. Complicating matters, even if third-party cookies are disabled, a tracker may be a first-party website at some point. Mozilla Firefox's cookie settings are featured prominently in its "Privacy" menu, with a checkbox to either allow sites to set cookies or to block this behavior. An additional checkbox specifies whether or not third-party cookies should be accepted. On the other hand, Google Chrome's cookie settings are buried in the "Under the Hood" menu's "Content Settings" submenu. Chrome's stated recommended setting is to allow cookies to be set, although cookies can be restricted to the current browsing session, restricted to first-party sites or blocked entirely. Chrome independently allows a user to choose to delete both cookies and plug-in data, such as LSOs, when the browser is closed.

In contrast to other browsers, Microsoft Internet Explorer's cookie settings provide users with a slider on which they can choose their privacy level. Settings for directly disabling third-party cookies, or disabling all cookies, are buried in an "Advanced" menu. A user's preferences based on this slider are evaluated using websites' Platform for Privacy Preferences Project (P3P) tokens. P3P is a machine-readable language with which websites can express their privacy practices, such as the information that they collect and how this information is used. Microsoft Internet Explorer uses P3P policies to decide whether to accept or block a cookie from a particular site. Thus, cookie decisions can be made on the basis of how cookies will be used. The default setting in the Internet Explorer 6 through 10 web browsers blocks third-party cookies when they do not have P3P tokens and when they have P3P tokens, indicating a privacy policy considered "unsatisfactory" by Microsoft's criteria. Although P3P is a World Wide Web Consortium (W3C) standard, Internet Explorer is the only major web browser that uses P3P, and P3P has not been widely adopted by websites. Furthermore, some sites misrepresent their privacy policies by using nonsensical or sample P3P tokens, rendering P3P unreliable.[44] Microsoft has sought to combat this loophole by including a "Strict P3P Validation" feature in Internet Explorer 10. If a user enables this feature, which is off by default, the browser will block "cookies from third-party sites that don't have valid P3P policies."[45]

In contrast to privacy-protection mechanisms that attempt to disallow or circumvent tracking technologies, an idea that has gained momentum in recent years is a "Do Not Track" header that requests that potential trackers not track a user. Do Not Track (DNT) is an HTTP header that is sent alongside requests for web content. This header can indicate that the user has requested not to be tracked, that the user has actively chosen not to make this request or that no preference has been set. However, the exact details of both the meaning and mechanism of Do Not Track are currently in flux as the W3C works to define these concepts, and the end date for this process has been repeatedly pushed back, leading to skepticism that the process will be completed successfully.[46] For instance, one debate about the Do Not Track proposal centered on whether enabling this feature would mean that trackers could not collect information about a user, or whether they could collect information but not use the information to target advertising. Since Do Not Track does not actually block communication with a particular tracker, a user who has enabled this feature relies on companies to honor this request. As this book went to press, only a small number of companies had committed to do so.

Despite the uncertainty about the meaning of Do Not Track, Firefox, Safari, Internet Explorer and Chrome have all implemented the feature. However, browsers differ in the user experience of enabling DNT. For instance, Microsoft automatically enables Do Not Track as the default setting in Internet Explorer 10, which led to protracted debate among industry and standards-body groups about whether or not trackers may ignore such default settings.[47] In Internet Explorer 9, enabling the "Tracking Protection List" feature also enables DNT. In Firefox, DNT may be enabled by clicking the checkbox "Tell sites I do not want to be tracked," which is the first option available in the browser's privacy menu. Similarly, Safari's privacy menu contains the option "Ask websites not to track me." Well after the other major browser vendors, Google implemented DNT in Chrome in late 2012, yet buried the setting in an advanced menu and provided a message discouraging users from activating DNT.[48]

In addition to cookie controls and Do Not Track, web browsers often include other privacy features. For instance, Internet Explorer 9 includes Tracking Protection Lists (TPLs). With TPLs, third parties can curate lists of domains, and users can download these lists, which specify whether or not requests to particular domains should be blocked. In contrast to DNT, TPLs don't require users to rely on websites to honor their requests since communication to those sites is actually blocked.[49] Furthermore, all major browsers offer private browsing modes that disable the storage of browsing data on a user's computer while the mode is enabled. However, a 2010 study demonstrated that, at best, these modes offer minimal protection from tracking and surveillance, the privacy protections provided by these modes often differ from users' expectations and the implementation of these modes is sometimes flawed.[50]

5.3.1.2 Web-Based Privacy Tools

Beyond using software tools already available on their computers, users can take advantage of web-based tools to control tracking. Among the most visible web-based tools is a system of opt-out cookies offered by a number of companies engaged in tracking. Opt-out cookies are HTTP cookies indicating that a consumer has opted out of receiving behavioral advertising. Although users who have opted out will not receive targeted ads from a particular company, some companies will still track those users' online activities. A primary way that consumers can learn about opt-out programs and set opt-out cookies is through industry-standardized icons and taglines. However, a 2012 study found that these icons and taglines poorly communicated to consumers that advertisements were being targeted to them or that consumers could click on these icons as a step in choosing not to receive targeted ads.[51] Opt-out cookies are also problematic from a usability perspective since users who delete their cookies, as many privacy-conscious users might, also delete their opt-out cookies. Furthermore, setting opt-out cookies for each of the hundreds of tracking companies a user might encounter would take a long time. Centralized websites organized by industry groups offer a single place at which a user can opt out from many companies at once.[52] However, research has identified major usability problems with these centralized websites.[53]

Some companies that track users also provide web-based dashboards through which users can view and sometimes edit the profiles these companies have constructed of their interests. For instance, Google, Microsoft and Yahoo! all provide dashboards for advertising preferences, and Evidon's Open Data Partnership allows additional trackers to show users the behavioral profiles they have created.[54]

An informed consent requirement for cookies that is part of European Union law has prompted many websites to provide prominent notices about cookie options. As a result of updates in 2009 to the European Data Protection Directive, implicit consent is no longer considered sufficient notice to consumers in certain cases when websites wish to set cookies.[55] As a result, in 2012, some sites began providing consumers with conspicuous notices about the use of cookies, often with options to disallow certain types of cookies on that site.

5.3.1.3 Third-Party Browser Add-ons

Browser add-ons designed for privacy purposes are an additional mechanism for stopping web tracking. A number of companies offer tools specifically designed to stop web tracking conducted by advertising networks, social networks and other companies interested in collecting what websites a user visits. For example, the company Evidon offers Ghostery, while the company Abine makes DNT+. These tools generally work by blocking, to varying extents, the mechanisms used for tracking. Some tools, such as DNT+, maintain a blacklist of domains or resources tied to tracking and completely prevent the user's browser from communicating with those domains or trying to download those resources.[56] In contrast, other tools, including Ghostery, allow the request to go through, yet prevent the request from including cookies. Other subtle modifications to requests, such as removing the HTTP referer field, can also protect the user's privacy in limited ways.

Some general-purpose browser add-ons can limit web tracking to an extent. For instance, the popular Firefox and Chrome add-on Adblock Plus, designed to block nearly all advertising on the web, blocks requests to the domains of a number of advertisers and thereby limits the collection of tracking data by those particular advertisers. Similarly, NoScript, a Firefox add-on designed to prevent websites from executing JavaScript code and plug-ins like Flash, can prevent tracking that occurs using those plug-ins. Notably, HTTP cookies are sometimes created using JavaScript, and blocking the Flash plug-in can prevent LSOs from being set.

A major dilemma with all of these tools is the burden they impose on users, who must take a number of steps to protect their privacy. Generally, these tools first require a user to install the tool, either from the developer's website or from a centralized repository. Following installation, tools often ask a user to choose configuration options. Over time, the tool may automatically update itself, or user intervention may be required to install the newest version.

Unfortunately, neither specific privacy tools nor general-purpose add-ons are necessarily easy for an average consumer to use. For example, a 2012 study of web tracking privacy tools revealed serious usability flaws in all nine of the popular tools it tested.[57] Pervasive usability flaws identified by the authors included nonprotective default configurations incommensurate with the goals of a privacy tool, confusing interfaces and jargon. In addition, their study participants found it difficult to make decisions required by the tools about what advertising companies to block, what blacklists or whitelists to choose and what tracking technologies to disallow.

5.3.1.4 Deciding What to Block

The majority of tools ask users to configure settings and decide what to block. However, a user's decision about what to block can be fraught with complexity. Based on interviews with 48 nontechnical users, a 2012 study concluded that users have great difficulty reasoning about tracking technologies and evaluating companies to block, and hold major misconceptions about how behavioral advertising works.[58] However, users are not alone in facing this difficulty. Software designed for blocking also must decide what to block. If a tool blocks too little, it will be ineffective. However, if it blocks too much, it may break web functionality, leading users to be annoyed and potentially abandon the tool. Furthermore, widespread adoption of a tool that thoroughly blocks existing tracking methods might lead trackers to adopt increasingly surreptitious and subtle methods of tracking.

Some tools use partially automated metrics for determining what to block. For instance, Microsoft Internet Explorer uses P3P tokens specified by websites in order to determine what to block. Furthermore, some versions of Internet Explorer determine when to block cookies from a domain using frequency counts, which are running totals of the number of different first-party domains on which a particular tracker has been seen by that user's browser.[59] Other tools are designed simply to help users visualize this sort of frequency information. For instance, Mozilla's Collusion tool presents a visualization of which third parties track users across particular websites.[60]

Instead of asking the user to make a decision about each potential tracker, organizations or individual experts can compile a list of domains or patterns to block. Precompiled lists have been used by tools ranging from Internet Explorer Tracking Protection Lists to the Adblock Plus browser plug-in. Although they can ease the decision-making process for users, lists have their own drawbacks. First of all, users need to be aware that they must select a list, and they also must be able to evaluate potential choices, both of which have been shown to be difficult in past research.[61] Furthermore, by their nature, lists will not conform exactly to an individual user's privacy preferences, which tend to be complex. It is also possible for lists created by one organization to cause competitors' pages to be blocked or to serve business interests, further complicating the compilation of lists. The advantage of lists is that they provide users a simple one-size solution that may later need to be tailored to fit their needs.

Tools' differences in the extent to which they block tracking add more complexity to users' efforts. A tool that blocks too little leaves the user easily vulnerable to tracking, whereas a tool that blocks too much can break the functionality of the websites that the user hopes to visit. Some tools, including the general-purpose script-blocking tool NoScript and web-tracking-privacy tool Ghostery, break functionality on websites in ways that may be obvious or opaque to users. To proceed with their browsing, users might try to unblock specific elements until a page loads, disable the tool entirely or adopt ad hoc solutions, such as using a different browser without the privacy tool.

Researchers have coined the term "functional privacy" to capture users' willingness to aim for as much privacy as they can get without breaking the functionality of what they hope to accomplish on the web.[62] However, it remains to be seen whether such a conception would incentivize trackers to break the functionality of pages intentionally. Along these lines, tools that aim to provide privacy without breaking website functionality have been proposed. For example, ShareMeNot blocks social widgets on websites until a user actually wishes to use the widget, which is a promising direction for the design of privacy tools.[63]

In place of a web-based tool or software, some users create ad hoc strategies or adopt overriding strategies. For instance, some users might use different browsers with different privacy settings, using a less privacy-protective browser when a site's functionality breaks with a more privacy-protective setup. In contrast, other users employ privacy-preserving proxies that are designed to scrub their web requests from potential identifying information, such as cookies, HTTP headers and their IP address, along with tunneling requests from many users through the same channel. Like all other solutions, proxies are not a silver bullet and can certainly still leak information about a user. They can also break web functionality.

Implicit among the challenges of protecting user privacy against web tracking is the complex nature of privacy decision making. Past research has demonstrated that privacy is often a personal process in which different users will have very different preferences.[64] Furthermore, privacy depends on context, which is a notion currently unsupported by major privacy tools.[65] Overall, a user has many tough choices and few easy solutions when attempting to stop web tracking.

5.3.2 Blocking Tracking of Web Searches

Users who wish to protect their privacy when using search engines also have a handful of mechanisms available. However, this task is more complex since most privacy tools for limiting web tracking focus on third-party tracking, and disabling certain tracking mechanisms on first-party sites will often break those sites' functionality. As a result, the simplest and most secure way for a user to minimize having private information leaked through web searches is to use a search engine that promises not to track the user. Alternatively, users can download tools that help them obscure their searches by inserting a large number of decoy requests, or they may use proxies or other general-purpose tools to make their searches more private, although only to an extent.

In recent years, a handful of search engines have begun to use privacy-protective practices as a competitive advantage. The most popular search engines generally save a user's search history, including his or her search queries, when these queries occurred and information such as the user's IP address and unique identifiers from cookies. In contrast, privacy-protective search engines, such as DuckDuckGo, promise to neither collect nor share a user's personal information. By default, DuckDuckGo does not use HTTP cookies except to save preferences about the page layout a user has chosen, nor does it allow the HTTP referer field to contain information about the search query. However, users must trust DuckDuckGo and similar sites to fulfill their privacy promises.

Users who wish to hide their search history can also download a tool to assist them, although few tools exist for this purpose. TrackMeNot, an add-on for Firefox and Chrome, protects a user's privacy by issuing decoy queries to major search engines.[66] As such, it operates by achieving security through obscurity, creating ambiguity about whether a particular query was issued by a user, or whether it was issued automatically by the program. The plug-in's behavior is meant to mimic that of a real user. For example, it sometimes performs a large number of queries in a short amount of time, and it selectively chooses whether or not to click through to a link.

Users can also use general or ad hoc techniques to prevent their searches from being tracked. For instance, a proxy or an anonymizing network such as Tor can strip some or all of the identifying information from web traffic, making a user's searches more difficult or impossible to track. However, it is possible for private information to leak even when using techniques such as the TrackMeNot plug-in and anonymizing services. Researchers have shown that users who enter their own name or other personally identifiable information in searches can still be vulnerable to having their searches tracked even if they would otherwise be anonymous.[67]

5.3.3 Blocking E-mail Tracking

In contrast to web tracking, the issue of e-mail tracking has become a less pervasive problem in recent years without direct user intervention. A number of modern e-mail clients block beacons, images and other content loaded from external sites since this external content could be used for tracking. This behavior disables one of the most widespread techniques for determining whether or not an e-mail has been read.

However, since tracking can still be accomplished through URL rewriting, it is important that a privacy-conscious user not follow links contained in e-mails. If a user does not follow links contained in e-mails, tracking using URL rewriting cannot succeed. Furthermore, due to the threat of phishing attacks, it is generally considered good practice not to follow links in e-mails whenever the user must enter information at the destination. Even if a link in an e-mail does not seem to contain any type of unique identifier, users who follow the link or otherwise access that information on a site are subject to web-tracking techniques.

Finally, a common ad hoc technique to prevent e-mail tracking is for a user to maintain multiple personas online. As it is often free to create an e-mail account, many users have multiple e-mail accounts. If a user has created an account exclusively for receiving e-mail solicitations, he or she may not mind if a company knows when that account has read an e-mail since the account may not be tied to any real-life identity. Of course, subtle information leaks are possible. For instance, the date and time that the e-mail has been read, as well as a user's IP address, browser configuration and HTTP cookies, can tell a company substantial amounts of information about that user. In addition, a person who uses a separate e-mail account and then makes a purchase tied to that e-mail address from one company is at risk for having his or her identity tied to that account, even by other companies with whom this purchase data is shared or to whom this data is sold.

5.3.4 Effective Practices

Currently, a user who hopes to prevent his or her activities on the web from being tracked is put in a difficult position. To protect against the myriad different tracking threats, a privacy-conscious user must often use a patchwork of tools. Even with substantial effort, it is unlikely that the user can feel fully in control of his or her privacy. For instance, there are always potential tracking mechanisms that a researcher or newspaper may soon reveal have been put into use, and the data that has been collected about a user's activities is rarely made available to the user. Furthermore, whereas some tools provide a technological solution by blocking one or more mechanisms used for tracking, other tools require a user to trust that a company or website will respect a preference that has been set or follow a practice the company has advertised.

While there are no perfect solutions for users to protect themselves against tracking, there are many effective practices that should be followed by the companies or organizations providing users with tools to protect their privacy. The inclusion of a graphical user interface and colorful icons does not magically make a privacy tool easy to use. Rather, to craft a tool that actually does help consumers protect their privacy, careful consideration and substantive feedback from user studies is essential, albeit often overlooked.

It is important for users to be made aware of tracking in the first place. User education can take many forms, ranging from prominent disclosures from trackers themselves to media stories warning of privacy risks. Regardless of the type of communication, it is essential that communication be both clear and prominent. This issue has taken on particular importance following debate over the European Union's disclosure requirements for cookies, in which regulators deemed it insufficient when a user is considered to have implicitly consented to tracking after being informed of this practice only by a lengthy privacy policy. In contrast, it is considered effective practice to provide users with conspicuous, clear and understandable notice about tracking, and to give them the opportunity to choose not to be tracked. Unfortunately, the implementation of this notice in practice has been of questionable usability and utility for users.

Of course, the mechanisms for allowing users to choose not to be tracked have their own effective practices. First of all, users should not be expected to make decisions about particular technologies. When a user decides he or she does not wish to be tracked, the developer should understand whether the user wants to block tracking accomplished using LSOs, or only tracking using HTTP cookies, or both. This wish is often technology-neutral, and it is essential that privacy tools match this expectation to the greatest extent possible. Furthermore, privacy-protective default behaviors should be chosen when they won't interfere with desired functionality. For instance, in the case of preventing beacons from tracking whether an e-mail has been read, e-mail clients automatically block these requests without requiring the user to do anything. Any actions for which user intervention is required should be able to be completed quickly, and any interfaces presented to the user should be tested extensively in usability studies to ensure that they can be used with few or no errors.

5.4 Location Tracking

As more people carry mobile phones with location tracking capabilities, the ability to draw on constant location information is becoming increasingly prevalent. Social networking applications, employee-tracking systems and location-enabled media (such as photos) are among the technologies that use this location data to enhance their systems.

Location tracking also extends beyond the mobile phone. RFID chips are increasingly embedded in smart cards as well as in consumer products. If an RFID reader detects a particular RFID chip at a given location, a particular user's location can be revealed. GPS and other tracking technologies are emerging in consumer hardware like cars and cameras. In such an environment, those deploying such technologies should be aware of their capabilities as well as their potential privacy implications.

This section outlines location tracking technologies and services, techniques for blocking location tracking and effective practices for those employing location-tracking technologies.

5.4.1 Location-Tracking Technologies

Devices can contain a wide variety of location-tracking technologies, each of which relies on slightly different types of underlying systems. We will describe several of the most common location-tracking technologies: Wi-Fi and cell tower triangulation, GPS, RFID chips, phone tracking and the use of location data stored in content metadata.

5.4.1.1 Wi-Fi and Cell Tower Triangulation

Wi-Fi and cellular signals can be used to allow a device that is enabled for Wi-Fi or cellular communications to determine its location.

Cellular phones communicate with cellular towers that receive their signal and connect phones to a global network. The time it takes messages from a particular cell phone tower to arrive to a phone, the strength of the signal from that tower and, most simply, which towers a phone can communicate with all reveal information about the phone's location. After determining the phone's position relative to a handful of towers whose locations are known by the cellular provider, the position of the phone can then be determined geometrically through triangulation.

In addition to signals from cell towers, the Wi-Fi signals a phone receives can help determine its location. Wi-Fi signals have a shorter range, allowing for more fine-grained location information. Cell towers provide a more permanent location marker but less granular location data.

Wi-Fi and cell tower triangulation require the creation of a preexisting database of Wi-Fi access points and cell tower locations that cover the region over which the location tracking will occur. Thus, this type of location tracking is primarily beneficial in urban areas where there is a high density of Wi-Fi access points and cell towers.

5.4.1.2 GPS

Global positioning system (GPS) satellites can also be used to determine location, specifically the device's longitude, latitude and altitude. Many consumer devices, including mobile phones, are equipped with GPS capabilities for location tracking. Cameras and similar devices can also include GPS capabilities for tagging the location of photographs taken, and automobile infotainment systems can include GPS capabilities to pull regional content, such as weather and news-related information, into the vehicle's navigation system.

GPS calculates a device's location using signals received from at least four of a set of dozens of geosynchronous satellites positioned in space and run by the U.S. government.[68] Based on the differences in time it takes messages from these different satellites to arrive to a receiver, a GPS receiver can determine its position relative to the satellites. Since these satellites' positions are known and constant relative to the earth, the GPS receiver can determine its own position geometrically. Because devices receive and do not transmit any signals in the GPS process, devices do not automatically reveal their location by using GPS. However, devices with GPS can also include transmitters that can be used to reveal the device's location to other parties and services.

5.4.1.3 RFIDs

Radio frequency identification (RFID) chips are tiny microchips that can reach a size of 0.4mm square. Each microchip is identified by a unique serial number and contains an antenna with which it transmits information, such as its serial number, to an RFID reader.

RFID chips can be placed on products or cards or implanted in animals (such as household pets) for tracking purposes. They are commonly used in supply chain management to allow companies to track inventory. Passive RFID chips, which do not contain their own power source, are the most common. When power is applied by an RFID reader, these chips transmit a signal encoding their identifier. Active RFID chips contain their own power source, which allows them to transmit farther than passive chips. Depending on the type of chip and its power, particularly whether it contains its own power source, the signal can be picked up at varying distances. RFID chips transmitting at low frequencies have a range of about half a meter; those that transmit at ultrahigh frequencies can reach readers located dozens of meters away.[69] The unique serial number associated with each RFID tag allows for location tracking. Tagged items are tracked as the readers pick up the tag IDs at different locations. If additional information is stored on the tag, the reader is also able to pick up that information and associate it with the tag's location.

5.4.1.4 Phone Tracking

The location of a mobile phone and the individual to whom the cell phone belongs can be tracked using receivers installed within a building complex. The FCC also requires that phone companies be able to track phones when an emergency (911) call is placed.[70]

An application of phone-tracking technology came to light during the 2011 holiday shopping season when two U.S. shopping malls tested a system to track shoppers within the mall based on the location of their cell phones as part of a "mobile phone survey." Signs notified the shoppers that the tracking was taking place, and shoppers had the option to opt out by turning off their cell phones. The malls ended the survey early after concerns about shopper privacy and the legality of the survey were raised.[71]

5.4.1.5 Metadata

Location information can also be automatically stored in the metadata of content, like photos. Metadata is information that is automatically or manually added to content and that can be later accessed and used during processing or by applications.

For photos taken with GPS-enabled devices, like cell phones or GPS-capable cameras, location is often automatically stored in the camera metadata. When the photos are loaded into photo browsing or editing applications, this information is then accessible to the user or application.

5.4.2 Location-Based Services

Location-based services draw on the data provided by location-tracking technologies to augment a variety of systems, including social media and other location-based applications. Emerging uses of location-based services include tracking individuals, such as employees or children, and location-based advertising. Location-based information can also be combined with other data to create new applications.

5.4.2.1 Social Media

A variety of social media applications use location tracking as the basis for, or to augment, their services.

Some applications are primarily focused on allowing a user to notify others of his or her location and to track others' locations. One such application is Foursquare, a mobile app that allows users to "check in" at locations and view their friends' check-ins. Users are further motivated to check in by the ability to earn badges and receive coupons for participation. Similarly, Find My Friends is an Apple application (for iPhones, iPads or iPods) that shows the location of a user's friends who use the service.[72]

Other applications include location-based features to augment their services. Facebook Places allows users to check in at locations as well as tag shared items with location data.[73] Yelp, a site that allows users to rate restaurants and other services, includes a feature with which users can physically check in to the locations of the service providers.

5.4.2.2 Location-Based Applications

A variety of other applications rely on location-based services for functionality. These include applications that provide maps and directions on cell phones or GPS units, local weather applications and applications that query a user's location to provide information on nearby services, items or individuals.

Applications that provide maps or directions typically rely on location-based services to pinpoint a user's location. The application then provides a map of the user's current location based on a database. GPS navigation is often used in car-based units to help users navigate street maps. The user's location is provided using GPS, and maps are provided based on a database of street maps. In both examples, direction routing is performed based on mapping algorithms.

Smartphones also often provide map and direction functionality, which can use a combination of GPS and Wi-Fi and cell tower triangulation to calculate a user's location. Google Maps for mobile devices is one example of such a mapping application.

Other applications use location information to provide location-specific content. For example, weather applications track a user to provide location-specific weather alerts or updates. iMapWeather Radio is one such application; it uses location tracking to localize weather forecasts and critical weather alerts for a user.[74]

Other applications provide information about services, items or individuals in a user's vicinity. Many mapping applications allow users to search for the nearest restaurants, gas stations or other services.

5.4.2.3 Tracking Kids and Employees

Location-based services can also allow users to explicitly track others. Parents can use the GPS in their children's cell phones to perform location tracking. Online services allow them to see where their children are throughout the day using either a specialized cell phone or a normal calling plan.[75]

Just as employers can use online surveillance to monitor employee computer usage, so can they use location tracking to monitor or track employee whereabouts. This can be done to reduce company liability, address potential threats to security and track operational efficiency. Employee tracking can be performed using RFID chips or GPS trackers carried by the employees.[76]

5.4.2.4 Location-Based Ads

Location-based information also provides a rich data source to advertisers, allowing them to create advertising that specifically takes an individual's location into account. Advertisers can offer advertisements or marketing offers tailored to a specific location based on data from mobile devices with location identification or a user's self-identified location on services like social networks.

Advertisers can take advantage of user location in a variety of ways. The first is to specifically identify the consumer's physical location, often by determining the location of the consumer's smartphone. An advertiser can either constantly track the consumer's phone or use a "geofence" to determine when the consumer is in the vicinity of a specific, targeted location. Advertisers can also use consumer's location check-ins on various services like Facebook or Foursquare to determine the consumer's location and offer targeted advertising.

Mobile devices equipped with near-field communication (NFC) are another technology that can support location-based advertising. NFC allows devices in close proximity, or that are touching, to transmit information via radio waves. This allows consumers to access content when at a specific location.[77]

However, location-based advertising presents privacy concerns. In 2011, a study of theoretical sharing preferences by Kelley et al. found that users had significant privacy concerns about sharing their location with advertisers, but found these concerns were somewhat mitigated when users had the ability to restrict sharing based on their location or the time of day.[78]

5.4.2.5 Combining with Data from Other Sources

Location information drawn, for example, from mobile devices, can be combined with data from other sources to allow inferences that would not be possible with each data source taken individually. For instance, the "Please Rob Me" website gained media attention in 2010 for its possible privacy implications. This site aggregated information from users' Foursquare and Twitter accounts to create a list of people who were likely not at home since they were currently checked in elsewhere. Controversy over the privacy implications of combining location data with data from other sources erupted again in early 2012. This time, the "Girls Around Me" phone application used the gender information from accounts provided to Foursquare, as well as location information provided by check-ins, to allow users to search for women in their vicinity. Foursquare found that the app violated their policies and shut off the developer's access to Foursquare data.[79] However, this scenario provides an example of how inferences can be drawn from location-based data and can lead to privacy concerns.

5.4.3 Geographic Information Systems

A geographic information system (GIS), such as a computer database or imaging tool, is a technology used to view and manipulate stored geographic information. Such geographic content could relate to any quantities associated with a particular location, including maps, population or other census statistics, or data about a specific resource at a location.

Uses for GIS are wide-ranging. They can include logistics systems used for businesses, such as airlines, that need to track passengers, and utility companies, which need to direct crews, as well as agricultural applications for planting decisions.[80]

5.4.4 Preventing and Controlling Location Tracking

The range of location tracking technologies and the uses for location tracking can present privacy concerns. It is possible to block some types of location tracking on mobile devices. However, even when a mobile phone is turned off, it is often still possible to use the triangulation techniques discussed in this chapter to track its location as long as the phone's battery is connected. Furthermore, it is not always preferable to block location tracking, as the addition of location data can augment a service. Thus, systems are also being developed to allow more granular control over location sharing for location-based applications. Additionally, current research examines ways to preserve privacy in location-sharing technologies.

5.4.4.1 Blocking Tracking

Depending on the type of location-tracking technology, users can block or limit tracking to varying degrees.

For location-based services that automatically include location data or include it when the user opts in (e.g., checks in on a social network), a user can either opt out of location tracking or remove location data from content after the fact. The mechanism for opting out of location tracking varies based on the technology used. For some services, like location-based services that rely on check-ins, users are opted out by default and are required to check in to be tracked. For other services, like adding location data to tweets on Twitter, the user can choose to turn location tracking on or off. Still other services, like some smartphone applications, require that users decide whether or not to enable location tracking when they download the application. In this case, a user can opt out only by choosing not to use the service.

Users can also remove location data from some content after it has been added by the application. For example, location data can be automatically added to photo metadata on a GPS-enabled camera or mobile phone. It is possible to use photo-editing applications, like iPhoto or Picasa, to delete the location metadata from the photos after they are taken. Other location-based services, like Google Latitude, also allow users to view the information that was tracked about them and remove data, like location, after the tracking has occurred.

Tracking through RFID chips can be physically blocked, or in some cases, the RFID chip can be physically removed. Because RFID chips rely on a radio wave signal for tracking, a protective sleeve can be placed over an item that contains an RFID chip to prevent the chip from being read until the user desires the chip to be readable. This is useful for items like passports that include chips containing information that the user does not want to be accessible until a certain time. RFID chips can also be removed from items like clothing or other products to prevent tracking, although such techniques prevent the use of the information on the RFID chip at a later time.

5.4.4.2 User Controls

Although it is possible to block tracking to various degrees, sometimes it is more desirable to control who has access to different types of location data at different times. On location-based applications, the interface allows users to set privacy settings with various degrees of granularity that control who is able to access their location information. Technologies like geofences let users control the boundaries of location tracking using geographic guidelines.

Location-based services can enable users to set privacy settings to different levels of granularity, giving users control over who has access to their location information at what times. At a basic level, Foursquare[81] allows users to prevent anyone they have not accepted as a "friend" from viewing their check-in location data. This is known as setting a whitelist, or a priori setting up a group of people who always have access to the data.

It is also possible to allow privacy settings along more granular dimensions. Researchers found that users' location-sharing preferences varied based on the type of information that they planned to share, the type of group they planned to share with, time of day, day of week and the location.[82] Loccacino, a prototype based on these findings, permits constant location tracking.[83] It allows users to control their location-sharing preferences based on the people who can view them, where they are located and the time at which the location is being viewed.

5.4.4.3 Research into Privacy Protections for Location

Beyond methods for controlling location sharing, there is research into methods for providing the benefits of location sharing while preserving a level of user privacy.

Privacy-preserving location-based services are difficult to achieve. It is difficult to completely de-identify an individual's location trace. Patterns in an individual's location, such as home and workplace, can uniquely identify many people.[84]

In 2011, a group of researchers prototyped a system for detecting, in a privacy-preserving manner, whether two users of a location-based service were near each other. They used "location tags," which are signatures associated with a location, to allow a user to detect whether he was in proximity to another user without giving away the user's own exact location, detecting the other user's exact location or revealing locations to any other users.[85]

5.4.5 Effective Practices

There are numerous location-tracking technologies and opportunities to include them in location-based applications. Additionally, there are a variety of potential uses for such location-based applications. However, when creating and using systems that use location-tracking technology, it is necessary to keep in mind the privacy implications of tracking an individual's location.

As was apparent when the shopping malls attempted to implement a customer tracking system, privacy is an important issue when including location-tracking technology in an application. It should be included only if it provides a direct benefit, and, wherever possible, should be an opt-in rather than opt-out. Once data is collected, users should be able to easily see what has been stored about them and delete or update any past location data.

Collected location data should also be considered privacy-sensitive. Users should be informed, through a privacy policy or other means, of how their location information will be used. If it is going to be used in an unexpected manner, it is effective practice to ensure that users know about this ahead of time. Additionally, before making location data more publicly available, it is effective practice to carefully consider how it might be reused or combined with other datasets. Combining location data with other sources can provide a rich dataset, as many GIS systems show; however, as the Foursquare "Girls Around Me" application demonstrated, it can also be privacy-invasive.

When using location-based applications to track others, such as in a workplace setting, it is effective practice to limit such tracking to instances where there is a clear need and to inform employees about the tracking whenever possible. Additionally, tracking should take place only while the employee is working. If tracking is done through a mobile phone that an employee also carries during nonwork hours, tracking should be limited to the workday. Once tracking data is collected, it should be used only for necessary purposes and access should be minimized.

5.5 Audio and Video Surveillance

In this section, we consider the role of audio and video devices in enabling surveillance.

5.5.1 Hidden Cameras and Microphones

Hidden cameras and microphones can provide video and audio surveillance without a person's awareness. Such devices can be very small or, like nanny cams, can be disguised in other objects. They can either record information wirelessly or transmit data back to the person performing surveillance.

Some emerging examples of hidden camera and microphone technology involve smartphone and computer microphones and webcams. The devices contain microphones and cameras and allow an individual to perform remote surveillance on the area around the device.

5.5.1.1 Smartphones as Hidden Cameras and Microphones

An individual's smartphone can be transformed into a hidden camera and/or microphone. Smartphones contain microphones and cameras that can be remotely activated, as well as a connection to the Internet that allows for the remote activation and transmission of the surveillance data. This use of a remotely activated smartphone microphone is called a "roving bug."

Under the federal Wiretap Act, it was found legal for the FBI to use remotely activated cellphone-based audio surveillance in the case of *United*

States v. Jon Tomero.[86] In the example that led to this case, the FBI used roving bugs on two mob bosses' cell phones to provide surveillance on conversations that occurred near the phones.[87]

Through malware on the phones, remote attackers can also install roving bugs. Smartphones have little anti-malware protection, and smartphone malware is a growing attack vector.[88] Through smartphone malware, an attacker can gain control of the microphone and camera and capture surveillance on an individual.[89]

5.5.1.2 Monitoring Through Laptop and Desktop Computers

Laptop and desktop computers also allow for audio and video surveillance. Like smartphones, computers typically have microphones and cameras with network connections. This makes them vulnerable to eavesdropping.

Similar to smartphones, surveillance can occur after a user inadvertently installs malware on his or her computer, allowing an attacker to take control of the camera and/or microphone. Farley and Wang describe an example of how malware can be uploaded onto a computer, take control of a user's microphone for audio surveillance and simultaneously hide its own existence.[90]

Surveillance through computer cameras or microphones can also arise when the computer is owned by one entity and used by another, such as when computers are distributed by an employer or school. However, the use of hidden surveillance has legal implications that are still becoming apparent as privacy issues emerge.

A recent case illustrates this issue. In 2010, it was discovered that a Pennsylvania school district was using the webcam feature on district-owned laptops to remotely take pictures while the laptops were in student homes. This remote monitoring became apparent after pictures taken at a student's home were used to confront the student about potentially inappropriate behavior in his home. While the district claimed that the purpose of this feature was to track lost laptops, they had not informed the parents or students that they were able to remotely perform video monitoring using the laptops, despite using the feature 42 times over a 14-month period.[91]

The parents of the student whose surveillance photo initiated the case sued the school district for violation of privacy, leading to a settlement of over $600,000.[92] There were additional federal and state investigations of whether the district had violated federal wiretap, or other privacy, laws.[93]

5.5.2 CCTV

Closed-circuit television (CCTV) is a type of video monitoring system that is commonly used by governments for preventing crime or terrorism, but it can also be used in private environments for purposes such as preventing shoplifting, providing security for a private facility or tracking employees in a workplace.[94]

In CCTV systems, cameras are set up allowing images to be transferred to a remote destination where footage is available to law enforcement or security personnel for either real-time or post-hoc monitoring. CCTV can encompass a variety of different types of cameras of different levels of sophistication (including both mobile and permanently mounted cameras) and can capture images of varying quality.[95]

Examples of systems that use CCTV include traffic enforcement, such as red light cameras and license plate recognition programs, and terrorism prevention efforts. CCTV analysis systems can also be augmented with additional technology. For example, biometrics and other facial recognition capabilities are used to try to recognize terrorists in a crowd or in an airport. In the United States, general use of CCTV in public spaces by the government is legal, as long there is not a "reasonable expectation of privacy."[96]

CCTV can also be used for workplace surveillance, such as for employers to observe employees within the workplace. In this environment, use of video surveillance is legal as long as it is limited to public areas.[97]

5.5.3 Tracking VoIP Conversations

In recent years, voice over IP (VoIP) technologies like Skype have become a popular way to make voice or video calls. These VoIP technologies, however, can also be tracked in both unintentional and intentional ways. Like computer systems, VoIP systems can suffer from vulnerabilities that unintentionally enable eavesdropping.[98] Researchers have demonstrated that simply having access to the encrypted version of a message may be sufficient for using linguistic techniques to reconstruct the call if certain types of encryption are used.[99]

A number of intentional mechanisms can also be used to surveil VoIP communications. In the United States, the FCC has interpreted the 1994 Communications Assistance for Law Enforcement Act (CALEA), which requires companies to be able to intercept communications in response to authorized legal requests, to include VoIP services. Although Skype had made "affirmative promises to users about their inability to perform wiretaps," Skype was among the services revealed to be accessible as part of the PRISM program in the United States.[100]

5.5.4 Protecting Against Audio and Video Surveillance

User protection against audio and video surveillance on computers and smartphones can take place on several levels. First, it is possible to prevent potential surveillance by avoiding the malware that would allow attackers to take over a camera or microphone by using antivirus software. Additionally, malware is often delivered through untrustworthy downloaded software, especially on smartphones. Avoiding such software can help lower the risk of an attacker implementing audio or video surveillance.

It is also possible to try to avoid audio and video surveillance by blocking the hardware and software features necessary for surveillance to occur. For example, on a computer, it is possible to physically turn off or block a webcam when it is not being used. For instance, some laptop users keep a sticky note over the built-in camera lens when not using the camera. Using firewall software to track incoming and outgoing network connections and block any suspicious activity can also help prevent surveillance.[101]

5.5.5 Effective Practices

When performing audio or video surveillance, especially within a work environment, it is effective practice to ensure that the minimal amount of surveillance is being performed for the necessary objective and that it is conducted in a legal manner.

Video and audio surveillance can be very privacy-invasive and should not be performed unless a necessary objective (e.g., security or efficiency) outweighs the privacy drawbacks. Wherever possible, those under surveillance should be informed about the system to lower the impact of the privacy violation. Additionally, a group should check local privacy laws before putting surveillance in place. In the United States, a first step for employers is making sure that the surveillance is not taking place in an environment in which employees have an expectation of privacy (e.g., inside a bathroom stall).

Once audio and video surveillance data has been gathered, it is effective practice to take proper measures to maintain data security and limit exposure of the content. Whenever possible, use automated systems to analyze the data or employ a separation of duties, where the analyst examines the audio or video and only reports the finding to others; this avoids exposing the raw audio and video to unauthorized repurposing or snooping. In these situations, it is important to securely retain the raw audio or video in the event the finding is ever challenged. To ensure that the data is not misused, one should track access to the data and limit it to necessary personnel. A clear policy should be put in place for who has access to the data and under what circumstances, and for how long the data will be retained. Data should be purged when no longer needed for the intended purpose.

5.6 Chapter Summary

In this chapter, we presented an overview of tracking and surveillance techniques and countermeasures. We began by explaining how the packets that encapsulate communication over the Internet can be surveilled on a large scale, at the edge of a workplace or school or over a wireless connection. We then demonstrated how surveillance of low-level communications over the Internet can be made more difficult by encrypting web requests using the HTTPS protocol, by sending traffic through an encrypted VPN tunnel or by using an anonymizing network, such as Tor, to separate the identity of the sender of a message from the message itself.

We then discussed numerous technologies that can be used to collect information about the websites that a particular user has visited, often for the purpose of better targeting advertisements to that person. While we explained in depth how HTTP cookies enable this sort of tracking, we also introduced technologies that can be used either as alternatives to HTTP cookies or in conjunction with HTTP cookies in order to respawn deleted cookies. These technologies include LSOs, DOM Storage, and more subtle techniques, such as browser history stealing and browser fingerprinting. We then explained a number of ways in which users can block certain types of web tracking. For instance, we introduced the cookie controls built into web browsers, illuminated the debate over a proposed Do Not Track mechanism, discussed opt-out cookies that some advertising companies offer and delved into third-party browser add-ons for blocking web tracking. Alongside these methods, we explained their shortcomings, as well as effective practices in the design of privacy tools. We also briefly described ways to prevent tracking of web searches and e-mail messages.

Next, we provided an overview of location-tracking technologies, describing how the location of a phone can be triangulated based on the signal from cell towers and how devices can use GPS to determine their location. We also explained the complex interaction between utility and privacy as users share information about their location on social networking sites, in addition to proposals for limiting the privacy perils of these disclosures. Finally, we touched briefly on methods for audio and video surveillance. In addition to more canonical examples of surveillance, such as placing hidden cameras and microphones in public or private locations, we demonstrated how both smartphones and personal computers can be co-opted by malware to surveil users.

Endnotes

1 Charlie Savage, Edward Wyatt and Peter Baker, "U.S. Confirms That It Gathers Online Data Overseas," New York Times, June 6, 2013, www.nytimes. com/2013/06/07/us/nsa-verizon-calls.html.

2 Barton Gellman and Laura Poitras, "U.S., British Intelligence Mining Data from Nine U.S. Internet Companies in Broad Secret Program," Washington Post, June 6, 2013, www.washingtonpost.com/investigations/us-intelligence-mining-data-from-nine-us-internet-companies-in-broad-secret-program/2013/06/06/3a0c0da8-cebf-11e2-8845-d970ccb04497_story.html.

3 Daniel J. Solove, " 'I've Got Nothing to Hide' and Other Misunderstandings of Privacy," San Diego Law Review 44 (2007).

4 Peter Whoriskey, "Every Click You Make," Washington Post, April 3, 2008, www. washingtonpost.com/wp-dyn/content/article/2008/04/03/AR2008040304052.html.

5 Robert Sheldon, "The Situation Is Under Control: Cyberspace Situation Awareness and the Implications of China's Internet Censorship," Strategic Insights 10, no. 11 (2011).

6 Federal Communications Commission, "Commission Orders Comcast to End Discriminatory Network Management Practices," Federal Communications Commission: News Media Information, August 1, 2008, http://hraunfoss.fcc.gov/edocs_public/attachmatch/DOC-284286A1.pdf.

7 www.wireshark.org/.

8 www.kismetwireless.net; www.baurhome.net/software/eavesdrop/.

9 http://codebutler.com/firesheep.

10 David Streitfeld, "Google Concedes That Drive-By Prying Violated Privacy," New York Times, March 12, 2013, www.nytimes.com/2013/03/13/technology/google-pays-fine-over-street-view-privacy-breach.html.

11 Nikita Borisov, Ian Goldberg and David Wagner, "Intercepting Mobile Communications: The Insecurity of 802.11," in Proceedings of the 7th Annual International Conference on Mobile Computing and Networking (MobiCom), 2001.

12 CERT, "WiFi Protected Setup (WPS) PIN Brute Force Vulnerability" (Vulnerability Note VU#723755), Vulnerability Notes Database, December 27, 2011; revised May 10, 2012, www.kb.cert.org/vuls/id/723755.

13 G. Daryl Nord, Tipton F. McCubbins and Jeretta Horn Nord, "E-Monitoring in the Workplace: Privacy, Legislation, and Surveillance Software," Communications of the ACM 49, no. 8 (2006).

14 American Management Association, "Over Half of All Employers Combined Fire Workers for E-Mail and Internet Abuse," 2007 Electronic Monitoring & Surveillance Survey, February 28, 2008, http://press.amanet.org/press-releases/177/2007-electronic-monitoring-surveillance-survey/.

15 Federal Communications Commission, Children's Internet Protection Act, www.fcc.gov/guides/childrens-internet-protection-act.

16 John Schwartz, "Schools Get Tool to Track Students' Use of Internet," New York Times, May 21, 2001, www.nytimes.com/2001/05/21/business/schools-get-tool-to-track-students-use-of-internet.html.

17 Michael McCardle, "How Spyware Fits into Defense in Depth," SANS Institute: InfoSec Reading Room, 2003.

18 https://anonymous-proxy-servers.net/.

19 David M. Goldschlag, Michael G. Reed and Paul F. Syverson, "Hiding Routing Information," in *Proceedings of the 1st Workshop on Information Hiding*, Lecture Notes in Computer Science, 1174 (1996): 137–150, Cambridge, UK.

20 https://www.torproject.org/index.html.en.

21 Charlie Savage, Edward Wyatt and Peter Baker, "U.S. Confirms That It Gathers Online Data Overseas," *New York Times*, June 6, 2013, www.nytimes .com/2013/06/07/us/nsa-verizon-calls.html.

22 Gellman and Poitras, "U.S., British Intelligence Mining Data."

23 Cloud Security Alliance, Government Access to Information Survey Results, July 2013, https://cloudsecurityalliance.org/research/surveys/#_nsa_prism.

24 Michael Barbaro and Tom Zeller, Jr., "A Face Is Exposed for AOL Searcher No. 4417749," *New York Times*, August 9, 2006, www.nytimes.com/2006/08/09/technology/09aol.html.

25 Aleecia McDonald and Lorrie Faith Cranor, "The Cost of Reading Privacy Policies," *I/S: A Journal of Law and Policy for the Information Society* 4, no. 3 (2008).

26 Balachander Krishnamurthy and Craig E. Wills, "Privacy Diffusion on the Web: A Longitudinal Perspective," in *Proceedings of the 18th International Conference on World Wide Web* (WWW), 2009.

27 Federal Communications Commission, Children's Internet Protection Act; White House, "Consumer Data Privacy in a Networked World: A Framework for Protecting Privacy and Promoting Innovation in the Global Digital Economy," February 2012, www.whitehouse.gov/sites/default/files/privacy-final.pdf.

28 Jennifer Valentino-DeVries, "Facebook Defends Getting Data from Logged-Out Users," *Digits* (blog), *Wall Street Journal*, September 26, 2011, http://blogs.wsj .com/digits/2011/09/26/facebook-defends-getting-data-from-logged-out-users/.

29 Ashkan Soltani et al., "Flash Cookies and Privacy," Social Science Research Network, August 10, 2009, http://papers.ssrn.com/sol3/papers.cfm?abstract_id=1446862.

30 Thomas Frank, "Session Variables Without Cookies," January 20, 2008, www.thomasfrank.se/sessionvars.html.

31 Mozilla Developer Network, DOM Storage Guide, https://developer.mozilla.org/en-US/docs/DOM/Storage; accessed August 15, 2012.

32 W3C, Web SQL Database, W3C Working Group Note 18, November 2010, www.w3.org/TR/webdatabase/.

33 Aleecia McDonald and Lorrie Faith Cranor, "A Survey of the Use of Adobe Flash Local Shared Objects to Respawn HTTP Cookies," CMU-CyLab-11-001 Technical Report, January 31, 2011; Soltani et al., "Flash Cookies and Privacy."

34 Mika Ayenson et al., "Flash Cookies and Privacy II: Now with HTML5 and ETag Respawning," Social Science Research Network, July 29, 2011, http://papers.ssrn .com/sol3/papers.cfm?abstract_id=1898390.

35 Samy Kamkar, "Evercookie—Never Forget," October 11, 2010, http://samy.pl/evercookie/.

36 Jeremiah Grossman, "I Know Where You've Been" (blog post), August 11, 2006, http://jeremiahgrossman.blogspot.ro/2006/08/i-know-where-youve-been.html.

37 Peter Eckersley, "How Unique Is Your Web Browser?" in *Proceedings of the 10th international conference on Privacy enhancing technologies* (PETS), 2010.

38 European Parliament, Directive 2009/136/EC of the European Parliament and of the Council of 25 November 2009.

39 Tanzina Vega, "Code That Tracks Users' Browsing Prompts Lawsuits," *New York Times*, September 20, 2010, www.nytimes.com/2010/09/21/technology/21cookie

.html; Tanzina Vega, "New Web Code Draws Concern Over Privacy Risks," *New York Times*, October 10, 2010, www.nytimes.com/2010/10/11/business/media/11privacy.html.

40 Blase Ur et al., "Smart, Useful, Scary, Creepy: Perceptions of Online Behavioral Advertising, " in *Proceedings of the Eighth Symposium on Usable Privacy and Security* (SOUPS), April 2, 2012; revised July 13, 2012.

41 McDonald and Cranor, "The Cost of Reading Privacy Policies"; Mark A. Graber, Donna M. D'Alessandro and Jill Johnson-West, "Reading Level of Privacy Policies on Internet Health Web Sites," *Journal of Family Practice* 51, no. 7 (2002); Blase Ur, Manya Sleeper and Lorrie Faith Cranor, "{Privacy, Privacidad, Приватност} Policies in Social Media: Providing Translated Privacy Notice," in *WWW Workshop on Privacy and Security in Online Social Media* (PSOSM), 2012.

42 Ryan W. Neal, "Mozilla Firefox 'Do Not Track' Feature Coming, But Advertisers Object," *International Business Times*, June 22, 2013, www.ibtimes.com/mozilla-firefox-do-not-track-feature-coming-advertisers-object-1318663.

43 Steve Lohr, "The Default Choice, So Hard to Resist," *New York Times*, October 15, 2011, www.nytimes.com/2011/10/16/technology/default-choices-are-hard-to-resist-online-or-not.html.

44 Pedro Giovanni Leon, Lorrie Faith Cranor, Aleecia M. McDonald and Robert McGuire, "Token Attempt: The Misrepresentation of Website Privacy Policies Through the Misuse of P3P Compact Policy Tokens," in *Workshop on Privacy in the Electronic Society*, September 10, 2010.

45 Microsoft, Internet Explorer 10 Privacy Statement for Windows 7, last updated December 2012, http://windows.microsoft.com/en-US/internet-explorer/ie10-win7-privacy-statement.

46 W3C Tracking Protection Working Group, www.w3.org/2011/tracking-protection/; Robert X. Cringely, "The Myth of Do Not Track—and the Tragedy of Internet Privacy," *InfoWorld*, July 31, 2013, www.infoworld.com/t/cringely/the-myth-of-do-not-track-and-the-tragedy-of-internet-privacy-223827.

47 Peter Bright, "Microsoft Sticks to Its Guns, Keeps Do Not Track on by Default in IE10," *Ars Technica*, August 7, 2012, http://arstechnica.com/information-technology/2012/08/microsoft-sticks-to-its-guns-keeps-do-not-track-on-by-default-in-ie10/.

48 Michael Muchmore, "Google Chrome's Sham 'Do Not Track' Feature," *PCMAG*, November 9, 2012, www.pcmag.com/article2/0,2817,2411916,00.asp.

49 Lorrie Faith Cranor, "A First Look at Internet Explorer 9 Privacy Features," *Technology|Academics|Policy*, March 16, 2011, www.techpolicy.com/Blog/March-2011/A-first-look-at-Internet-Explorer-9-privacy-featur.aspx.

50 Gaurav Aggarwal, Elie Bursztein, Collin Jackson and Dan Boneh, "An Analysis of Private Browsing Modes in Modern Browsers, " in *Proceedings of the 19th USENIX Security Symposium*, 2010.

51 Pedro Giovanni Leon et al., "What Do Online Behavioral Advertising Privacy Disclosures Communicate to Users?" in *Proceedings of the 2012 Workshop on Privacy in the Electronic Society*, 19–30, New York: ACM Press, April 2, 2012.

52 Network Advertising Initiative, www.networkadvertising.org/choices/, accessed August 9, 2013; Digital Advertising Alliance, www.aboutads.info/choices/, accessed August 26, 2012; Evidon, Profile Manager, www.evidon.com/consumers-privacy/opt-out, accessed October 7, 2013.

53 Pedro Giovanni Leon et al., "Why Johnny Can't Opt Out: A Usability Evaluation of Tools to Limit Online Behavioral Advertising," in *Proceedings of the SIGCHI*

Conference on Human Factors in Computing Systems (CHI), October 31, 2011; revised May 10, 2012.

54 Google, Ads Settings, https://www.google.com/settings/ads/onweb/, accessed August 27, 2012; Microsoft, Your Privacy and Microsoft Personalized Ads, https://choice.microsoft.com/en-US, accessed August 9, 2013; Yahoo! Ad Interest Manager, http://info.yahoo.com/privacy/us/yahoo/opt_out/targeting/details.html, accessed August 1, 2012; Evidon, Profile Manager, www.evidon.com/consumers-privacy/manage-your-online-profile, accessed October 8, 2013.

55 Information Commissioner's Office, "Guidance on the Rules on Use of Cookies and Similar Technologies," V.3, May 2012, www.ico.gov.uk/~/media/documents/library/Privacy_and_electronic/Practical_application/guidance_on_the_new_cookies_regulations.ashx.

56 Abine, "Frequently Asked Questions About DNT+," www.donottrackplus.com/faqs.php, accessed August 27, 2012.

57 Leon et al., "Why Johnny Can't Opt Out."

58 Ur et al., "Smart, Useful, Scary, Creepy."

59 Jennifer Valentino-DeVries, "How to Use Microsoft's InPrivate Filtering," Digits (blog), Wall Street Journal, August 1, 2010, http://blogs.wsj.com/digits/2010/08/01/how-to-use-microsofts-inprivate-filtering/.

60 Mozilla, "Introducing Collusion: Discover Who's Tracking You Online," www.mozilla.org/en-US/collusion/, accessed August 9, 2013.

61 Leon et al., "Why Johnny Can't Opt Out."

62 Robert J. Walls, Shane S. Clark and Brian Neil Levine, "Functional Privacy or Why Cookies Are Better with Milk," in 7th USENIX Workshop on Hot Topics in Security (HotSec), 2012.

63 Franziska Roesner, Tadayoshi Kohno and David Wetherall, "Detecting and Defending Against Third-Party Tracking on the Web," in Proceedings of the 9th USENIX Symposium on Networked Systems Design and Implementation (NSDI), 2012.

64 Ur et al., "Smart, Useful, Scary, Creepy."

65 Helen F. Nissenbaum, "Privacy as Contextual Integrity," Washington Law Review 79, no. 1 (2004).

66 Daniel C. Howe and Helen Nissenbaum, "TrackMeNot: Resisting Surveillance in Web Search," in Ian Kerr, Carole Lucock and Valerie Steeves, eds., Lessons from the Identity Trail: Anonymity, Privacy, and Identity in a Networked Society (New York: Oxford University Press, 2009), 417–436.

67 Christopher Soghoian, "The Problem of Anonymous Vanity Searches," I/S: A Journal of Law and Policy for the Information Society 3, no. 2 (2007).

68 Federal Aviation Administration, "Navigation Services—Global Position System," 2010, www.faa.gov/about/office_org/headquarters_offices/ato/service_units/techops/navservices/gnss/gps/, accessed July 22, 2012.

69 Ari Juels, "RFID Security and Privacy: A Research Survey," IEEE Journal on Selected Areas in Communications 24, no. 2 (February 6, 2006).

70 Joel Johnson, "Is Your Carrier Tracing You via GPS and 911 Calls?" Popular Mechanics, October 1, 2009, www.popularmechanics.com/technology/how-to/4258805.

71 Sean Gallagher, "Mall Owners Pull Plug on Cellular Tracking (For Now)," Wired, November 29, 2011, www.wired.com/business/2011/11/mall-pull-plug-cell-tracking/; Sean Gallagher, "We're Watching: Malls Track Shoppers' Cellphone Signals to Gather Marketing Data," Wired, November 28, 2011, www.wired.com/business/2011/11/malls-track-phone-signals/.

72 http://itunes.apple.com/us/app/find-my-friends/id466122094?mt=8.

73 www.facebook.com/about/location/.

74 http://itunes.apple.com/us/app/imapweather-radio/id413511993?mt=8.

75 David Pogue, "Cellphones That Track the Kids," New York Times, December 21, 2006, www.nytimes.com/2006/12/21/technology/21pogue.html.

76 Gundars Kaupins and Robert Minch, "Legal and Ethical Implications of Employee Location Monitoring," in Proceedings of the 38th Hawaii International Conference on System Sciences, 2005.

77 Frost & Sullivan, "Location-based Advertising—Relevant Trends and Technologies," February 16, 2012, www.frost.com/sublib/display-report.do?id=9838-00-31-00-00.

78 Patrick Gage Kelley, Michael Benisch, Lorrie Faith Cranor and Norman Sadeh, "When Are Users Comfortable Sharing Location with Advertisers?" in Proceedings of the SIGCHI Conference on Human Factors in Computing Systems (CHI), 2011.

79 Andrew Dowell, "Tracking Women: Now There's Not An App For That," Digits (blog), Wall Street Journal, March 31, 2012, http://blogs.wsj.com/digits/2012/03/31/tracking-women-now-theres-not-an-app-for-that/.

80 Michael F. Goodchild, "Unit 002—What Is Geographic Information Science?" NCGIA Core Curriculum in GIScience, 1997, www.ncgia.ucsb.edu/giscc/units/u002/, accessed July 29, 2012.

81 https://foursquare.com/privacy/.

82 Michael Benisch, Patrick Gage Kelley, Norman Sadeh, and Lorrie Faith Cranor, "Capturing Location-Privacy Preferences: Quantifying Accuracy and User-Burden Tradeoffs," Personal and Ubiquitous Computing 15, no. 7 (2011).

83 http://locaccino.org/.

84 Yves-Alexandre de Montjoye, César A. Hidalgo, Michel Verleysen and Vincent D. Blondel, "Unique in the Crowd: The Privacy Bounds of Human Mobility," Scientific Reports 3 (March 25, 2013), http://dx.doi.org/10.1038/srep01376.

85 Arvind Narayanan et al., "Location Privacy via Private Proximity Testing," in Proceedings of the 18th Annual Network and Distributed Systems Symposium (NDSS), 2011.

86 Lewis A. Kaplan, United States District Court, S. D. New York, United States of America v. John Tomero et al., Defendants, No. S2 06 Crim. 0008(LAK), November 27, 2006.

87 Declan McCullagh and Anne Broache, "FBI Taps Cell Phone Mic as Eavesdropping Tool," CNET, December 1, 2006, http://news.cnet.com/2100-1029-6140191.html.

88 Neal Leavitt, "Mobile Phones: The Next Frontier for Hackers?" Computer 38, no. 4 (2005).

89 Ryan Farley and Xinyuan Wang, "Roving Bugnet: Distributed Surveillance Threat and Mitigation," Emerging Challenges for Security, Privacy and Trust. IFIP Advances in Information and Communications Technologies 297, 2009.

90 Ibid.

91 Suzan Clark, "Pa. School Faces FBI Probe, Lawsuit for Using Webcams on Laptops to Watch Students at Home," ABC Good Morning America, February 22, 2010, http://abcnews.go.com/GMA/Parenting/pennsylvania-school-fbi-probe-webcam-students-spying/story?id=9905488.

92 John P. Martin, "Lower Merion District's Laptop Saga Ends with $610,000 Settlement," The Inquirer, October 12, 2010, http://articles.philly.com/2010-10-12/news/24981536_1_laptop-students-district-several-million-dollars/2, accessed August 27, 2012.

93 Clark, "Pa. School Faces FBI Probe."

94 Joyce W. Luk, "Identifying Terrorists: Privacy Rights in the United States and the United Kingdom," *Hastings International and Comparative Law Review* 25, 2002; Electronic Privacy Information Center, "Workplace Privacy," http://epic.org/privacy/workplace/#technologies, accessed August 27, 2012.

95 Martin Gill and Angela Spriggs, *Home Office Research Study 292: Assessing the Impact of CCTV* (London: Home Office Research, Development and Statistics Directorate, 2005).

96 Luk, "Identifying Terrorists."

97 Electronic Privacy Information Center, "Workplace Privacy."

98 Robert Westervelt, "Cisco Warns Serious VoIP Vulnerability Enables Eavesdropping," CRN, January 11, 2013, www.crn.com/news/security/240146127/cisco-warns-serious-voip-vulnerability-enables-eavesdropping.htm.

99 Andrew M. White, Austin R. Matthews, Kevin Z. Snow and Fabian Monrose, "Phonotactic Reconstruction of Encrypted VoIP Conversations: Hookt on fon-iks," in *Proceedings of the 32nd IEEE Symposium on Security and Privacy*, May 2011.

100 Glenn Greenwald et al., "Microsoft Handed the NSA Access to Encrypted Messages," *The Guardian*, July 11, 2013, www.theguardian.com/world/2013/jul/11/microsoft-nsa-collaboration-user-data.

101 Farley and Wang, "Roving Bugnet."

CHAPTER 6

Interference

Aaron Massey, Travis Breaux, CIPT

Interference is an act that prevents or obstructs a process from continuing or being carried out properly.[1] For individual privacy, interference can be informed by Warren and Brandeis' privacy right "to be let alone" and Alan Westin's notions of solitude and reserve, wherein an individual's preference not to be used, avoiding outside interference from others.[2] Surveillance and tracking technologies, such as those described in Chapter 5, enable interference because they provide access to the individual's physical person as well as to information about the person's behaviors and preferences. Society's need to protect itself from nefarious individuals sometimes justifies the use of surveillance and tracking technologies.

Similarly, businesses need to create accurate information models about individuals in order to ensure routine and reliable business activities. However, the risk of interference for individuals increases with the amount of information collected and maintained. Example activities include an individual's ability to use transportation and banking services, to earn a living wage by finding employment or to exercise a vote in a democratic society. These activities rely on establishing a person's identity and authorization to use services or perform actions—for example, establishing that a person is licensed to drive, is creditworthy or is not a criminal felon. If an error exists in a person's credit report, or if a person is incorrectly placed on a "no-fly" list, this individual would suffer from interference with his or her private matters. In this chapter, we begin by introducing interference in the context of current legal views, definitions and privacy harms. We then examine interference from different technological perspectives, such as spam, mobile applications and other software APIs, behavioral advertising, cyberbullying, social engineering and lastly remote desktop administration. We conclude with recommendations that IT professionals may follow in the context of their professional responsibilities.

6.1 Framework for Understanding Interference

Unlike ensuring that an IT system keeps personal information confidential, which can often be achieved using a cryptographic system such as those described in Chapter 3, interference is a threat to privacy that culminates from a sequence of steps in an IT system. Some of these steps may be innocuous, such as collecting a person's zip code, whereas others are more prone to missteps, such as determining a person's life stage based on his or her purchase history.[3] Finally, other actions can lead to a process obstruction or unwanted attention, such as sending advertising to a person based on an attribute inferred from data. Whether the attribute is accurate or not does not lessen the perception of the intrusion. However, whether the act is welcome or unwelcome often depends on the person's privacy preferences. For some pregnant women, advertising can introduce them to products that increase daily comfort. For others who wish to control the time, location and circumstances for revealing their pregnancy, their status is a private family matter; in this case, advertising can interfere in a woman's personal affairs by circumventing her ability to control access to her personal information.

In this chapter, we introduce a framework that classifies three general types of interference by the object that IT interferes with, whether that object is a decision, a personal feeling or a social engagement. The three types borrow heavily from the work by Daniel Solove and William Prosser, which we discuss.

- *Obstruction or decisional interference* is any action that interferes with decisions that affect the person's daily life, such as whether to allow the person to travel, to borrow money or to obtain lawful employment. This form of interference is difficult to detect as it can be concealed in complex business or IT processes. Consequently, this form is not easily recognizable by the person about whom the decision is made: He or she may be unaware of the decision-making process or the decision itself may be hidden from the person.

- *Intrusion into physical, psychological or informational spaces* is any action that affects individuals' solitude, including their desire to be alone or to be among a few confidantes of their choosing, and their desire to control who has access to their visual and thoughtful attention or who has access to their information. Such actions include searches of private spaces, curfews or other restrictions of movement, and alerts and notifications that grab and divert the attention of the person. While these actions may constitute objective harms under Calo's classification, the act of surveillance is a psychological intrusion and subjective harm, because it can affect whether people feel comfortable behaving as they otherwise would without persistent monitoring.[4]

- *Interference with representation of self* is any action that alters how an individual is represented, such as a person's marriage, financial or employment status, race, gender or sexual orientation, political views or any other affinity toward specific ideas or social groups. Regardless of whether the representation is accurate, individuals may wish to control access to the representation to avoid unwanted attention.

The act of interference may be direct or indirect. An act of direct interference involves the person whose privacy is most affected by the interference. An act of indirect interference is significantly removed from the effects of the act. Type 1 interference can be indirect, if the decision occurs without directly involving the person (e.g., a decision of creditworthiness). Type 2 interference can be direct, if the act interacts with the person's physical, psychological or informational space, such as by reading a person's contact list from a mobile phone.

The three types of interference are not orthogonal. Intrusion can influence obstruction: For example, surveillance of a person's movement can interfere with that person's feeling of oppression, and thus affect their decision about whether to meet their counterparts. Assumptions about the same person's associations, which lead to a negative representation of that person, may be used to interfere with the person's movement— for example, by prompting the person to take a different path or by detaining the person for questioning. Last, misrepresentation can influence obstruction: If a person is misrepresented as a convicted felon, then that person may be denied certain types of employment, which is a decision made by a prospective employer.

The three types of interference are based on privacy scholarship, which lends credibility to their application in information technology. William Prosser, a scholar on tort law, codified specific types of interference from hundreds of civil privacy cases in his law review article, "Privacy."[5] This analysis resulted in four distinct torts that appear in Table 6-1. In 2002, Daniel Solove expanded upon Prosser's torts in his own taxonomy of privacy harms; we compare Prosser's and Solove's categories in Table 6-1.[6]

Table 6-1: Comparing Prosser's and Solove's Classifications of Interference-Related Privacy Acts

William Prosser's Four Kinds of Torts	Daniel Solove's Taxonomy of Privacy
Intrusion upon seclusion or solitude	Intrusion, decisional interference
Public disclosure of private facts	Breach of confidentiality, disclosure, exposure, increased accessibility
Presentation of an individual in a false light	Distortion
Use of an individual's name or likeness without permission	Appropriation

Solove's taxonomy distinguishes between different categories of intrusion and information disclosure, which results in multiple categories mapping to a single tort in Prosser's view on privacy. For example, intrusion is recategorized into two forms of invasion: decisional interference, which includes acts by a person to insert themselves into a decision-making process about another individual, and intrusion, which includes acts that disrupt a person's sense of solitude, whether physical or psychological.[7] We adopted this distinction separately in our framework Types 1 and 2, respectively. Solove further refines public disclosure of private facts through various means: Breach of confidentiality is a broken promise to keep facts private; disclosure is revealing private facts to yield negative consequences; exposure is a revelation resulting from revealing private facts; and increased accessibility results when otherwise obscure or hard-to-access public information becomes easier to access due to more pervasive collection, distribution and retention practices. We narrowly consider the second tort and corresponding taxonomic categories as they relate to interfering to obtain a person's private information under Type 2. Whereas these four taxonomic categories are about revealing private facts, the activities of disclosure can also lead to factual inaccuracies about a person, which Solove labels distortion. Last, the intentional use of a person's likeness without permission is called *appropriation*. We consider the last three torts narrowly as they relate to interfering with a person's self-representation. While Solove appropriately distinguishes the subtleties between these categories, the end result is similar for an IT professional: interference can affect how a person is perceived.

The challenge for IT professionals is that technology does not inherently interfere with individual privacy, and the technological advantages to the individual may outweigh the harms. Telemarketing calls may be welcome or unwanted depending on the person's privacy preferences. Creditworthiness allows banking institutions to make better decisions, which makes it

easier for higher-risk individuals to obtain loans or use bank accounts fo
safeguarding money. Similarly, public safety in aviation depends upon
prohibiting dangerous individuals from boarding aircraft. In situations
where the risk exceeds the harm, we recommend in Chapter 2 that IT
professionals use a risk strategy to identify specific harms and avoid, transfer
or mitigate those risks with appropriate privacy controls. Furthermore,
after discussing real-world scenarios where interference occurred, we offer
several recommendations that the IT professional may use to specifically
evaluate how any technology may contribute to interference.

6.2 Interference from a Technology Perspective

In this section, we examine different technological perspectives on
interference with user or consumer privacy. Table 6-2 summarizes the
perspectives and how they illustrate the three types of interference in
different situations and under different technologies. First, we quickly
review the familiar situation of unwanted messages. In the second topic,
we explore how software APIs can enable access to personal data and result
in unwanted disclosure and exposure. Behavioral profiling, the third topic,
leads to building complex representations of a person based on surveilling
his or her behavior and then using these profiles to make decisions about
the individual or to personalize his or her experiences. Similar to the
second topic, cyberbullying often requires exposing a person's private
details or recharacterizing the person beyond his or her control. Next, we
illustrate how social engineering directly interferes in security processes
to gain control of an individual's online persona. Finally, we conclude by
briefly discussing how administrative activities that manage IT systems can
intrude on personal privacy.

Table 6-2: Technology Perspectives and Their Classification in the Interference Framework

Technology Topic	Type 1: Obstruction	Type 2: Intrusion	Type 3: Self-representation
Unwanted messaging		✔	
Select software APIs		✔	✔
Behavioral profiling	✔	✔	✔
Cyberbullying		✔	✔
Social engineering	✔		✔
Administrative intrusions	✔	✔	

As we examine these cases, consider some of the following questions: How do companies learn about interference? Where does it come from? How does interference affect individuals? What can be done to prevent, mitigate or respond to interference? What are the differences between an action that causes interference and a failure to act to prevent interference?

6.2.1 Unsolicited Messages (Spam)

Unsolicited messages, also called spam, can be used to capture an individual's attention for advertising or other purposes. Spam is often restricted to e-mail, but increasingly unwanted messages can be sent using other means, such as SMS texts. Spam is estimated to be roughly 78 percent of the total volume of e-mail sent, and it has grown into a serious security and economic threat.[8] In 2003, the United States passed the Controlling the Assault of Non-Solicited Pornography and Marketing Act (CAN-SPAM Act) in an effort to regulate spammers, and the Federal Trade Commission (FTC) implemented the CAN-SPAM Act by providing guidelines for businesses that include offering individuals the opportunity to opt out.[9] Spam is often not directed at a specific individual any more than another individual, and response rates to spam are often extremely low compared to other forms of advertising. Under the CAN-SPAM Act, companies are required to provide one-click access within commercial bulk e-mail messages to unsubscribe from mailing lists and future bulk messages. The link to unsubscribe must be prominently displayed, and the receiving website must quickly allow the user to unsubscribe. This means that the receiving website cannot require collecting additional information from the user, nor can the website create obstacles to unsubscribing, such as requiring the creation of user accounts. Under other jurisdictions, such as Europe, companies must first obtain individual consent before sending marketing messages, called opt-in consent. Thus, organizations often collect a person's residency status in Europe to determine which mechanism must be applied to such communications.

Unwanted messages generally fall under the second type of interference, intrusion into psychological spaces. Depending on the type of message and time of day, the interference can affect individuals differently. Unwanted e-mail is generally easy to filter using Bayesian algorithms, which use statistical and probabilistic approaches to classify likely spam messages based on keywords and e-mail headers. E-mail users often customize Bayesian approaches to ensure a low false-positive rate so that desirable messages are delivered. Unwanted SMS texts, however, are more intimate as they arrive on a person's cell phone, which is typically used to receive personal calls. By employing the appropriate opt-in or opt-out mechanism, companies can more effectively communicate with potential customers while affording them control over unwanted interference.

6.2.2 Exposing Personal Data Through Software APIs

In early February 2012, a social networking application called Path made newspaper and blog headlines for interfering with users' control over their contacts. Path is a social network built primarily through mobile phone applications on the iPhone and Android devices.[10] Path focuses on photo sharing and competes with the Instagram network, which is owned by Facebook. A programmer from Singapore named Arun Thampi discovered the interference while creating a social networking application using the Path API.[11] He began investigating the Path API while using a man-in-the-middle proxy tool to examine specific API calls and learn how the calls operate.[12] As Thampi stated on his blog:[13]

> Upon inspecting closer, I noticed that my **entire address book (including full names, e-mails and phone numbers) was being sent as a plist to Path.** Now I don't remember having given permission to Path to access my address book and send its contents to its servers, so I created a completely new 'Path' and repeated the experiment and I got the same result—my address book was in Path's hands."
> (Emphasis in original.)

Thampi discovered that users signing up with Path would have their mobile address book copied to Path's servers without notification. Users responded to Thampi's discovery quickly. Many left negative reviews on Apple's App Store. The technical press picked up the story, and it eventually spread to larger media outlets like *USA Today* and the *New York Times*.[14] Dave Morin, the CEO and cofounder of Path as well as an early employee at Facebook, responded to Thampi's blog post by saying, in part, "We upload the address book to our servers in order to help the user find and connect to their friends and family on Path quickly and efficiently as well as to notify them when friends and family join Path." Eventually, Morin also apologized at length on Path's company blog:

> We believe you should have control when it comes to sharing your personal information. We also believe that actions speak louder than words. So, as a clear signal of our commitment to your privacy, **we've deleted the entire collection of user uploaded contact information from our servers.** Your trust matters to us and we want you to feel completely in control of your information on Path.
> (Emphasis in original.)

Path's privacy violation is strikingly similar to the 2010 violation by Google Buzz, which is a different social networking service.[15] Google users were invited to "Try Buzz in Gmail." Those who accepted the invitation found that Buzz had automatically begun following those Google users contained in the invitee's Gmail contacts, which were also made publicly available for others to see. Similar to Google Buzz, Path wanted users to connect *conveniently* with friends on their network. To that end, both Google and Path used contact information that was originally collected for one purpose (e.g., personal reasons of the e-mail sender and recipient) for another secondary purpose (e.g., bootstrapping social network relationships). Users formally complained about Google Buzz to the FTC, and the FTC found that Google had used deceptive business practices. As a part of the settlement, Google was required to have third-party companies audit its privacy practices for the next 20 years.

Consider one important difference between Google Buzz and Path's use of address book information: Who was responsible for the interference? Since Google maintained copies of both the contacts and the application that used the contacts for the secondary purpose, the Google Buzz violation is rather clear. However, the other case is not as simple. Path obviously created the application and infrastructure to upload users' contact information. However, as a part of Apple's App Store policies, Apple claims to verify that third-party applications meet their standards. Apple is also responsible for providing both the API platform that enables Path programmers to gain access to a user's contact list. It is reasonable to say that both companies, Apple and Path, share some of the responsibility for this interference and are exposed to litigation risks.

The FTC has received multiple complaints regarding mobile access to contact lists. A class action lawsuit was filed against more than a dozen mobile application makers, including Path and Apple, for their use of address book information without user consent.[16] At the time of this writing, the outcome of this lawsuit has not been decided. However, based on newspaper accounts of the situation, Path appears to have violated the first three Fair Information Practice Principles (FIPPs) recommended by the FTC: notice/awareness, choice/consent and access/participation.[17] Users were not aware of the collection, they were not provided a choice regarding whether they would like to share their contacts when they started using Path and they were not given appropriate access to all the information Path obtained about them. Each of these points has since been addressed as a part of the API calls that allow third-party developers to access address book information on Apple's iOS.[18]

While the Google Buzz and Path cases both illustrate a privacy violation, there are technologies that mine e-mail inboxes and contact lists to populate social networking sites in ways that conform to the FIPPs. Facebook and LinkedIn both use similar technologies where users choose whether to mine their contacts to expand their network. By offering a choice, these IT systems allow users to decide whether the advantage of easily improving their social networking experience through automated contact population is valued over the risk of exposing their personal information to unwanted contacts. Moreover, other safeguards could be used to ensure these services do not exceed their intended purpose, such as controls in the software to ensure the service does not collect complementary information, such as the dates, subjects or contents of e-mail messages, or dates when calls were placed on the mobile phone.

6.2.3 Behavioral Advertising as Decisional Interference

Electronic commerce on the Internet often depends on advertising-based revenue models. The FTC reported to Congress that Internet advertising revenues for 1996 totaled $301 million.[19] Only five years later, in 2001, Internet advertising revenues rose to $7.2 billion, and by 2007, this number reached $21.2 billion a year, with search-based advertising from companies like Google and Yahoo! comprising 41 percent of that total.[20] Advertisers spend billions of dollars every year on advertising, and increasingly they aim to target their ads to users whose behavior indicates they are more likely to purchase their products.[21] This can be a win for consumers and for advertisers: Consumers hear about new products that improve the quality of their lives, while advertisers are able to more efficiently spread the word about their products.

However, behavioral advertising technologies can raise concerns about interference. The FTC stated that some uses of behavioral advertising interfere with consumer expectations of privacy.[22] Government interest in protecting consumers from unfair interference has continued since those reports. In 2007 and 2009, the FTC issued separate documents with guidelines for balancing consumer interests and those of advertisers, both of which were based on discussions held by the FTC prior to release.[23] Unfortunately, the difficulty of estimating the value of privacy hampers efforts to balance economic interests with individual privacy expectations.[24] An empirical study on the effectiveness of behavioral advertising reported that it could improve advertising effectiveness by at least 670 percent.[25] This is a powerful economic motivator for advertising companies, and it resulted in scrutiny from the FTC, the U.S. Senate and the U.S. House of Representatives.[26]

Early Internet advertising consisted primarily of static banner ads placed on sites thought to have visitors who would be interested in the products being advertised. Google Gmail popularized *contextual advertising* that leverages user-provided content to deliver ads. Contextual advertising uses an algorithm to examine the content of a page and determine which ad is most relevant to that content. If you were reading an e-mail on Gmail about genealogy, then you might be served an advertisement for genealogy software. *Behavioral advertising* works differently, by constructing a *longitudinal profile* of an individual's interests and serving ads based on that profile rather than the content on the page. For example, a NASCAR fan might spend considerable time online reading about the latest NASCAR news, following the races and reading personal biographies of the drivers. Behavioral advertising would detect this trend and could select ads based on auto sports advertising across other websites, even when the user wasn't browsing sites related to that topic.

There are two approaches to behavioral advertising: first-party and third-party. In *first-party* behavioral advertising, the party with which the user initiated communication is also the party collecting user behavior to create the profile. There are many approaches to first-party behavioral advertising, and not all of them involve sophisticated technology.[27] Amazon.com's recommendation service illustrates first-party behavioral advertising.[28] Amazon monitors which products a user views before making a purchase, and its site recommends products to users who have demonstrated interest in related products. The assumption is that similar behavioral profiles will be interested in similar products, or that some products complement each other. Direct access to customer behavior and purchasing decisions is possible only in first-party behavioral advertising systems.[29]

In *third-party* behavioral advertising, the ad is delivered by a party different from the party with which the user initiates the communication. Websites regularly partner with third-party advertisers to support their website's business. Third parties may work with numerous first-party websites, collecting user profile data across multiple types of sites, such as news, weather, entertainment and travel websites, and delivering ads to users as they surf from one website to another. For effective third-party behavioral advertisers, the accuracy and relevance of the ads are assumed to improve as the number of websites with which a third-party advertiser works increases.[30] Last, behavioral advertising has also been shown to be more effective over short sessions than over long-term profiles.[31]

Advertisers using third-party behavioral advertising can use one of two techniques to construct behavioral profiles: web-based profiling or network-based profiling. *Web-based profiling* uses browser-based technology to track users as they surf the Internet. This technique can collect information only on websites with which the advertiser has partnered. *Network-based profiling* provides more access to user behavior by partnering with Internet service providers (ISPs) who provide users with connectivity to the Internet.

With this level of access and Deep Packet Inspection (DPI), these adver can create behavior profiles based on all of a user's network traffic. Netv based behavioral advertising provides ISPs with an additional revenue source to improve the quality of their infrastructure, but it poses the most serious risk of interference because of the exceptional level of access to user data.[32] Browser plug-ins that users may employ to obstruct behavioral advertisers from monitoring their website usage behavior are ineffective against network-based behavioral advertising. End-to-end encryption can be used to conceal the content of messages, but often not the original headers needed to route the information across the network.

When customers are aware of behavioral profiles and have control over the profiles, behavioral advertising can be mutually beneficial. Consider Amazon's recommendation service. Users often appreciate that they are introduced to products relevant to their interests.[33] Behavioral profiles can be used in numerous ways to personalize consumer experiences. For example, someone interested in true crime dramas may want product lists for television shows and fiction books to display those options more prominently. Personalization is explicitly not advertising. Individuals who have signed up for Netflix or a similar television and movie streaming service may want their behavioral profile to influence the options displayed to them simply for convenience and usability. Consider personalized web search engines that take into account the types of searches previously performed and the types of links the user has found useful. Some users may find such an engine far more efficient for their needs if the personalized search results more effectively address what they are looking for. These personalized services require the construction and maintenance of at least a minimal behavioral profile, even if it is as simple as grouping individuals into broad consumer groups or market segments.

The existence of behavioral profiles requires responsible organizations to follow safe privacy practices. If organizations maintain but never use the behavioral profile that they create, they should still notify users that the profile exists, explain the purpose of the profile and seek consent while providing users an opportunity to participate. The mere existence of a behavioral profile may constitute a subjective privacy harm under Calo's taxonomy.[34] When users are unaware that they are being profiled and have no control over it, many become concerned. In May 2008, Charter Communications, a U.S. Internet service provider, partnered with NebuAd, a behavioral advertising company, to create network-based behavioral profiles and to serve ads to their customers. Unfortunately, customers were mostly unaware of the program, and those who were aware complained to the U.S. Congress, which held hearings regarding the use of the technology. Although the hearings themselves did not directly result in damages, NebuAd lost its ISP partners, and the company eventually stopped developing behavioral advertising technologies.[35]

The 2008 U.S. congressional hearings on behavioral advertising technologies did not result in specific legislation; however, advertising has historically been the subject of extensive regulation designed for consumer protection.[36] It is worth noting that European regulation of behavioral advertising technologies has decreased consumer satisfaction with purchasing decisions based on advertising.[37] Losses in advertising effectiveness adversely affect smaller businesses that don't have the resources for larger, traditional advertising campaigns to promote their innovations.[38]

Behavioral advertising is regulated differently depending on the jurisdiction. In 2008, Dr. Richard Clayton from the University of Cambridge posted an analysis of Phorm's Webwise system, which tracks user behavior for the purpose of serving ads.[39] He argues that Phorm's system violated the UK's Regulation of Investigatory Powers Act of 2000, which makes interception of electronic communications illegal. Phorm's system intercepted communications using DPI and altered the way ads were served to the user. For this system to work, Phorm needed to partner with ISPs willing to provide access to their infrastructure and allow the modification of in-flight communications. In the UK, their partner was British Telecom, which eventually dropped Phorm as a partner because of the privacy concerns raised.[40]

Behavioral advertising technologies have been shown to be effective. What lessons can we learn from an examination of the history of behavioral advertising technologies? Amazon.com's success may suggest that providing users control over how they are tracked is more acceptable than, say, network-based approaches to behavioral advertising, such as those used by Phorm and NebuAd. In addition, behavioral advertising is a unique combination of interference-prone technologies: the behavioral model, which aims to represent who the person is (Type 2), thus enabling decision making (Type 1); and the sending of the personalized ad that describes this person's behavior and can reveal that behavior to others who see the ad, thus exposing this person to intrusions on his or her self-representation (Type 3). Because of these complex interactions, there are also multiple ways to reduce the risk of unwanted interference, which we discuss in Section 6.3.

6.2.4 Cyberbullying as Interference with Personal Identity

Warren and Brandeis were originally inspired to write their law review article defining privacy as "the right to be let alone" due to the invention of the snap camera, a then-new concept that allowed a photographer to quickly take a clear picture without requiring individuals to pose.[41] Today, such technology is common, and although it continues to enable interference with privacy, a culture has developed around the use of cameras that allows us to craft reasonably stable social policies to deal with violations. In this section, we examine a modern privacy concern involving remotely accessible web cameras.

On September 22, 2010, a freshman at Rutgers University named Tyler Clementi committed suicide. Three days prior, his roommate, Dharun Ravi, and Ravi's friend, Molly Wei, used a webcam to spy on Clementi one evening when Clementi asked to use the room privately. Ravi sought to confirm his suspicions that Clementi was gay and after seeing Clementi and another man kissing, Ravi tweeted about the incident stating, "Roommate asked for the room till midnight. I went into molly's room and turned on my webcam. I saw him making out with a dude. Yay."[42] Clementi read the tweet the next day and requested a room change because of the spying incident. One day later, Clementi requested the room again; Ravi attempted to spy on Clementi again and continued writing threatening tweets about his roommate. In the weeks leading up to the incident, Clementi had come out to his family before starting classes at Rutgers. He was not known to be gay in high school and, like many teenagers, he was socially awkward and appeared insecure.[43]

Clementi's suicide became an international news story about the seriousness of cyberbullying that was picked up by ABC News, CNN, *USA Today*, the BBC and numerous other major media outlets. Ellen DeGeneres said Clementi was "outed as being gay on the Internet and he killed himself. Something must be done."[44] Ravi and Wei were indicted on two charges of invasion of privacy, one for each spying incident. Ravi was additionally indicted on witness- and evidence-tampering charges. Wei reached a plea agreement for her testimony against Ravi. Ravi was convicted and sentenced to a 30-day jail term.[45]

In 2011, New Jersey enacted the Anti-Bullying Bill of Rights, which was prompted in part by Clementi's suicide.[46] This law was designed to address concerns that Ravi's trial and conviction were not adequate responses to his actions. In particular, it explicitly states that students have a right not to be bullied and that speech that "substantially disrupts or interferes with" a student's rights is a violation of the law.[47] Although the law may be overly restrictive of speech, it is clearly based in the traditional definition of privacy as the right to be let alone.[48]

Information technology enables a fundamentally different type of bullying: one that is no longer ephemeral or confined to the event or instance, but instead persists and compounds as others gain access to participate through the use of IT communications. Researchers Alice Marwick and danah boyd have written extensively about youth culture and bullying. They note that teenagers want to view themselves as in control of their lives, so teens downplay the things they cannot control as mere "drama" when those situations could actually be serious.[49] This was certainly true of Tyler Clementi. Shortly after Ravi tweeted about the first night he spied on Clementi kissing another man, Clementi spoke with Hannah Yang, a friend of his from high school.[50] When Yang suggested that the incident was a serious violation of Clementi's privacy, Clementi downplayed it.[51]

In this section, we observe how information collection, specifically surveillance, can be used to expose otherwise hidden details about an individual to a broader audience (a Type 3 interference). In an earlier case, Path used an API to gain access to the user's contact list. This activity was a design decision implemented as part of the company's product offerings. In this section, however, we have a situation where individuals use technology to interfere in the affairs of other individuals. When these cases arise, they may use a company's products to disseminate the covertly collected information. While companies may not be able to monitor all uses of their technology, they can include features that help good citizens report abuses that limit overall impact of the interference. In addition, they can contractually obligate users to conform to a code of conduct that requires them to respect the privacy of other users and avoid using the technology in inappropriate ways.

6.2.5 Social Engineering and Interconnected Systems

On August 6, 2012, a hacker used security flaws at Amazon and Apple to compromise Mat Honan's digital identity.[52] His Twitter account, Gmail account, AppleID and Amazon.com account all appeared to have been compromised.[53] He first noticed that his iPhone was rebooting; before he noticed that he wasn't able to connect to his Google calendar, his laptop rebooted and started asking for a four-digit pin that he hadn't set, and his iPad became inaccessible.[54] Meanwhile, his Twitter account, which was connected to a company Twitter account, was tweeting racist and homophobic messages.[55] Honan initially believed that his password had been cracked using a brute force attack, because the password he used was only seven characters long and rather outdated.[56] Instead, the hacker claimed to have gained access to the Twitter account by exploiting two flaws in Apple's and Amazon.com's account recovery services.[57] First, the hacker called Amazon.com by phone to add a credit card to Honan's account. At the time, Amazon.com allowed any caller to add a credit card by providing only the customer's name, e-mail address and physical address, all of which were easily obtained. In addition, Amazon.com required only the last four digits of a credit card on file to change the e-mail address on an account. Thus, the hacker called back a second time and used the last four digits of the credit card he had provided to reset the e-mail address. Once the e-mail address was changed to an account that the hacker had access to, he was able to reset the Amazon.com password and view the account details.

With complete access to Honan's Amazon.com account, the hacker was able to see the last four digits of the Honan's credit card on file. He assumed this was the same card that was on file with Honan's AppleID account, and he proceeded to use those digits to gain a temporary password for that account. Surprisingly, Apple reset the password despite the fact that the hacker was unable to correctly answer the security questions that Honan established for his AppleID; this was a violation of Apple's policies.[58] Using Honan's AppleID, the hacker was able to reset Honan's Twitter password and Gmail password through Honan's Apple-based e-mail service. At this point, the hacker had control of the Twitter account, so he proceeded to remotely wipe Honan's various Apple products to prevent Honan from recovering the Twitter account access.[59] To the credit of both Amazon.com and Apple, both companies remedied these security flaws after the story was published.[60] However, this section illustrates how social engineering tricks can be used to manipulate people and IT systems to gain access to a person's information, and in this case, the company Twitter account that is used to represent both Mat Honan and his company.

Social engineering is any means of using psychology to manipulate people to do something that divulges valuable information or provides access to valuable property. When combined with even rudimentary knowledge of technology, social engineering is a powerful technique that attackers can use to interfere with user privacy. Kevin Mitnick is famous for extensively using social engineering techniques to access computers and avoid capture by the FBI.[61] Mitnick would prey on people who wanted to be helpful. Most folks find it hard to say no to someone in need. The employees at Amazon and Apple didn't know that the hacker wasn't really Mat Honan, and the security measures required to prevent such an imposter were insufficient.

Malicious users can interfere with security processes to obtain access to another user's account and information. In Honan's case, social engineering was used to manipulate a human decision process in the customer service center, enabling the transfer of data needed to exploit an automated process and reset the account password. This form of interference was further used to gain access to a Twitter account, after which the malicious user made misrepresentations of the actual account holder. IT architects and other professionals should consider how their supported business processes (both human and machine-controlled) are vulnerable to exploitation by social engineering for conducting privacy attacks.

6.2.6 Administrative Intrusions into Personal Spaces

Organizations often use supervisors to ensure that employees or other members of the organization conform to organizational practices and procedures. This can occur within the workplace, schools and other environments affected by social and political power relationships. In 2010, the FBI investigated the Lower Merion School District in Pennsylvania for using webcams on school-issued laptops to spy on students at home.[62] School administrators had installed software on student laptops allowing them to remotely control the machine and ensure that students were not violating school rules. Although breaking school rules is generally less serious than committing a crime, students are usually not free to leave or to choose a competing school as a customer might in a traditional business environment. In most jurisdictions, education is compulsory for children of a certain age and students are considered to be a protected population. Similarly, employees have rights at a workplace that may supersede an employer's right to monitor their actions.

For students at Lower Merion, this administrative monitoring extended to outside the school environment because students were permitted to bring the laptops home. When an administrator claimed that a student had been involved in inappropriate behavior by observing the student in his home, the presence of this monitoring came to light. Parents and students brought a class-action lawsuit against the school district that was eventually settled out of court.[63] The idea of creating software to ensure students aren't misusing school-issued equipment is compelling to school administrators.[64] The challenge presented by mobile computing in these situations is that companies or schools that issue property to their employees or students may believe their policies now extend wherever these devices can be carried.

Consider the 2010 U.S. Supreme Court decision in *City of Ontario v. Quon*, which concerned employee privacy rights in the use of employer-provided mobile communications technology.[65] The Ontario, California, Police Department purchased electronic pagers for officers in its SWAT unit. These pagers were covered by an internal policy document that allowed some limited personal use of the device. When Sgt. Jeff Quon exceeded his messaging limit several times, the police department obtained transcripts of his messages to determine whether his overages were work related. Many of Quon's messages were personal and sexually explicit in nature, and he was disciplined. Quon sued, claiming the monitoring was an interference of his privacy. Eventually, the Supreme Court decided that the Ontario Police Department performed a work-related audit and therefore did not violate Quon's privacy.

While there are valid reasons for this kind of monitoring (e.g., protecting intellectual and physical property or auditing employee use of work-related equipment, as in the Quon case), organizations must assess the extent to which this kind of monitoring would interfere with the broader sense of privacy that their employees or students would normally enjoy. No organization should be eager to find itself in a legal battle over administrative monitoring of employees, students or other protected populations. Within our framework, administrative intrusions include encroaching on personal spaces (Type 2) and, potentially, decisional interference (Type 1), as the information obtained could be used to invoke policies that would otherwise govern individuals only under the administration of their organization.

6.3 Summary of Lessons Learned and Recommended Steps of Action

As noted in Table 6-2, each of the six cases illustrates different examples where interference has led to privacy harm. For IT professionals, the challenge is to design their systems and business practices in ways that can reduce the risk or negative outcome of privacy harm. We advise IT professionals to comply with the Fair Information Practice Principles or another set of accepted privacy principles as well as the following recommendations, which are based on our review of technological perspectives (note that this list is by no means complete).

Recommendation 1: Acquire insight into the privacy preferences of those individuals directly or indirectly impacted by your data practices. Focus groups, such as those discussed in Chapter 2, can be used to survey users and understand how they view privacy under different scenarios. Focus groups can be conducted anonymously so that the company's brand is protected and the data can be used to avoid consumer churn that may result for gross violations of privacy. In addition, consumer protection agencies, civil liberties groups and other nongovernmental organizations may be able to help define and codify privacy norms for individuals in various jurisdictions. For example, in the United States, the Federal Trade Commission maintains extensive recommendations for data privacy practices.

Recommendation 2: If data collection can be used for any kind of interference, notify the individual about the purpose and, if possible or required by law, allow the individual to opt in or opt out. Data collection processes exist in virtually every organization, and the data can be extremely sensitive and valuable. In addition to limiting the uses of data to the original purposes for which it was collected, the organization should engage with the person to ensure that uses are consistent with user preferences. In the second perspective, the repurposing of the contact list to provide new services was unwanted and could have been avoided for those users who would not have opted in. Avoiding unnecessary reuse of sensitive information or asking for permission to use collected data for new purposes can reduce interference.

Recommendation 3: Before intruding into a person's private affairs (physical, psychological or self-representation), ensure the technology provides an opportunity for the person to control or limit the intrusion to appropriate times. When a person is likely to engage with a technology in a physical location, attempt to understand the consequences of that engagement. Is the person at work, or attending an intimate event with family members? Understand how the engagement might affect the person emotionally. Would the engagement violate contextual integrity by expanding access to sensitive personal information?[66] Finally, consider how the engagement can affect a person's self-image and recognize that individuals control these personas by limiting who has access to different versions of themselves.

Recommendation 4: If data is used to make critical decisions that can deny individuals specific benefits, introduce safeguards to detect inaccuracies. Allow individuals to be aware of the decisions through notices and provide opportunities for them to review the data for accuracy. Increasingly, decision makers are finding novel ways to gain insight into people's behaviors. As we observed with behavioral profiling, data can be used to personalize services to individuals. Other examples of decision making include financial and employment decisions and decisions about granting access to private information. When data is inaccurate, such as in the altered e-mail address at Amazon.com, the effects of automated decisions can be unpredictable and prone to violate a person's privacy.

Recommendation 5: React quickly to customer concerns. Monitor customer reactions and events and take immediate action to reconcile unwanted interference. Path's reaction to customer complaints was swift and likely saved the company quite a bit of bad press. Similarly, Amazon and Apple reacted quickly to change the policies that led to Mat Honan's hacking. Understand that responding promptly to customer concerns requires preparation and planning. Reading about these technological perspectives in retrospect can inform the planning that is required to ensure that a company can quickly respond when a customer complains. Responding to a complaint reestablishes an individual's sense of control over the situation when that control is lost through interference.

Recommendation 6: Assume that interference will occur and plan for it. General-purpose technologies are likely to have both ethically "good" and ethically "bad" uses. No IT developer, designer or organization can prevent all forms of privacy violation or security breach. Therefore, it is critical to have a response plan in place and to practice implementing it. Conducting "interference response drills" can prepare people for potential privacy violations caused by their products and improve a company's awareness of how its existing policies and technology can help it respond to privacy threats. Consider the Tyler Clementi case. Ravi attempted to delete derogatory tweets and conversations. He was eventually convicted of evidence tampering. What policies and procedures needed to be put in place to ensure that Ravi's actions were not irreversible? How should employees of the university, Twitter and other organizations involved ensure that they can respond appropriately in the future? Answering these questions requires planning and practice.

6.4 Chapter Summary

In this chapter, we described privacy, and thus interference, as an inherently individualistic social concern. We have also shown that, given the nature of privacy, it is impossible to develop a finite list of clearly defined ways interference can occur. To address and mitigate interference, we discussed several technological perspectives and then generalized from these situations to recommend actionable steps that IT professionals can take. Because privacy is a social construct, however, no technological solution or mitigation indefinitely addresses interference concerns. Engineers must continually examine additional cases of interference, generalize from those cases and recommend new practices that they can take to address similar concerns in their products, and apply these recommendations diligently. By taking appropriate action, both engineers and lawyers can enable society to reap the benefits of information technology while limiting the dangers it presents to personal privacy.

Endnotes

1 *New Oxford American Dictionary*, 3rd ed., s.v. "interfere."

2 Samuel D. Warren and Louis D. Brandeis, "The Right to Privacy," *Harvard Law Review* 4, no. 193 (1890); Alan F. Westin, *Privacy and Freedom*. New York, NY: Atheneum, 1967.

3 In 2010, the retail store chain Target began inferring when a woman was pregnant by her purchase of unscented lotions, special vitamins and large tote bags, among other items: Charles Duhigg, "How Companies Learn Your Secrets," *New York Times*, February 16, 2012.

4 M. Ryan Calo, "The Boundaries of Privacy Harm," *Indiana Law Journal* 86, no. 3 (2010): 1131–1162.

5 William L. Prosser, "Privacy," *California Law Review* 48, no. 3 (1960): 383.

6 Daniel J. Solove, *Understanding Privacy* (Cambridge, MA: Harvard University Press, 2010).

7 Ibid.

8 Dan Fletcher, "A Brief History of Spam," *Time*, November 2, 2009, www.time .com/time/business/article/0,8599,1933796,00.html.

9 Federal Trade Commission, "CAN-SPAM Act: A Compliance Guide for Business," Bureau of Consumer Protection, September 2009, http://business.ftc.gov/ documents/bus61-can-spam-act-compliance-guide-business.

10 https://path.com.

11 Arun Thampi, "Path Uploads Your Entire iPhone Address Book to Its Servers," February 8, 2012, http://mclov.in/2012/02/08/path-uploads-your-entire-address-book-to-their-servers.html.

12 http://mitmproxy.org.

13 Thampi, "Path Uploads Your Entire iPhone Address Book to Its Servers."

14 Byron Acohido, "Apple Moves to Quell Path Privacy Gaff," *Technology Live* (blog), *USA Today*, February 16, 2012, http://content.usatoday.com/communities/ technologylive/post/2012/02/apple-moves-to-quell-path-privacy-gaff/1; Nicole Perlroth and Nick Bilton, "Mobile Apps Take Data Without Permission," *Bits* (blog), *New York Times*, February 15, 2012, http://bits.blogs.nytimes.com/2012/02/15/ google-and-mobile-apps-take-data-books-without-permission/.

15 Federal Trade Commission, "FTC Charges Deceptive Privacy Practices in Google's Rollout of Its Buzz Social Network," accessed 28 August 2012, www.ftc.gov/ opa/2011/03/google.shtm.

16 Elinor Mills, "Privacy Suit Filed Against Path, Twitter, Apple, Facebook, Others," CNET News InSecurity Complex, March 16, 2012, http://news.cnet.com/8301-27080_3-57399021-245/privacy-suit-filed-against-path-twitter-apple-facebook-others/.

17 Federal Trade Commission, "Fair Information Practice Principles," last modified November 23, 2012, www.ftc.gov/reports/privacy3/fairinfo.shtm.

18 John Paczkowski, "Apple: App Access to Contacts Data Will Require Explicit User Permission," All Things D, *Wall Street Journal*, February 15, 2012, http://allthingsd .com/20120215/apple-app-access-to-contact-data-will-require-explicit-user-permission/.

19 Federal Trade Commission, *Online Profiling: A Report to Congress (Part 1)*, 2000, www.ftc.gov/os/2000/06/onlineprofilingreportjune2000.pdf.

20 Interactive Advertising Bureau, "IAB Internet Advertising Revenue Report: 2001 Full Year Results," June 2002, www.iab.net/media/file/resources_adrevenue_pdf_ IAB_PWC_2001Q4.pdf; Interactive Advertising Bureau, "IAB Internet Advertising Revenue Report: 2007 Full Year Results," May 2008, www.iab.net/media/file/ IAB_PwC_2007_full_year.pdf.

21 Avi Goldfarb and Catherine E. Tucker, "Online Advertising, Behavioral Targeting, and Privacy," *Communications of the ACM* 54, no. 5 (2011): 25–27.

22 Federal Trade Commission, *Online Profiling: A Report to Congress (Part 1)*; Federal Trade Commission, *Online Profiling: A Report to Congress (Part 2): Recommendations*, 2000, www.ftc.gov/os/2000/07/onlineprofiling.pdf.

23 Federal Trade Commission, "Online Behavioral Advertising: Moving the Discussion Forward to Possible Self-Regulatory Principles," 2007, www.ftc.gov/os/2007/12/

P859900stmt.pdf; Federal Trade Commission, "FTC Staff Report: Self-Regulatory Principles for Online Behavioral Advertising: Tracking, Targeting, & Technology," February 2009, www.ftc.gov/os/2009/02/P085400behavadreport.pdf.

24 Solove, *Understanding Privacy*; Berin Szoka and Adam Thierer, "Online Advertising and User Privacy: Principles to Guide the Debate," *Progress Snapshot* 4, no. 19 (2008): 1–6.

25 Jun Yan et al., "How Much Can Behavioral Targeting Help Online Advertising?" in *WWW '09: Proceedings of the 18th International Conference on World Wide Web* (2009), 261–270.

26 Federal Trade Commission, *Online Profiling: A Report to Congress (Part 1)*; Federal Trade Commission, *Online Profiling: A Report to Congress (Part 2): Recommendations*; Federal Trade Commission, "Online Behavioral Advertising"; Federal Trade Commission, "FTC Staff Report"; U.S. House of Representatives, "What Your Broadband Provider Knows About Your Web Use: Deep Packet Inspection and Communications Laws and Policies," Hearing Before the Committee on Energy and Commerce, Subcommittee on Telecommunications and the Internet, 110 Cong. 1, 2008; U.S. Senate, "Privacy Implications of Online Advertising," Hearing Before Committee on Commerce, Science, and Transportation," 110th Cong. 1, July 2008.

27 Aaron K. Massey and Annie I. Antón, "Behavioral Advertising Ethics," in Melissa Dark, ed., *Information Assurance and Security Ethics in Complex Systems: Interdisciplinary Perspectives* (Hershey, PA: IGI Global, 2010), 162–182.

28 Ibid.

29 Ibid.

30 Ibid.

31 Yan et al., "How Much Can Behavioral Targeting Help Online Advertising?"

32 Massey and Antón, "Behavioral Advertising Ethics."

33 Ibid.

34 Calo, "The Boundaries of Privacy Harm."

35 Harlan Yu, "Lessons from the Fall of NebuAd," *Freedom to Tinker* (blog), October 8, 2008, https://freedom-to-tinker.com/blog/harlanyu/lessons-fall-nebuad/.

36 Massey and Antón, "Behavioral Advertising Ethics."

37 Goldfarb and Tucker, "Online Advertising, Behavioral Targeting, and Privacy."

38 Ibid.

39 Richard Clayton, "The Phorm 'Webwise' System," revised May 18, 2008, www.cl.cam.ac.uk/~rnc1/080518-phorm.pdf .

40 Richard Wray, "BT Drops Plan to Use Phorm Targeted Ad Service After Outcry Over Privacy," *The Guardian*, July 5, 2009, www.guardian.co.uk/business/2009/jul/06/btgroup-privacy-and-the-net.

41 Warren and Brandeis, "The Right to Privacy."

42 Ian Parker, "The Story of a Suicide: Two College Roommates, a Webcam, and a Tragedy," *New Yorker*, February 2012, www.newyorker.com/reporting/2012/02/06/120206fa_fact_parker?currentPage=all.

43 Ibid.

44 Ibid.

45 Ashley Hayes, "Prosecutors to Appeal 30-Day Sentence in Rutgers Gay Bullying Case," CNN, May 2012, www.cnn.com/2012/05/21/justice/new-jersey-rutgers-sentencing/index.html.

46 Derek Bambauer, "Cyberbullying and the Cheese-Eating Surrender Monkeys," *Concurring Opinions*, February 12, 2012, http://www.concurringopinions.com/archives/2012/02/cyberbullying-and-the-cheese-eating-surrender-monkeys.html.

47 Ibid.

48 Ibid.

49 Alice E. Marwick and danah boyd, "The Drama! Teen Conflict, Gossip, and Bullying in Networked Publics," (paper presented at A Decade in Internet Time: Symposium on the Dynamics of the Internet and Society, University of Oxford, September 2011), http://ssrn.com/abstract=1926349.

50 Parker, "The Story of a Suicide."

51 Ibid.

52 Mat Honan, "Yes, I Was Hacked. Hard," EMPTYAGE, August 3, 2012, www.emptyage .com/post/28679875595/yes-i-was-hacked-hard; Mat Honan, "How Apple and Amazon Security Flaws Led to My Epic Hacking," Gadget Lab, *Wired*, August 6, 2012, www.wired.com/gadgetlab/2012/08/apple-amazon-mat-honan-hacking/.

53 Honan, "Yes, I Was Hacked. Hard"; Honan, "How Apple and Amazon Security Flaws Led to My Epic Hacking."

54 Ibid.

55 Honan, "How Apple and Amazon Security Flaws Led to My Epic Hacking."

56 Ibid.

57 Ibid.

58 Ibid.

59 Ibid.

60 Nathan Olivarez-Giles, "Amazon Quietly Closes Security Hole After Journalist's Devastating Hack," Gadget Lab, *Wired*, August 7, 2012, www.wired.com/gadgetlab/2012/08/amazon-changes-policy-wont-add-new-credit-cards-to-accounts-over-the-phone/; Nathan Olivarez-Giles and Mat Honan, "After Epic Hack, Apple Suspends Over-the-Phone AppleID Password Resets," Gadget Lab, *Wired*, August 7, 2012, www.wired.com/gadgetlab/2012/08/apple-icloud-password-freeze/.

61 Kevin Mitnick and William Simon, *The Art of Deception* (Indianapolis, IN: Wiley Publishing, 2003).

62 Jacqui Cheng, "School Settles Laptop Spying Case to 'Protect Taxpayers,'" *Ars Technica*, October 12, 2010, http://arstechnica.com/tech-policy/2010/10/school-settles-laptop-spying-case-to-protect-taxpayers/.

63 Ibid.

64 Bruce Schneier, "Security and Function Creep," *IEEE Security and Privacy* 8, no. 188 (2010), DOI: 10.1109/MSP.2010.47, http://ieeexplore.ieee.org/stamp/stamp.jsp?tp=&arnumber=5403161&isnumber=5403138.

65 *City of Ontario, California, et al. v. Quon et al.*, 560 U.S. 130 S. Ct. 2619.

66 Helen F. Nissenbaum, "Privacy as Contextual Integrity," *Washington Law Review* 79, no. 1 (2004).

CHAPTER 7

The Roles of Governance and Risk Management in Driving a Culture of Trust

David Hoffman, CIPP/US, Malcolm Harkins

Today, companies depend on individuals to trust that their business practices, products and services will respect their privacy preferences. The current state of technology and data processing requires individuals to rely on companies to make and meet their commitments on how data will be processed and to safeguard individuals from harm. As we move toward using more digital devices that process and share data using remote data centers (sometimes referred to as "the cloud"), organizations need to have processes in place to responsibly manage data and thereby lay a foundation for trust. For IT professionals, developing a solid governance model and risk management processes is an essential component of this foundation.

An organization must identify the risks inherent in each of its activities, and it must reasonably anticipate and then mitigate these risks to acceptable levels. These risks arise when an organization fails to comply with a regulatory requirement, and are impacted by the degree to which the company aspires to have its brand convey trust to the individual. Currently, there are many situations where a company can comply with laws and regulations but still have substantial risk of eroding trust. A governance model and risk management process that takes into consideration both compliance and brand risks is one of the best mechanisms for preserving this trust. This chapter breaks these structures down into three components: people, policies and processes.

7.1 People

Within an organization, there can be many different positions, each with a separate and important role to play within the privacy context. The actual number of positions will vary from organization to organization, depending on the size and the unique needs of each entity. If an organization is small and has relatively few privacy needs, only a part of one employee's responsibilities may involve privacy. In contrast, a larger organization with greater privacy needs may utilize several departments in meeting its privacy requirements, each with routine interactions and meetings to coordinate privacy across the enterprise.

In large organizations, privacy responsibility starts at the top, with the board of directors and the chief executive officer (CEO). There must be recognition from the top that trust is an important value for the company, and that the privacy organization is a valued member of the business team. The board and the CEO should ratify the core principles of the privacy program, from which other policies can be derived. The board and CEO also provide the ultimate escalation opportunity for issues and facilitate corporate oversight of the privacy program.

It is also critical to have support from the business unit executives who oversee the day-to-day activities of the company. One effective model of governance is to form an executive management committee of those leaders whose business is most impacted by privacy (both as a risk and as a business opportunity). The committee composition should include those executives who will need to ratify a companywide policy impacting privacy (e.g., the heads of marketing, human resources, legal, government affairs, product groups). This management committee can act as a policy ratification mechanism for decisions that require management discussion but do not rise to the level of needing input from the CEO or the board.

The operational oversight of the program can be effectively managed by a partnership between the company's privacy leader, such as the chief privacy officer (CPO) or person with a similar title, and the lead information security employee, often called the chief information security officer (CISO). An organization cannot expect its privacy policies to function without an effective security program, and collaboration between the CPO's and CISO's organizations is critical for effective and responsible access and data management. Due to the frequent intersection of privacy and security issues, the CPO and CISO must be able to communicate and work together seamlessly. Responsibilities for these positions can include the creation and implementation of policies and controls as well as the evaluation or audit of their effectiveness.

It is important to have senior leadership from the legal department and the government affairs organization working along with the CPO and CISO. Depending on the company, some of these roles may be combined: For example, the CPO may also be the lead lawyer on privacy issues. Regardless of the number of people, bringing together the privacy, information security, legal and public policy disciplines into a well-functioning collaborative organization provides the best opportunity to drive a culture of trust internally and externally.

In addition to executives, privacy personnel within an organization may include IT staff, software developers, the legal department and department heads, and can even extend beyond organizational borders to contractors, affiliates, auditors or outside legal counsel. Examples of these entities and their potential duties include the following:

- *Privacy Compliance Staff:* Manage the structures and processes of privacy compliance from a centralized organization (e.g., incident handling, privacy impact assessment review, training development and deployment).

- *Privacy Champions:* Employees embedded in individual business organizations for whom privacy is either all or part of their jobs. These employees create a matrix organization that understands the privacy objectives, but are also close enough to the business to develop creative solutions that optimize for business value and privacy. See the area specialist in Chapter 2, who is the privacy champion in IT software development.

- *IT Staff:* Create and enforce IT privacy policies and oversee employee training in these policies. Ensure technical compliance with laws, regulations or standards governing the business. Implement proper authentication and authorization processes to access data.

- *Hardware and Software Developers:* Design in privacy at an early stage in the development process. Ensure that appropriate safeguards and reviewing procedures are in place to prevent privacy vulnerabilities from manifesting in code.

- *In-House Counsel:* Analyze applicable laws and regulations and ensure that organizational policies align with these legal requirements. Draft contracts for outside parties, create organizational policies and legally advise departments as necessary.

- *Department Heads:* Ensure departmental training in applicable privacy policies. Monitor compliance with these policies and emphasize their importance in all processes.

- *Contractors/Affiliates*: Contractually held to privacy standards deemed appropriate to mitigate risk to the primary organization.

- *Auditors*: Evaluate the adequacy of an organization's privacy policies and its performance under those policies.

- *Outside Legal Counsel*: Provide advice and expertise in a particular area of the law.

Each entity has an important individual organizational privacy role, but to be effective, all entities must work together. If, for example, software developers are unaware of the privacy policies being created by the CPO or legal department, the code being written is at a greater risk of not being in compliance with these policies. For this reason, management of policy communication between departments and adequate training are vital to ensure complete privacy protection for an organization.

7.2 Policies

Once the governance structure is provided to allow for the diverse skill sets to collaborate, the organization must decide what commitments it wants to make and what values it wants to operate under internally. These commitments and values are the basis for internal and external policies that articulate how the organization will process personal data. We take up external policies first and then internal policies.

7.2.1 External Policies

External policies can be included in various documents that communicate to suppliers, customers, business partners and individuals the extent of the commitments. What follows is a description of just some of these documents:

- *Codes of Conduct*: A good place to communicate high-level aspirational privacy goals of the organization.

- *Binding Corporate Rules (BCRs)*: An effective way to provide the basis for international data transfer, but also can serve as a resource for individuals who want a more detailed understanding of how the company thinks about privacy.

- *End-User Licensing Agreement (EULA)*: Generally, an agreement governing the use of computer software that potentially establishes purchaser rights, licensor restrictions and disclaimers of liability, as well as support or warranty provisions; violation of EULA provisions may be treated legally as a breach of contract.

- *Terms of Service (ToS) / Terms of Use (ToU):* Can be broader than EULAs, regulating consumer use of many services such as Internet service or search providers, shopping websites and online entertainment services. User violation of the stipulated terms may result in provider restriction or termination of the user's access to the service.

- *Application Programming Interface Terms of Use (API ToU):* Similar to ToS/ToU, except pertains specifically to the use of an application programming interface (API). An API is a specification allowing different software components to work together; for example, allowing pictures from an image-hosting site to be shared on a social networking site, or dynamic maps from a search engine to be embedded in a corporate website.

- *Privacy Notice:* Serves as a way for a company to provide notice to its users regarding its collection and treatment of personal information; privacy notices may appear within one of the agreements above, or may be presented separately as an independent agreement. Many companies now provide layered privacy notices, which can give individuals the information most relevant to them in an easy-to-read structure, while still allowing those who are interested to access more complete descriptions of the data processing practices.

Compliance with legal requirements serves to establish a bare minimum level of notice, which may not be sufficient; consumers generally react negatively upon discovering unexpected uses of their personal information by an organization. Depending on the individual consumer and the degree of surprise the organization's use of personal information has caused, repercussions may range from the consumer ceasing to use the organization's products or services to the filing of a class-action lawsuit against the company. To avoid these potential consequences, it may be prudent for an organization to go above and beyond what is legally required when providing notice to consumers, disclosing all of its data collection practices, both implicit and explicit, as well as any practices deemed sufficiently likely to surprise consumers. It may be helpful to explain not only what data is collected, but why the organization is collecting the data as well.

In addition to determining the content of the notice itself, it is also important for an organization to decide when the notice will be provided. Notice can be provided when the program is installed, the first time each user runs an application, or just prior to the moment when data is collected or shared. It is up to an organization to evaluate its unique situation and decide which time or times will provide the most meaningful notice to the user while creating the least amount of inconvenience or annoyance.

As with notice, an organization has varied options in implementing consumer choice. In many situations it may be unreasonable to provide individuals with an affirmative choice on whether the data should be processed (e.g., uses of the data for fraud prevention or for security purposes). These situations where consent is not required often fall in the same category as those for which consent is implied by the nature of the interaction. An example of this implied consent is the sharing of address information with a shipping company to fulfill an online retail transaction. However, when a use of data may surprise an individual, obtaining consent, or at least giving prominent notice at the point where information is collected, is often a good business practice to maintain the individual's trust. Continuing the shipping example, use of the shipping address to offer an information service allowing people to track down individuals might surprise the customer and damage the trust relationship. Because of this issue with unexpected secondary uses, an organization may choose to request consent for each specific use of information, re-obtaining consent for any new purpose. With so many options, an organization must be aware of legal and industry requirements as well as consumer expectations when deciding how it will implement choice. Also, how choice is implemented will make a significant impact on the user experience, so the privacy organization should consult with user experience designers.

7.2.2 Internal Privacy Policies

Sometimes, the terms *privacy notice* and *privacy policy* are used interchangeably. However, it is important to note the difference between notices and policies. As previously discussed, a notice can serve two functions. It can inform consumers about requirements regarding consumers' use of the organization's products and services, and it may also set forth the organization's standards governing its own use of consumers' personal information.

A policy, however, is the set of internal guidelines implemented within an organization upon which a notice is based. Organizations should have internal policies addressing privacy and security, data management and data loss prevention. To be functional, these policies should be documented and easily accessible, and they should be kept updated as dictated by evolving organizational needs. In addition, company employees must be familiar with the organization's internal policies and have ready access to the latest version. Perhaps most important, policies must be endorsed by executives and enforced by management; a company and its employees must adhere to internal policies in all activities.

7.2.2.1 Information Security Policies

Having information security policies is vital for the adequate protection of personal data. Providing adequate privacy protections depends heavily on the quality of the information security policies and how well they are put into practice. A basic internal security policy functions to prevent unauthorized or unnecessary access to corporate data or resources— protecting electronic and paper information from threats both outside the company and within. To perform this function, the security policy must be written with the organization's unique data lifecycle in mind. Whenever data is collected, transmitted, used or stored, procedures must be required to ensure that the information is physically secure and cannot be accessed or intercepted by an unauthorized party. A security policy should memorialize the principles for protecting personal data explored in Chapters 3 and 4, especially those concerning data encryption and user authentication. The policy should also go beyond these principles, dictating the physical securing and monitoring of both the devices and the premises where sensitive data is stored. Such information security precautions could include locks, safes, fences, security cameras and any imaginable security method deemed appropriate by the organization. The information security policies need to reflect how the employees of the company do their work, and communicate how the employees can best take advantage of tools and processes to secure sensitive company data, including intellectual property, financial data and personal data.

7.2.2.2 Privacy Policies

While an adequate security policy will guard against unauthorized data access, it often does not protect data from being used by authorized users in an inappropriate manner. Privacy policies build upon a security policy by governing the use and sharing of data by authorized users. These policies also provide the opportunity for the company to take positions on issues that can impact privacy. These policies will vary considerably depending upon the nature of the company's business, as the following list illustrates.

Employee privacy policies generally cover employee records, including benefits, salary and so on.

Personal devices at work policies cover phones, laptops, cameras, external media and other devices and the expectations around when, where and if these can be used in the environment.

Telecommuting policies cover the expectations raised when employees work remotely.

Photo and video recording policies cover when employees may make photo and video recordings at work.

Children's data policies cover the expectations on gathering and using data from children.

Unique identifiers in hardware and software policies cover the expectations on the use and deployment of identifiers that could be used to uniquely identify a device.

Social media privacy policies cover the expectations on the use of social media by employees.

Mobile application policies cover the expectations of developers of mobile applications for security as well as privacy purposes.

Cookie usage policies cover the expectations for the use of cookies on external websites.

Opt-in policies cover expectations for where and how to require opt-in consent.

Location-based data policies cover expectations for the collection and use of location-based data.

Genetic data policies cover expectations for the use of genetic data.

Trade show and events policies cover the expectations for the collection and use of information at shows and events.

7.2.2.3 Data Management and Loss Prevention

Data management and loss prevention policies should incorporate and expand upon the principles and procedures established by the organization's security and privacy policies. An organization must understand its business needs, focusing on what data must be collected and the degree of sensitivity of this data. After weighing the risk of data loss against business needs, policies can be made to guide the organization in collecting only the data it needs and securely disposing of the data when it is no longer needed. It may also be necessary to establish policies and procedures allowing data subjects themselves to access, modify or remove their own data.

While an organization's business needs are an important determining factor in the creation of data management policies, so too are national laws, local laws and regulations. Some regions have laws that specify types of information that cannot be collected by organizations, or data that cannot be retained for longer than a certain time period. These laws may also specify information that must be collected and retained for a certain time period. Sometimes these laws conflict; for example, one jurisdiction may require collection of certain data while another jurisdiction forbids collection of the same data, as is the case with racial information (required in some jurisdictions for reporting on employee diversity and prohibited from collection in other jurisdictions as an attempt to decrease discrimination). An organization should obtain legal advice in order to ensure that its policies comply with any applicable laws.

Another critical area of policymaking within an organization involves the organization's own employees. Policies should require employees, especially those handling sensitive data, to have their own user accounts, secured by an appropriate authentication mechanism. It may be advisable to require multiple-factor authentication for employees with access to extremely sensitive data. These user accounts should be granted only the privileges and security clearance necessary to perform the user's specific job functions, often referred to as role-based access. Finally, policies should require a segregation of duties: Privileges for sensitive procedures such as writing checks or processing credit card payments should be split among employees so that no single user performs all parts of a procedure.

Employees generally wish to perform their jobs with maximum efficiency, and may attempt to bypass policies in order to do so. These attempts may consist of sharing passwords, installing unauthorized applications or using private e-mail to bypass security filters. It is important to prevent such attempts to bypass policy, explaining why the data-protecting policies are necessary and establishing negative consequences for such behavior. Additionally, employees who work from home or any other business transaction occurring in more than one location—across state borders or between nations—may require further specialized guidelines from internal policies. Policymakers should preemptively recognize special circumstances such as these, which will require specialized rules to ensure that sufficient policies have been implemented to protect data and comply with applicable laws.

Internal policies must be designed to work together to prevent the loss or misuse of sensitive data. Comprehensive security and data management policies should minimize the risk of data theft by unauthorized parties, while a good privacy policy will guard against inappropriate use of data by authorized parties. An organization must understand and consider all of its business processes and its data lifecycle in order to create policies that will work together to prevent sensitive data from falling into the wrong hands.

7.3 Processes

Once a company has established its organizational structure and thought about its policies, it is time to put processes in place to systemize privacy protection.

7.3.1 Privacy by Design

Incorporating privacy early into the development process of products, services and programs is the best way to make certain to fulfill the privacy objectives of the organization. Privacy by Design (PbD) consists of seven foundational principles:[1]

1. *Proactive not Reactive; Preventative not Remedial:* Privacy by Design anticipates and prevents privacy events before they happen, rather than wait for privacy risks to materialize.

2. *Privacy as the Default Setting:* Privacy is built into systems by default—no action is required on the part of individuals to protect their privacy.

3. *Privacy Embedded into Design:* Privacy by Design is embedded into the design and architecture of IT systems and business practices, ensuring that privacy becomes an essential component of the core functionality being delivered.

4. *Full Functionality—Positive-Sum, not Zero-Sum:* Privacy by Design seeks to accommodate all legitimate interests and objectives in a positive-sum "win-win" manner, not through a dated zero-sum approach, where unnecessary trade-offs are made.

5. *End-to-End Security—Full Lifecycle Protection:* Privacy by Design, having been embedded into the system prior to any data collection, ensures secure end-to-end lifecycle management of information.

6. *Visibility and Transparency—Keep It Open:* Component parts and operations remain visible and transparent to both users and providers. Trust but verify.

7. *Respect for User Privacy—Keep It User-Centric:* The interests of the individual are kept uppermost by offering such measures as strong privacy defaults and appropriate notice and by empowering user-friendly options.

Privacy Impact Assessments are an effective tool to help fulfill those objectives.

7.3.2 Privacy Impact Assessments

A Privacy Impact Assessment (PIA), similar to an audit, is an evaluation performed to verify that a new or existing organizational process adheres to all appropriate privacy laws, regulations and policies. A PIA also assesses the risk to privacy associated with the business process that is being evaluated and examines potential methods of risk mitigation.

In the United States and Canada, government agencies are required to perform a PIA under certain circumstances. Other governments, such as those of the United Kingdom, Australia and New Zealand, have made official PIA guidance available. Though typically performed by government agencies, PIAs can be used by private-sector organizations as well. Generally, a PIA should be performed before any change or new development in information technology.

While PIA requirements and guidance vary from jurisdiction to jurisdiction, PIAs can generally be broken into four stages:

- *Preparation:* Analyze the proposed system or process to determine whether a PIA is required by law or as a best practice. Determine who will perform the analysis and when in the project's timeline the analysis will occur.

- *Data Analysis:* Analyze and document at a high level how personal information will be handled and why it will be done this way, within the project's data lifecycle: collection, use, disclosure, retention, and destruction.

- *Privacy Assessment:* Identify and document risks and vulnerabilities to privacy within the established data lifecycle, including legal or regulatory privacy requirements.

- *Reporting:* Evaluate any discovered risks or vulnerabilities and attempt to identify remedies. Describe the rationale for the ultimate project process choice.

It is an objective of a PIA to cause an organization to think about its process choices and their potential impacts on privacy. A PIA allows an organization to analyze and document not only the project's anticipated data lifecycle, but the reasons behind its treatment of data at each stage. Additionally, a part of the analysis involves contemplating remedies or alternative courses of action that will minimize identified project risks and vulnerabilities. While a PIA may not present an organization with the definitive solution to all privacy concerns, it serves as a valuable evaluative tool in identifying and mitigating potentially overlooked privacy risks within a project.

In large and complex organizations, it may be difficult to perform a PIA for all new products, services and programs. Many organizations have created quicker self-assessments that allow employees to assess whether there are potential privacy risks and whether a full PIA is necessary. These self-assessments allow an organization to gain from the knowledge of the employees closest to the business while reducing the bureaucratic burden on them.

The PIA and the self-assessments work best when integrated into existing business structures that require their completion. One method organizations use is to integrate them into the Secure Development Lifecycle, which some companies adopt to reduce the number of security flaws in their products. Where to best integrate the PIA and self-assessments will depend on the individual company and its existing business processes.

7.3.3 Risk Assessment

Organizations should have periodic risk assessments to determine how effective their existing structures are at minimizing risk. A risk assessment can be a powerful tool to prioritize resources and adjust to changes in the environment (both changes to the external landscape and changes within the company).

7.3.4 Complaint Handling

The privacy organization should have a formal process for handling privacy complaints. This process should be integrated into the existing mechanisms for how the company receives complaints and inquiries (e.g., customer support) and must allow all relevant stakeholders to be informed quickly enough to respond to the individual in a timely way.

7.3.5 Incident Response

Conducting incident response tests or drills is an excellent way to identify potential areas for improvement.

No matter how secure an organization is and how comprehensive its data policies are, there will always be some risk of a data breach. Therefore, in addition to proactively minimizing the risk of an incident, an organization must also formulate a procedure to follow in the event of a breach.

An incident response plan should contain the following items:

- *Discovering a Breach*: Before an organization can respond to an incident, it must discover that a breach has occurred! While this may seem obvious, data thieves can be sophisticated and sneaky; some breaches remain undetected for a long time. An organization may remain unaware that it has experienced a breach until the data that has been stolen has been fraudulently used elsewhere— and investigators have traced the data's origin back to the breached organization.

  Active monitoring of intrusion detection systems and system logs as well as examination of unusual system activity or changes is essential in order to discover breaches and breach attempts. While the details of breach discovery will vary depending on the specific circumstances of an organization, employee training, vigilance and active monitoring are key to both breach prevention and early detection (and possible minimization of the resulting damage) of a breach.

- *Gathering Information and Stopping the Breach*: In the event that a breach has occurred, or is occurring, it is imperative to stop the breach to prevent further data loss. At the same time, it is also important for an organization to gather as much information as possible about the breach. An incident response plan should contain guidance on how to quickly terminate a breach while simultaneously attempting to preserve as much evidence as possible of the affected data and the breach's origin.

  Stopping a breach may involve taking down production systems or otherwise affecting regular business activities until a solution has been found. An organization must be aware of this fact and balance the risk posed by potentially allowing the breach to continue against the loss of productivity or functionality that may result from rapidly containing the breach. A good incident response plan will contain contingency procedures that allow the organization to continue to function in some capacity while certain data or resources are locked down.

- *Legal Analysis*: Legal counsel should be included at the first opportunity to determine whether breach notification is legally required and to guide the response team.

- *Notification of Law Enforcement or Other Agencies*: It is critical for an organization to be aware of all the types of sensitive data it collects and stores, and the laws governing whom it must notify in the event of a breach of each type of data. While it is important to report a breach within a reasonable amount of time, certain regions may have additional legal requirements imposing deadlines by which an organization must notify the proper authorities. In addition to law enforcement personnel, notification to agencies such as state departments of insurance, the Federal Trade Commission (FTC) or the attorney general may be necessary. Private-sector entities frequently require notification as well; for example, affected financial institutions should be notified if a breach involves payment card information.

- *Notification of Affected Consumers:* Similar to notifying law enforcement or other agencies, an organization should also notify the consumers whose information has been breached. Again, local laws may set forth guidelines and penalties regarding which consumers to notify, how to provide notification and how quickly notification must be provided. Due to the complexity of the many nonharmonized breach notification laws, contracting with a vendor to provide breach notification services can be a good idea. The outside vendor can often stay up-to-date on changes in local laws more efficiently, and can bring additional resources to a situation if necessary.

- *Dealing with the Repercussions of a Breach:* In addition to the fines and lawsuits that may follow a breach of sensitive user data, other nonmonetary consequences may arise. For example, media coverage of the breach may adversely affect the organization's reputation; consumers directly and indirectly affected by the breach may cease to use the company's services; new consumers may be hesitant to entrust their sensitive data. An organization should have an idea of how it plans to deal with these and other potential repercussions of a breach. This strategy may involve hiring outside counsel or seeking aid from a risk consulting company.

- *Preventing Future Breaches:* After a breach has occurred, it is especially vital that an organization take steps to prevent similar potential breaches. Security holes should be patched, weak policies strengthened and employees trained as appropriate to minimize the risk of a future incident.

While internal policies play a pivotal role in reducing the risk of a data breach, a well-thought-out incident response plan can help to minimize direct and collateral damage resulting from an unforeseen breach. Training familiarizes employees with the organization's incident response plan and allows an organization to handle such events much more smoothly.

7.3.6 Training

An organization can have the strongest and most comprehensive plans and policies in the industry, but they will be all but useless without accompanying employee training. Employees must be familiar with any policies applying to them or the data they may be exposed to. They should understand the organization's security policy, privacy policy and any additional data management or loss prevention policies. Employees should know which information they will come into contact with in the course of their job and how to appropriately and securely handle it. Employees should also have an idea of what sensitive information they should never request or handle.

Training should be used not only to further employees' understanding of company policies, but also to educate employees about common threats to data security and how to respond appropriately. Employees should be trained in the organization's incident response plan. Additionally, adequate training may provide a defense against social engineering attacks; the mere awareness of the existence of such tactics allows employees to better guard against them. Training may also make it more likely that an employee will notice and report unusual system activity, increasing the chances of early detection of a breach or breach attempt.

Lastly, employee training can serve as notice to the employees themselves regarding their own privacy in the workplace. In many situations, organizations will find it advantageous to disclose their practices regarding both the treatment of their own employees' personal information and any workplace monitoring that is performed. In some locations, it is illegal to monitor certain employee activities without such notification. Types of workplace monitoring that may necessitate employee notification include e-mail, Internet use and telephone monitoring, security camera monitoring and GPS device monitoring. It is important to note that some types of workplace monitoring, especially telephone call monitoring or video surveillance in restrooms, may be illegal regardless of the degree of notice provided. Organizations are advised to consult with an attorney to become familiar with local rules before initiating or modifying a workplace monitoring program.

7.3.7 Asset Management

An organization has many assets in its possession, and these assets can assume different forms: electronic, physical or even intellectual property. To protect these assets, an organization must be able to properly manage them. On the most fundamental level, an organization must inventory these assets. Examples of these types of assets are:

- *Information Assets:* Customer and employee data, as well as all backup copies of this data. This data may reside on storage devices within the company, or outside of its borders.

- *Physical Assets:* Servers, workstations, laptops, portable storage devices, backup media, paper files.

- *Intellectual Property:* Software code, trade secrets.

Once an organization has a complete inventory of its assets, it may assign an owner to each asset. It is the responsibility of these asset owners to classify the assets under their control. This classification is done based on the owners' thorough understanding of the sensitivity of the information and the way it must move throughout the organization. From the greatest to the least sensitivity, three common classes of asset classification are confidential, internal use, and public information.

- *Confidential:* Information that, if disclosed, would cause the business to be severely compromised. It is absolutely essential that this class of information remain secure and private. Sensitive customer information, employee Social Security numbers and payment account information are all assets that may be classified as confidential.

- *Internal Use:* Important business information intended for internal use only. Examples of information that may be classified as internal use include company contact directories, business plans, sales revenue forecasts and its proprietary software code.

- *Public:* Information that may be safely shared with the public at large. Information classified as public includes a company's physical address, marketing materials and customer service contact information

Even if an organization decides not to assign an asset owner, it must still understand the sensitivity of its information assets and classify them accordingly. Once these assets have been classified, an organization must establish and enforce policies for granting and revoking access to these assets, as well as rules governing their use. Assets should also be regularly monitored and inventoried, with special attention paid to laptops and portable storage devices. Due to their ease of portability and the huge quantity of data they can contain, loss-prevention measures for portable assets are especially important. It is important to consider the lifecycle of both the device and the data that is stored on the device (and almost always on other devices). An organization needs to make certain it understands what data is on which device, but also other locations where the data may reside (e.g., backup tapes, storage facilities, cloud servers). Finally, it is also essential to update or upgrade assets as necessary; software updates or security patches may need to be applied and technology may become obsolete, requiring replacement.

7.3.8 Contracts

It is common for organizations to utilize outside vendors and contractors to perform various tasks within the company. However, it is still the responsibility of an organization to ensure that data under its control is treated consistently with its internal policies. One method of reconciling these two necessities is by preventing outside vendors and contractors from accessing any sensitive information altogether. This policy can be a secure way to protect sensitive data from outside access, but it may not always be practical. There are circumstances where the outside user must either work with a system that has access to sensitive data, or has been hired to perform a task with the sensitive data itself. It is important to note that if a data breach occurs in this situation, the organization that outsourced the task and data is likely to be held liable for the breach under applicable laws and regulations.

When an outside party must access sensitive data, it is important to conduct a review of the vendor or contractor. Also, contracts may provide a method of mitigating the risk. While an organization should thoroughly research all outside vendors' privacy and security policies, reputation and financial condition, this due diligence alone may not be enough to protect consumers' personal information. A contract between the organization and an outside party can be formed, requiring the outside party to adhere to the same standards and guidelines with regard to the data as the organization itself would be subject to. The contract should also detail clear expectations on roles and responsibilities for handling issues. There should also be provisions describing the lines of communication between the two companies, should an incident happen. It is critical then to have some mechanism to investigate (e.g., audit) whether the vendor is in compliance with the contractual commitments. Penalties for breach of this contract should be balanced against risk to sufficiently compensate the organization for the negative repercussions it would be subjected to as a result of a data breach. Of course, as with all legal devices, contracts may be subject to varying local and regional laws affecting their legality or enforceability.

7.3.9 Assessment of Laws and Standards

An organization may find itself subject to many different laws, regulations and standards depending on various factors, especially where it is located and with whom it does business. Organizations should be aware of the laws and regulations as well as their application under both the comprehensive and the sectoral models of law. Additionally, organizations should know whether their industry is subject to any self-regulatory standards. Once obtained, an organization can incorporate this information into its policies and procedures to avoid violations.

7.3.10 Program Assessment

Each organization should do a periodic assessment of the entire privacy program. This assessment should draw upon information from the risk assessment, but should also look at the effectiveness of each privacy process (e.g., the Privacy by Design process).

7.3.11 Internal Enforcement

Each company must hold its employees accountable for following its policies and guidelines. It is important to have a structure for enforcement. This structure usually will include the human resources and legal departments. What types of privacy violations will require warnings, penalties or termination of employment need to be thought out in advance.

7.4 Chapter Summary

Risk management and effective organizational structures are critical components that enable an organization to be trusted by its employees, customers, suppliers and consumers. Thinking through the people, policies and processes at the point of establishing a program can provide a solid foundation on which to build.

Endnotes

1 Ann Cavoukian, "Privacy by Design: The 7 Foundational Principles," revised January 2011, www.privacybydesign.ca/content/uploads/2009/08/7foundational principles.pdf.

Index

computer webcams, surveillance via, 201
concept of operations, in process
  models, 24
confidential information, 248
confidentiality, 8, 69, 96. *See also*
  identifiability
consent
    for data collection, 227–228
    explicit vs. passive, 12–13
    OECD Guidelines and, 10
    opt-in, 216
    secondary use and, 32
    for user tracking, 181
contextual advertising, 219–220
contextual integrity heuristic, 5, 34, 36
contractors, roles of, 236, 249
contracts, 249
cookies, 173–177
    blocking, 183–186
    opt-out, 185–186
    privacy policies covering, 240
COPPA. *See* Children's Online Privacy
  Protection Act of 1998 (COPPA)
counter mode (CTR), 111
coupling, in software design, 73
cracking encryption. *See* decryption
Cranor, Lorrie Faith, 67–68
Crowds, 155
cryptanalysis, 107–108
cryptographers, 93. *See also* encryption
cryptographic erasure, 115
cryptographic systems, 96, 100. *See also*
  encryption
currency, data, 70–71
cyberbullying, 215, 222–224

D

Daemen, Joan, 105
data aggregation, 32
data availability, 8, 70, 96
data breaches, responding to, 244–246
data collection, 12–14
    active vs passive, 12
    approaches to, 15
    consent for, 227–228

data integrity and, 71
  regulations, following, 240–241
  in taxonomy of privacy problems,
    27, 31
data controller, 12
data destruction, 15
data encryption. *See* encryption
Data Encryption Standard (DES), 101,
  107, 108–109, 110
    as block cipher, 105
    triple DES (3DES), 109
data governance. *See* governance model
data imputation, 151
data integrity, 8, 70–71, 96
data lifecycle, 11–15, 12
    completeness arguments and, 51–52
    privacy harms and, 33
data management policies, 240–241
data models, 63–65
data persistence, 70
data processor, 12
data quality principle, 10
data restoration, 71
data retention, 14
    approaches to, 15
    of audio/video surveillance, 203
    encryption and, 115
data storage, 14, 60–61
data transformation, 80. *See also*
  anonymization
data-at-rest protection, 104
database schemas, 64–65
databases, encryption of, 115
data-in-flight protection, 103–104
decisional interference, 33, 212, 214
decryption, 92, 98–99. *See also*
  encryption
    AES algorithm and, 105–106
    passphrases for, 113–114
    of public keys, 116
Deep Crack, 107
deep packet inspection, 167
defects, defined, 26–27
DeGeneres, Ellen, 223
department heads, 235

malware threats, 132–134
modes of operation, 110–111
public key, 75, 116–126
public key infrastructure (PKI), 126–132
secret key, 98, 105–116
secret sharing/splitting, 115–116
strength of, 93, 98–100
for wireless networks, 169
end-user licensing agreements (EULAs), 236
Enigma ciphers, 93
entity tags (ETags), 179
entropy pools, 112
erasing storage media, 115
errors, defined, 26–27
ETags (entity tags), 179
EU Data Protection Directive, 12
EV (extended validation) certificates, 129–130
Evercookies, 180
Evidon
Ghostery, 186–188
Open Data Partnership, 186
exclusion, 32
executive management committees, 234
explicit consent, 13
exposure, 32–33, 214
external threats, 70

F
Facebook. See also social media sites
conformance to FIPPs, 218–219
Places application, 195
user tracking by, 176
failure, defined, 26–27
Fair Information Practice Principles (FIPPs), 9, 29, 30, 218–219
false information (distortion), 32, 214
faults, defined, 26–27
feature-complete software, 81
federated architectures and systems, 62–63
FileVault, 104
Find My Friends application, 195

fingerprinting browsers, 148–149, 180
Firefox. See browsers; Mozilla Firefox
Firesheep extension, 168
first-party behavioral advertising, 220
first-party cookies, 175
first-party data collection, 12
Flash, blocking from websites, 187
Flash cookies, 177–178
flash drives. See mobile devices
flowcharts, as process models, 65
focus groups, 227
Foursquare, 195
privacy incidents, 197
user controls for, 198–199
frameworks, software, 75
frequency data, 153–154
Fried, Charles, 8
front-end architecture, 59–60
functional privacy, 188–189
functional requirements, 42

G
Gamma, Erich, 66
Garmisch report, 23
generalization of data, 150
generalizing preconditions, 53
Generally Accepted Privacy Principles (GAPP, 2009), 10, 41
genetic data policies, 240
geofencing, 196
GET requests, 166
Ghostery, 186–188
GIS (geographic information system), 197
glossary for software requirements specification (SRS), 44
Gmail
contextual advertising by, 219–220
HTML code and, 180–181
Google
Buzz, privacy violation by, 84, 218
digital certificate, 127
Maps API, 85
Privacy Policy, 50–51
Street View service, 57–58, 168

Q
quality attributes, 67–71
quasi-identifiers, 149
Quon, City of Ontario v. (2010), 226

R
radio frequency identification (RFID)
chips, 194, 196
random numbers, generating, 112
rate-limiting connections, 167
rationality, and privacy choices, 16
Ravi, Dharun, 223–224, 229
RC4 encryption algorithm, 105, 110
readers, software, 74
refrainments, 54
Regulation of Investigatory Powers Act
of 2000 (U.K.), 222
regulations, legal. *See* privacy
regulations
regulatory goals, identifying/analyzing,
55
related key attacks, 108
representations, software design, 63–67
object and data models, 63–65
patterns of, 66–67
process models, 65–66
repurposing data, 12, 13–14
requirements, 42–58
acquiring and eliciting, 45–47
analyzing, 49–58
documenting, 42–45
functional vs. nonfunctional, 42–43
glossary for, 44
implementation of law by, 47–49
incompleteness of, 50
preconditions, generalizing, 53
in process models, 23
template for, 43
trace matrices for, 47–49
visual models for, 45
requirements engineers, 20
reserve, as state of privacy, 4
resources, in URLs, 166
responding to risks, 39–40
restoring data, 71

retaining data. *See* data retention
RFID chips, 194, 196
Rijmen, Vincent, 105
risk assessments, 244
risk controls, 40–41
risk management, 28–41. *See also*
threats
assessing risk, 37–39, 244
categories of risk, 27
encryption algorithms and, 100
formulation of risk, 28
frameworks for, 35–41
assessment phase, 37–39
characterization phase, 35–37
control implementation phase,
40–41
monitor and review phase, 41
response determination phase,
39–40
threat identification phase, 37
identification and mitigation, 55–58
by individuals, 16
loss prevention, 240–241
malware countermeasures, 133–134
minimizing risk, 15
models for, 29–35, 29
combining models, 34–35
compliance model, 29–30
contextual integrity heuristic,
34, 36
Fair Information Practice
Principles (FIPPs), 9, 29, 30
identifying elements of, 37
subjective/objective dichotomy
model, 29, 30–31
taxonomy of privacy problems,
31–33, 37–39
process models and, 25–26
repurposing data and, 13–14
responding to risks, 39–40
risks, 6–7, 58. *See also* risk management
anti-goals, 55–57, 56
malware, 132–134
social engineering, 224–225
rounding, as data generalization, 151

About the Authors

Executive Editor
Travis Breaux, CIPT

Travis D. Breaux is an assistant professor of computer science at Carnegie Mellon University (CMU), where he teaches and conducts research to develop new methods and tools to build privacy-preserving, secure and trustworthy information systems. Courses include topics in privacy policy, law and technology and engineering privacy for undergraduate and graduate students in software engineering and information technology. Breaux has authored numerous papers in IEEE and ACM journals and conference proceedings. He is the director of CMU's Requirements Engineering Laboratory, which conducts sponsored research in privacy, and he is a cofounder of the IEEE International Workshop on Requirements Engineering and Law, which addresses challenges to aligning software requirements with regulatory codes. Breaux holds a PhD in computer science from North Carolina State University, a BS in computer science from University of Oregon and a BA in anthropology from University of Houston.

Contributors

Chris Clifton

Christopher Clifton works on data privacy, particularly with respect to analysis of private data. This includes privacy-preserving data mining, data de-identification and anonymization and limits on identifying individuals from data mining models. He also works more broadly in data mining, including data mining of text and data mining techniques applied to interoperation of heterogeneous information sources. Fundamental data mining challenges posed by these applications include extracting knowledge from noisy data, identifying knowledge in highly skewed data (few examples of "interesting" behavior) and limits on learning. He also works on database support for widely distributed and autonomously controlled information, particularly issues related to data privacy.

Clifton is now a professor in the Department of Computer Sciences at Purdue University. He was an assistant professor of computer science at Northwestern University before joining MITRE Corporation as a principal scientist in their Information Technology Division. He has a PhD and MA in computer science from Princeton University and bachelor's and master's degrees from the Massachusetts Institute of Technology.

Lorrie Faith Cranor

Lorrie Faith Cranor is an associate professor of computer science and of engineering and public policy at Carnegie Mellon University, where she is director of the CyLab Usable Privacy and Security Laboratory (CUPS) and codirector of the master's program in privacy engineering. She is also a cofounder of Wombat Security Technologies, Inc., and previously was a researcher at AT&T Labs–Research. She has authored over 100 research papers on online privacy, usable security and other topics. She has played a key role in building the usable privacy and security research community, having co-edited the seminal book *Security and Usability* (O'Reilly 2005) and founded the Symposium on Usable Privacy and Security (SOUPS). She has served on a number of boards, including the Electronic Frontier Foundation board of directors and the editorial boards of several journals.

Simson Garfinkel

Simson L. Garfinkel is an associate professor at the Naval Postgraduate School. His research interests include computer forensics, the emerging field of usability and security, personal information management, privacy, information policy and terrorism. He holds six U.S. patents for his computer-related research and has published dozens of journal and conference papers in security and computer forensics. Garfinkel received three BS degrees from MIT, an MS in journalism from Columbia University and a PhD in computer science from MIT.

David Gordon

David Gordon works on engineering and public policy matters at Carnegie Mellon University. His research has been focused on developing methods and tools to reconcile privacy requirements across multiple legal jurisdictions to help software developers build privacy-preserving systems. Gordon holds an MBA from the University of Buffalo and bachelor's degrees in computer science and music from SUNY Geneseo.

Malcolm Harkins

Malcolm Harkins is vice president and chief security and privacy officer (CSPO) at Intel Corporation, where he is responsible for managing the risk, controls, privacy, security and other related compliance activities for all of Intel's information assets, products and services. Before becoming Intel's first CSPO he was the chief information security officer reporting to the chief information officer.

In 2010, he received the Excellence in the Field of Security award at the RSA conference. He was recognized by *Computerworld* magazine as one of the top 100 Information Technology Leaders for 2012. In addition, the International Information Systems Security Certification Consortium (ISC)2 recognized Harkins in 2012 with the Information Security Leadership Award. Harkins is a frequent speaker at industry events. He is also an author of many white papers and recently published his first book, *Managing Risk and Information Security, Protect to Enable* (Apress 2012).

Harkins received his bachelor's degree in economics from the University of California at Irvine and an MBA in finance and accounting from the University of California at Davis.

David Hoffman, CIPP/US

David Hoffman, CIPP/US, is director of security policy and global privacy officer at Intel Corporation, in which capacity he oversees Intel's privacy compliance activities, legal support for privacy and security and all external privacy and security policy engagements. Hoffman was a member of the U.S. Federal Trade Commission's Online Access and Security Committee. In 2005, Hoffman was appointed to the Department of Homeland Security's Data Privacy and Integrity Advisory Committee. He also serves on the Center for Strategic and International Studies Cyber Security Commission. Hoffman holds an AB from Hamilton College and a JD from the Duke University School of Law, where he was a member of the *Duke Law Journal*.

Aaron Massey

Aaron Massey is a postdoctoral fellow at Georgia Tech's School of Interactive Computing and the associate director of ThePrivacyPlace.org. His research interests include privacy, computer security and regulatory compliance software engineering. Massey earned a PhD and MS in computer science from North Carolina State University and a BS in computer engineering from Purdue University. He is a member of the ACM, IEEE, IAPP and the USACM Public Policy Council.

Stuart Shapiro, CIPP/US, CIPP/G

Stuart S. Shapiro is a principal information privacy and security engineer and a member of the Privacy Community of Practice at the MITRE Corporation, a not-for-profit company performing technical research and consulting primarily for the U.S. government. At MITRE, Shapiro supports a variety of security and privacy activities, including critical infrastructure protection, policy frameworks, risk and control assessment and incident response. He has led multiple projects in enterprise privacy-enhancing technologies and methodologies for privacy risk management. He has also held several academic positions and has taught courses on the history, politics and ethics of information and communication technologies. His professional affiliations include the IAPP, the Advisory Board of the Ponemon Institute's Responsible Information Management Council and the Association for Computing Machinery's U.S. Public Policy Council, where he currently serves as co-vice-chair.

Manya Sleeper

Manya Sleeper is a PhD student at Carnegie Mellon University in the School of Computer Science. Her research focuses on usable security and privacy, specifically improving access control and privacy decision making. She is advised by Lorrie Faith Cranor. She received her undergraduate degree in computer science and government from Dartmouth College.

Blase Ur

Blase Ur is a PhD student in the School of Computer Science at Carnegie Mellon University, advised by Lorrie Faith Cranor. His research focuses on usable security and privacy, including passwords, online behavioral advertising, access control and privacy decision making. He received his undergraduate degree in computer science from Harvard University.

The CIPT:
The Privacy Certification for Technologists

The Certified Information Privacy Technologist (CIPT) is the global standard in privacy certification for IT professionals.

The CIPT is the only certification for technologists that effectively addresses the role and importance of privacy protection in developing, engineering and managing IT products and services.

Subject matter areas covered include:
- IT privacy risks
- Foundational elements for embedding privacy in IT
- Privacy considerations in the information lifecycle
- Privacy in systems and applications
- Online privacy
- Technologies with privacy considerations

Who should have a CIPT credential?
- Enterprise system architects (CTO, CIO)
- Business process professionals (purchase decision-makers for IT services and products)
- Designers, developers, engineers and administrators of software, network or database systems
- IT managers
- Website operators
- Desktop support specialists
- Risk and regulatory compliance managers
- Information security professionals (CISO, CSO)
- IT compliance and auditing professionals (CISM, CISA)

Whether you're new to the field or you're an experienced professional, achieving a CIPT will demonstrate to your colleagues, peers and employer that you have achieved a foundational knowledge of the essential privacy concepts, practices and principles that impact IT and security.

Learn more about the IAPP certification programs at www.privacyassociation.org/certification.